WORDS OF LIFE

This Teacher's Guide was designed for teachers of Pre-adolescent Children (9 to 11 years old)

**TEACHER'S GUIDE
YEAR 1**

I0161808

Corresponds to Year 1 of the cycle of three years of WORDS OF LIFE (Pre-adolescent Children) Teacher's Guides.

SUNDAY SCHOOL AND DISCIPLESHIP MINISTRIES

Pre-adolescent Children, Year 1 - Teacher's Guide

Published by:

Mesoamerica Region Discipleship Ministries

www.SdmiResources.mesoamericaregion.org

Copyright © 2017 - All rights reserved

ISBN: 978-1-63580-081-4

Reproduction of this material is permitted only for local church use.

All of the scripture verses quoted are from the NIV Bible.

Translated into English from Spanish by:

Bethany Cyr, Monte Cyr, Amanda Englishbee (Lessons 1-10, 41-52), Emily Raquel Gularte Oliva (11-30, 33-40), Nancy Mong (31-32)

Printed in the United States

LESSON CONTENT

I. OVERVIEW

Biblical Base

Points out the Biblical passage from which the lesson has been taken. It can make reference to a single book of the Bible or a scripture passage. You should read the entire passage and be familiar with it.

Memory Verse

A single Bible verse has been chosen to use for the entire unit with the purpose of emphasizing the Biblical truth.

Biblical Truth

Each lesson has a Biblical truth that will develop the overall purpose of the unit.

Lesson Objective

To clarify where to guide your students understanding and what should be accomplished through the teaching-learning process.

II. TEACHER PREPARATION

This section is provided to aid you in reference to the Bible study; it will expand your knowledge about the topic. For better effectiveness, you should take into consideration the following:

Pray and ask God for Direction

Read the Bible passage several times and take notes so you can remember the main ideas that you find.

Consult other versions of the Bible, Bible commentaries, Bible dictionaries, etc . . .

Compare your ideas with those that are presented in this book.

Meditate on each of them, reflect on how each passage applies to your own life.

III. LESSON DEVELOPMENT

Here you will identify how the lesson can be developed so that your students will attain a better understanding of the lesson material.

Introduction

This is the key moment when you will capture the interest of your students; it gives the children the first ideas of what the theme of the lesson will be. You will also find different activities, such as review questions about basic knowledge of the story or topic, reflection questions, activities from the student's workbook, etc...

Developing the Bible Story

The Bible story is developed using methods that give students the opportunity to have an active role. Make sure that the key points are clear in their minds. You can practice your presentation of the topic at home so that you are better prepared in front of the students. Be encouraged, the work is the Lord's and you are an instrument in His hands to carry it out.

Life Application

This is time for your students to reflect on their daily lives, the moment to guide them and ask how their lives are compared to what the Bible teaches.

Usually, these are activities that ask for personal answers. Direct the children towards reflection and don't manipulate their answers, since these should be sincere and individual.

IV. ACTIVITIES

In this section you will find activities that will reinforce the key points of the lesson, give ideas for verse memorization, etc.

Suggestions:

- Each unit begins with a Unit Guide where you will find what you need to develop each lesson under the section titled "Suggestions".
- Keep in mind that the lesson is not limited to the day of the class; it's beneficial to prepare throughout the week.
- Visit your students at least once every semester.
- Pray and communicate with your students through letters, phone calls, invitations or visit them at home if they miss class.
- Send a note or mention in class, special occasions in the student's life, such as birthdays, graduation from school, etc.
- Motivate your students through contests to encourage their attendance, learning, verse memorization, to invite their friends, etc.
- Arrive early to each class to prepare the classroom.
- When preparing your lessons, take into consideration your students ages, needs and any problems the students may have.

Table of Contents

SUGGESTIONS FOR BIBLE MEMORIZATION

1. WHAT DOES THE VERSE SAY?

Have your students express what the verse says by using their senses.

See
In the Bible.
Visual Aids: on the chalk/white board, signs, posters, flashcards, etc.

Hear
Read it out loud
Record it and play it back

Speak
Repeat it after listening to it
Read it together and individually
Sing it

Touch
Write the verse.
Fill in the blank.
Solve a crossword
Use hand motions

2. WHAT DOES IT MEAN?

Explore the definitions.
Let the kids express what they understand about each Bible verse.
Explain words they don't understand.

Discuss the context.
For more explanation, use Bible commentaries, dictionaries and other resources.
Investigate the background of the verse.
Who is speaking and to whom are they speaking?

Illustrate it.
Show pictures/illustrations of the text.
Create your own drawings.
Use hand motions, sign language or act it out.

3. HOW DO I APPLY IT TO MY LIFE?

Discuss the following:
The daily life application of this verse.
In which circumstances will it be useful and what effect will it have on your life and others' lives.

Remember a Bible verse:
When you are being tempted.
When you are troubled.
When you want to encourage others.

1. Understand Your Students and Allow For Normal Behavior.

Children are active and curious.
They are not miniature adults: we must always differentiate between bad behavior and immaturity.

2. Create An Atmosphere That Promotes Good Behavior.

Let children know that you love them and appreciate them.
Show interest in what happens to them outside of class.
Be organized in how you handle the students.
Provide clear and consistent guidelines; let the children know what you expect of them.
Don't show favoritism.

3. Acknowledge Your Position As A Teacher.

Be in charge of the class.
Be a figure of authority that students can follow.
Become a friend to your students.
Explain to them what is expected of them and give them good examples.

4. Use Methods That Involve the Children and Capture Their Interest.

Be prepared and get to the classroom before any of the children.
Provide a variety of activities that are appropriate for your students' ages.
Use activities that capture their interest and ability.
Allow children to choose some of the activities.

5. Focus on Positive Behavior.

Limit the number of rules.
When you correct a child, discuss it with their parent, guardian, or the person responsible for them.

WHAT DO YOU DO WHEN A CHILD MISBEHAVES?

1. Find the Cause of the Problem.

Does the child have learning or medical problems that prevent their participation in class?
Does he try to control the class?
Is he academically talented and therefore bored with the class?
When you know the cause of the problem, you may be able to correct it after talking with the child's parents.

2. Take Control of the Situation.

Ignore behavior that doesn't interrupt the class.
Include the child in learning activities.
Let him see that you are observing his misconduct.
Approach the child in a loving manner.
Tell the child, quietly, what you want him to do.
Teach students the consequences of continued misconduct.

3. Talk to Parents or the Person Responsible for the Child.

If you know that you will most likely have to talk to his parents or guardian, do it.
Start by telling the parents what you appreciate about their child.
State the problem and ask for their ideas of how to resolve the problem..

Dear Teacher:

We have prepared a series of teaching resources that will improve the dynamic of your class. Each lesson has an activities section; please use these materials to encourage your students to use their motor skills as well as help them gain a deeper understanding of the lesson. Prepare extra activities and crafts for the kids who visit your class.

LET'S MEET THE PRE-ADOLESCENT STUDENT

This is an age of discoveries.
  » They want to express their ideas.
  » They are physically and mentally "mature" enough.
  » They enjoy doing new activities.
  » They enjoy discussions that require complete answers.
  » They don't like "yes" and "no" answers anymore.
  » They enjoy working as a team.
  » They enjoy listening to stories, especially stories about Jesus.

As a teacher, encourage them to daily discover their life in Christ. Challenge them to do God's will.

Recipes for Play Dough or Molding Clay

Flour and Salt Dough
Ingredients:
2 or 3 Cups of Flour
¾ Cup Fine Salt
½ Cup Warm Water
Food Coloring

Instructions:
Mix the flour with the salt and add the warm water little by little as you stir. If you want it to be colorful, add drops of food coloring as it thickens. The consistency of the dough will depend on the amount of water you add. Store in a closed container in the fridge.

Cooked Dough
Ingredients:
2 Cups of Flour
1 Cup Salt
1 Tablespoon Vegetable Oil
2 Teaspoons
Food Coloring

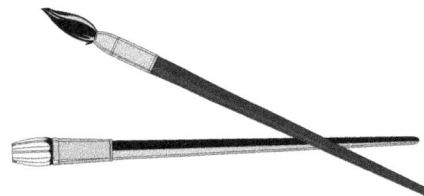

Instructions:
Mix the dry ingredients and then add the water and the vegetable oil. Cook the mix over low heat until it thickens, stirring it constantly. Take it away from the heat and let it cool. To make it the color you want, add drops of food coloring while you mix the dough. If kept in a closed container, it should last for over a month.

Mud Dough

Ingredients:
2 Cups of Dirt
2 Cups of Sand
½ Cup of Salt
Water

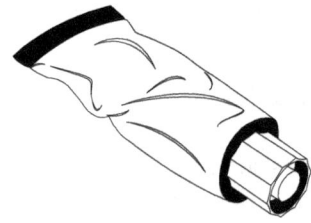

Instructions :
Mix the dirt, sand, and salt, and then add water a little at a time until you get a consistency that is good for molding.

Finger Paint

Ingredients:
1 ¼ Cup Corn Starch
½ Cup Powdered Soap
3 Cups Boiling Water
1 Tablespoon Glycerin
Food Coloring

Instructions:
Dissolve the starch in cold water. Pour it into the warm water slowly as you stir to avoid clumps. Add the soap and the glycerin. To add color, use food coloring. This recipe is not toxic. If stored in plastic cups, it should last several days.

White Glue

Ingredients:
4 Cups Water
1 Cup Wheat Flour
½ Cup Sugar
½ Cup Vinegar

Instructions:
Boil 3 cups of water. Meanwhile, in a container, mix one cup of water, flour, sugar, and vinegar. When the water starts to boil, add the mix and stir slowly over the heat. If there are clumps, stir it more. If it's too thick, add water. If it's too thin, boil it for longer. Store in a jar with a lid.

PAPER FOR CARDS AND CRAFTS

1. Soak 6 sheets of paper or pages from a magazine torn into small pieces in hot water.
2. Put it in the blender with half a cup of oatmeal or flowers or vegetables such as carrots or celery.
3. Strain the mixture and add 4 tablespoons of glycerin and 6 tablespoons white glue.
4. Spread the paste on a plastic sheet/tray with a rolling pin or stick until thin and even.
5. Let it dry in the sun for two days.
6. You can use this paper to make cards, bookmarks, letters, etc.

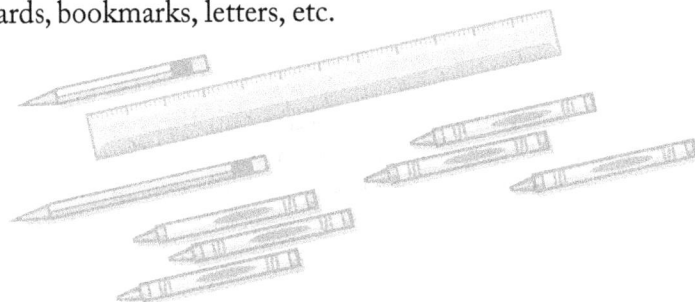

WOMEN OF FAITH

BIBLE TRUTH: Your students will get to learn about the lives of three women: Martha, Priscilla and Lydia; and they will see the example of faith and service these women were in spreading the gospel during the first years of the early church.

UNIT OBJECTIVE

- ❧ Students will understand that God uses women, as well as men, who fully trust in him to testify of their faith to other people.

- ❧ Students will be motivated to serve Jesus, testifying of their faith to the people that surround them.

- ❧ Students will learn different ways that they can present their testimony of faith to other people.

UNIT LESSONS:

- » **Lesson 1** - Martha Reaffirms Her Faith In Christ
- » **Lesson 2** – Priscilla Testifies Of Her Faith.
- » **Lesson 3** - Lydia, A Woman Of Faith In Action

UNIT MEMORY VERSE: *"Yes, Lord," she replied, "I believe that you are the Messiah, the Son of God, who is to come into the world."* (John 11:27)

This verse relates to all of the lessons in this unit, because they are Martha's words that acknowledge Jesus as the Christ, the Savior of the world. If there is no conviction of who Christ is in our lives, we won't be able to testify to others of his love and salvation. Therefore, the basis for giving a testimony of faith is to have faith in God.

Suggestions:

1. It is important that you make sure that the students have already received Christ as their Savior. If this is not the case, you can use evangelistic methods from lesson 3 and use them in the first class.

2. In lesson 2, the students will write the names of people for whom they can pray and present the plan of salvation to. Motivate them to write the names on a piece of paper.

3. Work in advance with the evangelistic method for children. Practice how to use it, and in lesson 3 teach it to the students.

4. During this unit you can ask the students to prepare a mural for the classroom. Every class session, the children can draw and write things that will illustrate the most important lesson points.

5. Verse of the Month Club: The goal is to motivate your students to learn a memory verse during each unit that will give them a Biblical truth to remember. Write it on a poster board and place it in a visible place for the students to see. Before they memorize the verse, it is important that they read it and then can explain the meaning of the verse. If it is possible, use a more modern version of the Bible such as the New International Version. Using hand-motion games or songs to help your students learn the verse makes it more fun and easier to remember.

6. For lesson 1, write the word TRUST on a poster board.

7. Prepare the following and take them to class for lesson 3: a piece of purple cloth for the development of the Bible story. And in order to explain how to make the evangelism booklet (activity number 2), make one ahead of time and have it ready to show your students so they can see how to make it.

MARTHA DECLARES HER FAITH IN CHRIST

I. OVERVIEW

Biblical Base: John 11:1-44.

Memory Verse: *"Yes, Lord," she replied, "I believe that you are the Messiah, the Son of God, who is to come into the world."* (John 11:27)

Biblical Truth: People who trust in God remain firm in spite of having difficult times, and they show it by testifying of their faith and security in God to other people.

Lesson Objective: To help students trust in God despite the problems they may suffer, and to teach them that trust in the Lord allows them to share their testimony with others.

II. TEACHER PREPARATION

In John 11:1-44, we see Jesus taking control in a death situation; in this scenario he shows his power and great glory.

We know that Jesus had a close relationship with Lazarus and his sisters. So, when he gets sick, they go to him, their great friend. It's surprising that Jesus doesn't go immediately after their call. Instead, he waits four days. Even though the petition was made, he had to wait for God's timing for the answer.

Martha is the first one to approach Jesus after he arrives; maybe she was sad and at the same time, a little upset. She complained to Jesus that he had arrived too late. "Master, if you would have been here, my brother would not have died" (v. 21). She felt that Jesus could have helped them. Then she reflects and says full of faith, "But I also know that everything you ask God, God will give to you" (v.22). Jesus answers with encouraging words, "Your brother will live" (v.23).

The previous phrase opens the conversation to speak about the theme of the resurrection. Martha believed, like many Jews, that the resurrection would happen at the end of the world. Jesus Christ clarifies that this could happen that very same day, because he is the resurrection and the life, and everyone who believes in him won't die eternally. Even though he is speaking of a spiritual resurrection and not just physical, these words encourage and give hope to Martha's sad heart. She makes a valuable statement, "Yes, Lord, I have believed that you are the Christ, the Son of God that has come to the world" (v.27).

With these words, Martha reaffirms her faith in Christ in spite of her sadness. Not knowing that Jesus would resurrect her brother Lazarus that very moment, however, her words, "I have believed" mean that she continues to believe in Him in spite of the adversity she is going through.

Today, many people believe in Christ and follow him, but when they have a difficult situation, they get mad at God; they distance themselves from him and even blaspheme his name. Martha is a good example of a woman of faith. She loved Jesus like a great friend, but didn't really know about his power as the son of God. She believed with a lot of faith during a very difficult moment that only Jesus could help her. She didn't doubt why he didn't respond to her call; on the contrary, this trial helped her to reaffirm her faith and to trust Christ in a full way.

Her faith was rewarded when Jesus resurrected her brother. She then believed more and more, and not only that, that miracle helped her to understand that she should tell others what God had done in her life and in the life of her family. It's believed that Martha and Mary were true followers of Jesus, even after his death and resurrection.

III. LESSON DEVELOPMENT

Introduction

Activity: Trust

We'll start the class by studying the word **"TRUST."** (Before class, write the word "Trust" on poster board.) Start a discussion with your students asking them what they believe the meaning of the word "Trust" is. Let them participate, and come to a conclusion. Then have everyone write down the answer on their worksheet entitled "Martha Declares Her faith in Christ" (under the word "Trust"). Then ask them who they trust (let those who haven't participated answer this). Tell them to write down the names of those they trust on their worksheets.

Let your students unscramble the words that show when we need to trust in someone (when "I feel lonely", "I am sad" or "I am afraid"). Say, "Think of a time when you needed to trust in someone. Now, draw in the blank circles a face that expresses those feelings."

Before they finish this activity ask: "If someone whom you trust breaks your trust, would you continue trusting in that person?" (Let several students answer.) Tell them that today they will study a Bible story where something similar happened to a woman. But before you tell the story, have them fill in the blanks at the bottom of their worksheets. Ask them: "Who is the one who never fails and who we can always trust?" (God) Tell them that people might fail us but we can always trust in the Lord.

Developing the Bible Story

Ask some of your students to represent the people in the story and have them read the dialog while the rest of the class listens:

Martha: (Say to the messengers): You have to find Jesus! He is the only one that can help Lazarus. When you find him, tell him, "Lord, the one you love is sick." He will know what to do.

Narrator: The messengers took the news to Jesus and came back with an important answer.

Messenger: Jesus said that this disease is not deadly, but for the glory of God, so that the son of God may be glorified by it.

Narrator: *"Now Jesus loved Martha and her sister and Lazarus. So when he heard that Lazarus was sick, he stayed where he was two more days"* (John 11:5-6).

Martha: Where is Jesus? Why didn't he come? He knows that Lazarus is sick. I hope he comes soon. It hurts me to see my brother suffer!

Narrator: But Jesus didn't come. Lazarus sisters were confused and dazed; when he died, they said, "If Jesus would have been here, this would not have happened." Meanwhile, Jesus said to his disciples,

Jesus: *"Our friend Lazarus has fallen asleep; but I am going there to wake him up."*

Narrator: Jesus said this about Lazarus' death, but they thought he was talking about natural sleep. Then Jesus clearly said, *"Lazarus is dead."*

Four days later, after Lazarus was buried, the news came that Jesus was coming to the city. When Martha heard this, she went to meet him. She didn't understand why he didn't come any sooner. Didn't Jesus know that they needed his help?

Martha: (Jesus comes near and Martha meets him saying,) *"Lord, if you had been here, my brother would not have died. But I know that even now God will give you whatever you ask."*

Jesus: *"Your brother will rise again."*

Martha: *"I know he will rise again in the resurrection at the last day."*

Jesus: *"I am the resurrection and the life. The one who believes in me will live, even though they die; and whoever lives by believing in me will never die. Do you believe this?"*

Martha: *"Yes, Lord, I believe that you are the Messiah, the Son of God, who is to come into the world."*

Narrator: She returned to her house and told her sister Mary that Jesus was in town and wanted to see her; when Jesus saw how Mary and the Jews with her were weeping because of Lazarus' death, he was deeply moved in spirit and troubled. He asked,

Jesus: *"Where have you laid him?"*

Narrator: When they showed Jesus the grave, Jesus wept. Then the Jews said,

Jews: *"See how he loved him!"* (Referring to Jesus)

Some Other Jews: *"Could not he who opened the eyes of the blind man have kept this man from dying?"*

Narrator: Then Jesus went to the grave and said, *"Take away the stone."* But Martha said,

Martha: *"But Lord, by this time there is a bad odor, for he has been there four days."*

Jesus: *"Did I not tell you that if you believe, you will see the glory of God?"*

Narrator: When they removed the stone from the grave, Jesus looked up and said,

Jesus: *"Father, I thank you that you have heard me. I know that you always hear me, but I said this for the benefit of the people standing here, that they may believe that you sent me."*

(When he had said this, Jesus called in a loud voice,) "Lazarus, come out!"

Narrator: *"The dead man came out, his hands and feet wrapped with strips of linen, and a cloth around his face."*

Jesus: (walks towards some people and says,) *"Take off the grave clothes and let him go."*

Life Application

Activity: Trust or Distrust?

Give your students the worksheet entitled Trust or Distrust? Say: "Martha trusted in Jesus because she could see him and talk to him. We can learn to trust in God even when we don't see him, through the things we experience every day. Our trust grows when we pray and see God answer those prayers. For example, we may pray for God to heal us when we are sick, or we may ask God to give us focus when we are going to take a test so that we can remember what we've studied, etc."

Say: "Lets answer the questions that are written on the hand". When is it easy to trust in Jesus? (Let the children express their answers.) When is it difficult to trust in Jesus? (When he doesn't answer like we want him to; when we are afraid; when we get in trouble for telling the truth, etc.)

Ask the students to draw a star next to the items that are more difficult for them to trust in Jesus. Pray with them and ask God to help them to trust in him, in spite of what they are going through. You can end by singing a song that talks about the topic of faith or trust in God. Then pray for the needs of each student.

IV. ACTIVITIES

Review Game:

Write the name of each student on pieces of paper and place them in a container. If possible, have your students sit in a circle. While you clap, have your students pass the container around the circle. When you stop clapping, the student that has the container will take out a piece of paper and read the name of the student that is on the paper. Then, you will ask a question about the story to that student. If they don't know that answer, give another student the opportunity to answer. Continue passing the container until you have asked all the questions.

Suggested Questions

1. How did Martha express her trust in Jesus before Lazarus' death?
2. After Lazarus died, what doubts or questions do you think Martha had about Jesus?
3. In spite of her doubts and questions, how did Martha show that she trusted in Jesus?
4. What was it that helped Martha continue to trust in Jesus, even though it seemed like he let her down?

You can ask more questions that you think are relevant.

Memory Verse

Write the memory verse on a piece of card board or poster board so that your students can learn it during the course of the unit. Teach them how to find the verse in the Bible. After they have read it, explain it's meaning to them and why it's important that they remember it.

Encourage the children to memorize it. You can play the invisible word game to help them learn the verse. Start by writing the verse on a chalkboard or white-board. Say the verse together, out loud. Then erase a word and say the verse again, inserting the erased word in the appropriate place. Continue erasing one or two words and repeating the verse until all the words are erased. You could give a small prize to the student(s) who can say the verse once all the words are erased.

(If you don't have a chalk or white-board, write the verse on sheets of paper, one word on each sheet and tape it to the wall. Then, instead of erasing a word, take a word off the wall.)

NOTES:

PRISCILLA TESTIFIES OF HER FAITH
I. OVERVIEW

Biblical Base: Acts 18:10-28.

Memory Verse: *"Yes, Lord,"* she replied, *"I believe that you are the Messiah, the Son of God, who is to come into the world."* (John 11:27)

Biblical Truth: A Christian should testify of his faith to others, and help them understand Jesus Christ's message.

Lesson Objective: To help the students discover that those of us who are Christians have a responsibility to help others grow spiritually.

II. TEACHER PREPARATION

In Acts 18:18-28, we read about an immigrant named Priscilla, and her husband, Aquilla. Around the years 49-50 A.D., the emperor Claudius exiled all the Jews from Rome to end all the disturbances that were happening there. Some of the problems arose when the Christian Jews announced their faith in Jesus Christ in the synagogues.

Priscilla and Aquilla lived in Corinth when they met the apostle Paul. They made tents and Paul helped them. Because of this connection between them, they shared a very strong friendship which, of course, carried over into their ministry. Later, when Paul traveled to Ephesus, Aquilla and Priscilla went with him. Paul started a church in their home and when he went to another city to evangelize, they stayed in Ephesus.

One day they heard about a man name Apollo who spoke in the synagogue and knew about the Old Testament. The Bible says that he taught about the baptism of John with truth. He also taught about repenting for your sins and the coming of the Messiah, but he didn't know that the dead and risen Jesus WAS the Messiah. He wasn't aware of the baptism in the name of Jesus or knew what being filled with the Spirit meant.

Priscilla and Aquilla invited him to their house, gave their testimony of faith and showed him all they knew about Jesus; the result being that Apollo grew in his faith and converted into a great evangelist. He took the message of salvation to many places along with other disciples.

Priscilla was very busy, since she was a wife (we're unsure if she had any children). On top of that she helped her husband in his shops. In this time, women weren't allowed to know much about anything, much less about God. But Priscilla, on top of her responsibilities and regardless of the prejudices at this time, decided to serve God and she took the necessary time to teach Apollo about God and show him her faith in Jesus.

To testify and show our faith to others is not just a responsibility but also a privilege that brings blessings to our lives – while we are teaching others of our faith, we are learning ourselves.

III. LESSON DEVELOPMENT
Introduction

Start the class by asking your students what the key word was from last week (confide/confidence), and if it was easy for them to confide in Jesus during the week. Ask them if they talked to Him when they were worried or during difficult moments (let a few kids recount their experiences).

Say: "Today we are going to study another lady from the Bible, but first let's talk about who is a witness." (Write down their answers and ideas on the whiteboard/chalkboard.) Then talk about how important it is to be a witness for Jesus Christ. Ask: "What does a Christian witness about?" (Give them an opportunity to answer.)

Developing the Bible Story

Have the students follow along in their worksheets while you tell the Bible story:

Priscilla and her husband Aquilla lived in the city of Ephesus, and they made tents. They also happened to be great friends with Paul and he also made tents when he wasn't too busy with his missionary work.

They were Jews who knew and believed in Jesus Christ as their personal savior and they all wanted others to know Him too. One day they heard that a man name Apollos was preaching at their local synagogue. They went to hear him speak; he knew a lot about John the Baptist and his disciples and he told stories from the Old Testament with clarity and preciseness. He taught them that the Savior would come someday.

Priscilla loved to hear him speak, even though Apollos

didn't know much about Jesus.

After Pricilla and Aquilla had heard him preach, they invited him to their house and taught him everything they knew about Jesus. They told him that Jesus died on the cross for the sins of the world and three days after his death he rose again.

Apollos was a good student. He was anxious to tell the other disciples of John the Baptist what he had learned. Afterwards he traveled to many places to share the Good News.

Pricilla and Aquilla continued making tents, but they also opened their home to teach others about their faith in Jesus Christ. This began one of the first early churches. They were happy to be able to teach Apollo about Jesus.

To finish off the story, play "hot potato" with your students. The game consists of passing an object from hand to hand while you have some music playing in the background. When the music stops, whoever is holding the object in their hand must answer a question. Whether the question is answered correctly or not, keep the game going until all four questions are answered correctly:

- How did Priscilla and Apollos give their testimony?
- How important was it for Apollos to hear the testimony of these Christian brothers – how did it help him?
- What will happen to the people that never hear the Good News?
- Will you give your testimony and witness to your friends, classmates and family?

Life Application

Activity: Do you know them?

For this activity, the students can write on their worksheets the names of people who live near them or who they may interact with on a daily basis (the bus driver, lunch lady, etc). If they don't know their names, they can refer to them by their job. Have them put a cross next to the people they know are Christians and encourage them to pray for those that are not.

At the bottom of the page: What will you do so that Jesus is not a secret? Have your students think about how they can share the gospel of Christ with those who don't know him:

- Invite a friend to watch a Christian movie
- Listen to Christian music
- Hang up Christian posters in your room
- Read Bible stories to little kids
- Give your testimony at church
- Pray before you eat
- Read Christian books and magazines
- Wear shirts that have a Christian theme
- Love God and others as yourself.

Remind them that what we do is more important than what we say. An important way we show that we are Christians is to love God with all our heart, soul and mind, and others as ourselves.

IV. ACTIVITIES

Make sure your students have the worksheet entitled "Accept the Challenge". If they have already identified someone that is close to them who doesn't know Christ, help them finish the exercise by making a plan to present them with their testimony. Remind them about how firm and clear Priscilla and Aquilla's testimonies were that they gave to others. Ask: "How can we have the same effect?" (Talk about the ways that God has helped them spiritually; challenge them to remain faithful to Jesus; pray for each other; mention new teachings that God has shown you in your Christian walk, etc.)

Memory Verse

Ask your student to show their classmates the text they learned in the last class and explain the drawings that each one used to illustrate it. Once this is finished let each student take their drawings home to hang up somewhere so they can see it and continue memorizing the verse over the week. After repeat the verse a couple times, have a contest to see who knows it better, the boys or the girls.

Pray for the students, that God gives them courage and the words to witness to their friends and family about Christ like Priscilla and Aquilla did. If some of them are nervous, or they don't feel like they can do it, challenge them to do it this week. Tell them that next week you'll discuss their experiences with this challenge.

NOTES:

LESSON 3
LYDIA, A WOMAN OF FAITH IN ACTION
I. OVERVIEW

Biblical Base: Acts 16:11-15.

Memory Verse: *"Yes, Lord," she replied, "I believe that you are the Messiah, the Son of God, who is to come into the world."* (John 11:27)

Biblical Truth: Christians want their family and friends to come to know and love Jesus.

Lesson Objective: To help students share the message of salvation with their friends and family through a method of evangelism.

II. TEACHER PREPARATION

Acts 6:11-15 talks about a woman named Lydia who lived in Philippi and was the first person in Europe who converted into a Christian. This story is about a business woman who was very influential in a prosperous town in northern Greece. Even though she held a great economic position, she still needed a large influx of money to establish another business of purple thread (which was very expensive in that day).

Lydia was a gentile woman who adored the god of the Jews. She learned of him in her native land of Thyatira; however, there wasn't a Jewish synagogue in Philippi where she could learn more about the Lord.

When there wasn't a synagogue, the Jews would come together on the river shore to carry out their washing ceremonies. So, Paul, Silas, Timothy and Luke walked to the shore to look for a place to praise God one Sabbath day, and they found a group of women praying.

They sat with them and started to preach and evangelism to them about Jesus. Lydia was sensitive to the voice of God and she believed. And even though the Bible doesn't specifically say, we believe that she preached this message to her family, because it DOES say that her whole family believed and was baptized.

We don't know who exactly her family was, and it doesn't mention that she had a husband or kids, etc. Perhaps she was a widow or was a single lady; or maybe her family included her kids, parents and other adults, like servants and slaves. But as the head of her house, without a doubt, she exercised profound influence over them; because of her testimony and her change of life – all of them began to believe in Jesus too.

After being baptized, Lydia begged Paul and the other missionaries to stay in her home. It's believed that it was there that the Philippine church began. It was a very evangelical and generous congregation. Paul spent a lot of time with them, until he felt they were cemented enough in the stories of Jesus and their faith in Him. From there, he left with Silas, but Luke stayed in Philippi to continue to minister to them. When we read the letter to the Philippians, we can see that Paul felt great appreciation for this church, and he mentioned them often in his ministry.

Lydia was a woman of great sensitivity towards the Message. From the first time she heard about Jesus, she believed and her life changed. From then on she was a faithful disciple and helped convert her family. We also believe she converted many others – people that came to her business, other friends and other family members.

We should be brave like her and witness to others about Jesus Christ; we worry about our family members, friends, coworkers… Economic levels or education or anything else like that don't matter. Those who don't know Jesus need a message of hope and love; and we can be the one that God uses to preach that to everyone around us.

III. LESSON DEVELOPMENT
Introduction

Start the class by asking your student if they shared their testimony with any of their neighbors or friends. Let a few of them tell their stories.

Give each student a worksheet entitled "I'll tell Them" and have them write the names of their friends and family members that they are closes to that don't know Christ inside the heart. Tell them: "Today we are going to learn about a woman who loved her family and friends very much, just like we love our friends and family."

Developing the Bible Story
Lydia's Wise Decision

There was a woman named Lydia who lived in Philippi. She dedicated her life to selling a very special kind of fabric that was purple. (Try to find a piece of purple fabric or something else that is purple to demonstrate.) Explain to them the importance of this color in Biblical times: why this tint was so expensive: they extracted it from sea mollusk that was very difficult to find and only people who had a lot of money were able to buy fabric of this specific color, like royalty and other rich people.

One of Paul's friends said, "There is no synagogue here and it's the day of rest. Where should we praise and worship God?" Paul answered, "In cities that don't have

15

a synagogue, the people go to the river to praise Him. Perhaps we could find one near here to worship."

They all left the city and went to the shore of the river to join with other Jews to praise God. They hoped to teach them the truths about Jesus, the Messiah that all the Jews waited patiently on who had already come and gone.

"There! There is a group; it looks like we came to the perfect place!" said one of Paul's disciples.

Paul and his friends sat near a group of women; they wanted to hear what Paul and his friends said. One of them was Lydia, a business woman from the city of Thyatira (she sold very expensive purple cloth). Lydia and her friends listened to Paul's words while he told about how Jesus came to earth and died on the cross. Also, how God resurrected him on the third day.

Lydia thought about it. "It's possible that the Messiah has already come! It's everything I have been hoping for forever! I believe in Jesus! Can I be baptized? Also, I want my friends and my family to know about Him." When her family heard the message, they also believed and they were baptized.

Lydia didn't want Paul and his friends to leave because she wanted to know more about Jesus Christ. So, they stayed for quite a while at Lydia's house.

Life Application

This lesson emphasized the responsibility that all Christians must witness and testify of Jesus' life and love to others, like our friends and family. Sometimes it's difficult, especially for students of this age.

Occasionally, some parents who aren't Christians impede their children's attendance at church, or they try to change their convictions.

But, even though witnessing can be difficult, God can give us the courage and bravery that we need to complete the task. Here we find a method of evangelism which might help your students to share the message of salvation to family members and friends.

IV. ACTIVITIES

Give your students the worksheet entitled "Do you know my friend?" On the worksheet they can see the most important events of Jesus' life. Let several students explain the illustrations. Afterwards have them cut out the page along the solid lines, fold the page in the middle and make an eight-page book. (Bring one already completed so the kids can follow your example.) Staple the pages together in the middle. Next, have them write the corresponding Bible verse on each page. Explain to them that this book is called "Do you know my friend? His name is Jesus." They can use it to share the gospel of Jesus with their family members and friends who they love.

Show them how use it by asking the following questions:

Cover: Do you know my friend? His name is Jesus.

Page 2. Do you celebrate Christmas? If you do, you are celebrating my friend Jesus' birthday. (Luke 2:7)

Page 3. God became a man and was born as a baby. He grew up and was an obedient child of God and His earthly parents. (Luke 2:40)

Page 4/5. My friend Jesus taught people to love God; He healed the sick, fed the hungry and brought the dead back to life. (Matthew 5:1-2)

Page 6. My friend Jesus died on the cross because there were people who didn't like him. He knew that he had to die to pay the ultimate price for our sin. He did it because he loves us so much. (Mark 15:25-26)

Page 7. But, my friend Jesus, even though He was dead, was resurrected on the third day; He conquered death and sin! He lives forever! (Luke 24:6)

Page 8. My friend Jesus wants to be your friend too. He went up to Heaven, but he's also wants to be in your life. He can forgive you for all of the bad things you've done. If you believe in him and repent of your sins, he will forgive you and make you a child of God. (Acts 1:9-11)

If your friend accepts the story of Christ and wants to have a relationship with Jesus, pray for them that Christ will forgive them of their sins and they, too, can become a child of God.

Let the kids test out their new method of evangelizing so they know how to use it.

Memory Verse

Write the verse on a piece of poster board and cut it up. Mix up the pieces so that the students can put it back in order. You can do this several times. Remind them that this Bible verse invites us to be sure of our faith in Christ Jesus. (Give some sort of incentive to the students who have learned their memory verse.)

Ask the students to remember the people that they noted on their worksheet; and put a star next to the name of the friends or family that they want to talk to about Jesus. Challenge them to use their new book to help them share with their friends and family about Jesus. Also tell them that in the next class they will get to share their experiences with the class.

HOW TO MAKE GOOD DECISIONS

BIBLICAL TRUTH: That students will learn that to make good decisions in their daily lives, they need God's help.

UNIT OBJECTIVE
- That students understand that God is very interested in the fact that they make good decisions.
- Through the Bible lessons, students will learn to analyze and ask themselves if their decisions are right or wrong.
- That students will learn that by making good decisions, they honor God and their parents.

UNIT LESSONS
- **Lesson 4** – Take Responsibility For Your Decisions!
- **Lesson 5** – Use Your Talents For God!
- **Lesson 6** – Stop! Beware Of Bad Decisions.
- **Lesson 7** – Do What Is Right And You'll Be Different.
- **Lesson 8** – Decide To Move Forward!

UNIT MEMORY VERSE: *"So whether you eat or drink or whatever you do, do it all for the glory of God."* (1 Corinthians 10:31)

The activities throughout the lessons will help the students learn the verse.

UNIT EXPLANATION

Every day, students must make decisions. Most of them are more and more independent from the adults in their lives as they learn to make decisions on their own. They choose friends, activities, how to spend their time and how to spend their money. They also come face to face with important choices about their bodies and how to live peacefully with their family. Your students need to know how to make wise decisions to be happier and more productive in their lives. Bad decisions cause problems and unhappiness. This unit emphasizes that God can help them make positive decisions in every aspect of their lives.

Verse of the Month Club

Challenge your students to continue being part of the Verse of the Month Club. In each unit, the student will have the chance to learn a memory verse. Encourage your students to use their time wisely to learn it. They can be part of this club when they've learned the Bible verse by memory.

Suggestions:
1. In Lesson 4, for the "Lesson Development", you should bring in two cardboard boxes that are the same size and two pieces of fruit; 1 that is good and ripe and one that is bad (maybe even a little bit rotten).
2. In the same lesson, in "Activities", write out 3 or 4 examples of decisions that children must make.
3. For Lesson 5, in the "Memory Verse" section, bring the verse, written on cardboard with the words cut apart so that your students can work on reassembling it.
4. In the "Lesson Development" section in Lesson 7, you'll need to bring two plates. On one put fruit and vegetables and on the other put candy, chips and chocolates. You'll present these to the students after you finish the Bible story.
5. Lesson 8 is the last lesson of this unit. Give a small prize to all the students who have learned their memory verse.

TAKE RESPONSIBILITY FOR YOUR DECISIONS!

I. OVERVIEW

Biblical Base: Genesis 13:1-13, 19:12-26, 2 Peter 2:4-9.

Memory Verse: *"So whether you eat or drink or whatever you do, do it all for the glory of God"* (1 Corinthians 10:31).

Biblical Truth: It's important to know how to make good choices that honor God because they help determine what will happen from day to day in your life.

Lesson Objective: To help students understand that everyone is responsible for their own decisions. And, above all, there will be consequences whether good or bad.

II. TEACHER PREPARATION

In Genesis 13:1-13 and 19:12-26, we see Abraham and his nephew Lot with a big problem; there were too many people and livestock in one small place. Their shepherds fought over the water and the pastures where they fed their sheep and cattle. The time for them to separate had come…

Abraham let Lot decide where he wanted to go first. This not only showed his generosity, but it was also a sign of his complete faith in God. And Lot, the good business man that he was, saw the Jordan Valley and the benefits of a very rich land. However, there in the valley were two cities, well known for their evil. But blinded by the fertility of the land, Lot ignored the danger that existed there and decided to move his family there anyway.

Lot's decision to move close to such a perverse city, and then later into it, meant that Lot would pay a very high price. God would send two angels to warn them that He would destroy the city. Lot encouraged his sons-in-law to leave, but they didn't pay any attention to him. He really didn't want to leave either; the angels had to take him by the hand, along with his wife and daughters and take them to a safe place.

From the time we are little, we are constantly making decisions, some small and others more important, like what clothes we wear, what time to wake up, what TV shows we watch, what we spend our time on, and so forth.

We must learn that every decision comes with a consequence. We are free to make those decisions, but we are responsible for the consequences that come our way. Lot made a split-second decision, he didn't even think about it, didn't even talk to God about it, and this brought death and other consequences to his family.

III. LESSON DEVELOPMENT
Introduction

In general, people make decisions based on what looks the best to them. Prepare two boxes in the same exact way except put a good piece of fruit or a vegetable in one and a piece of fruit or vegetable that has gone bad in the other. Then wrap them in the same wrapping paper. Say "Do these boxes look the same? Well they also look the same inside, what do you think is inside? (Let several kids answer.)

Then have one group of kids unwrap one and another group unwrap the other. Show everyone what was inside both boxes. Emphasize that many times things look the same on the outside but what is important is what is on the inside. Have your students do the "Take Responsibility for Your Decisions" worksheet - it goes with this demonstration.

Developing the Bible Story

Talk to your students about the choice that Abraham made when God asked him to leave his home and family to go to an even better place that he would give him. Say, "What do you think Abraham did? When God decided it was time for him to leave, He promised to bless Abraham and make his family a great nation. Also, Abraham's nephew decided to go with him."

Ask them, "Do you want to hear more of the story?" Then ask your students to get into 3 groups; 1 group will read the part of Lot, 1 group 2 the part of Abraham and the other group will read the part of the Angels. You'll be the Narrator.

Lot's Decision

Lot: Uncle Abraham! Uncle Abraham! Our shepherds are fighting again! (Lot runs into the shop where Abraham was working.)

Abraham: Fighting over pastures again?

Lot: Isn't that what it's always about?! Your shepherds are saying there's not enough grass for your herds AND mine. They won't let my sheep or cows eat here. What are we going to do to solve this problem?

Narrator: Abraham thought for a moment. He owned a lot of sheep and cows, but so did his nephew Lot. And there was not enough grass and water for all of the animals if they wanted to stay together. And since he loved Lot, he didn't want to fight with him, so he said,

Abraham: "*Let's not have any quarreling between you and me, or between your herders and mine, for we are close relatives. Is not the whole land before us? Let's part company. If you go to the left, I'll go to the right, if you go to the right, I'll go to the left.*"

Lot: Wow! Abraham is letting me choose which area I want. Even though He is older and my uncle, and he has the right to choose, he is letting me decide. This is great!

Narrator: He looked around and saw the whole plain of the Jordan; it had lots of water, like the garden of the Lord. But there was still a problem – the people who lived in the cities in the valley were evil and perverse. But there's so much grass and water . . . Then Lot chose for himself the whole plain of the Jordan.

Abraham: All right, you go and live in the valley. I'll go to the hills.

Narrator: The two men parted company. Abraham stayed in the land of Canaan, while Lot lived in the cities in the valley. Years later, Lot's herds of sheep and cattle had grown a lot because they had eaten well on the grass of the lowlands. So, Lot became very rich and didn't want to live in tents anymore. He decided to move to the city of Sodom. But the inhabitants of Sodom were evil and they committed horrible sins against Jehovah. Their wickedness was so terrible that God decided to destroy the city. But since Lot was Abraham's nephew, God sent two angels to rescue him and his family.

Angeles: Lot, we are going to destroy this place, because the evil of the people of this city has gone up before Jehovah. Therefore, Jehovah is going to destroy it. Go and tell your family what is about to happen.

Narrator: Lot spoke to his sons-in-law, the husbands of his daughters and said:

Lot: Get up, get out of this place, because Jehovah is going to destroy this city.

Narrator: But his sons-in-law thought he was joking. The angels hurried to Lot saying:

Angeles: Get up, take your wife and your two daughters so that they don't perish in the punishment of the city.

Narrator: Because Lot delayed, the men seized his hands, his wife and his two daughters, because of Jehovah's mercy towards them; The angels took Lot and his family out of the city. And when they got away from the city, they told Lot:

Angeles: Flee for your lives; Don't look back or stop anywhere in the valley.

Narrator: When Lot and his family were safe, the Lord rained sulfur and fire on Sodom and Gomorrah from the heavens ... then Lot's wife looked back behind her and became a pillar of salt.

(This Bible story is found in Genesis 13:6-13, 19:14-17, 19, 24 and 26.)

Activity: Which Apple Looks Better?

Ask the students to draw a star under the apple that looks the best. Have them fold their worksheet up along the dotted line and they'll see that sometimes what appears to be the best, isn't!

Ask them: "What choices did Lot make?" Let some kids answer and then investigate further. "What consequences did Lot have to face because of his choices?" Write the response on the board. "If Lot had known everything that was going to happen in the valley, do you think he would have made the same decision?"

Life Application

Give your students the worksheet entitled "Decisions, Decisions, Decisions." Lead them in a discussion about some of the decisions that they've made. God gives us all the privilege and responsibility to make choices. What kinds of decisions do kids their age make? Have them put an X by the hardest ones:

- -What do kids think about when they make decisions?
- -How can they know if the decision they make will have good or bad consequences?

Explain to your students that we can't know in advance what will happen when we make decisions, but if we ask for God's help, he will give us the wisdom to know how to choose what is best for us.

IV. ACTIVITIES

Learning Activity

Case Studies:

Bring in writing, three or four examples of children who had to make decisions. Organize your students in teams, read the cases and then have them comment on the decisions that those children made. Were their decisions good or bad, and what were the consequences of their choices?

Memory Verse

Review the memory verse again to help your students memorize it; invite your students to write it down at home to help them remember it better. Tell your students that praying, reading their Bible and asking their parents for advice will help them make good decisions.

Pray for your students and make sure to pray that God will help them make good decisions in their lives.

USE YOUR TALENTS FOR GOD!

I. OVERVIEW

Biblical Base: Exodus 25:1-9, 31:1-11, 1 Peter 4:10.

Memory Verse: *"So whether you eat or drink or whatever you do, do it all for the glory of God."* (1 Cor. 10:31)

Biblical Truth: God gave all of us talents and abilities to use for his work.

Lesson Objective: To help students identify some of their talents and encourage them to use those talents for the service of the Lord.

II. TEACHER PREPARATION

In Exodus 25, all of the materials that God wanted for the construction of His Tabernacle are mentioned. Then He describes to Moses the specific measurements and designs for everything that should be in the tabernacle. Maybe Moses asked, "Who can do all of this?" He was the political, religious, and military leader, but he had no artistic talent to do everything God asked.

It wasn't God's purpose to just miraculously build his temple. No, He wanted people to build it, using their God-given talents. God chooses, prepares and directs His servants to complete daily tasks. God chose Bezalel and Oholiab as Bezalel's helpers to create beautiful pieces for the tabernacle.

God called these men specifically to make artistic objects with gold, silver, precious stones, metals, fabric, wood, animal skins, etc. And He equipped them to make different things like banisters, carpentry, carved jewelry, clothing, etc.

In addition to their natural talents, God also gave them the Holy Spirit so they could work with wisdom, intelligence and science. What a privilege for those two men. They didn't do all the work by themselves; they had many artists who they directed until they finished making the beautiful sanctuary in which to praise God.

It's interesting to discover that serving God isn't a result of having sufficient talents or abilities; it's because we've been chosen by God and directed by the Holy Spirit. Many times, we serve God because he chose us. But sometimes we serve because we just like to; we might not have made sure that what we are doing is really what God has called us to do. When this happens, that which is said in 1 Peter 4:10 is fulfilled: *"Each of you should use whatever gift you have received to serve others, as faithful stewards of God's grace in its various forms."*

III. LESSON DEVELOPMENT

Introduction

Review Activity: Who Am I?

To remember the lesson, divide the class into two teams; read each of the following statements and then ask, 'who am I?' The team that chimes in first should be able to say who said the phrase. Each correct answer is worth 10 points and the team that has the most points at the end wins.

1. Let's not have any quarreling between you and me. (Abraham)
2. We require this pasture for the game and flocs of our master. (the Shepherds)
3. I choose the Jordan plain. (Lot)
4. God has sent us to destroy the city of Sodom. (Angels)
5. If you go towards the left, I'll go to the right; if you go towards the right, I'll go to the left. (Abraham)
6. Get up, leave this place' because Jehovah will destroy this city. (Lot to his sons-in-law or Angels to Lot)
7. We are going to move to Sodom. (Lot)

After the review, talk to your students about the talents and abilities that God has given them. Explain that God has given human beings talents to be used in specific areas like music, math, business, manual labor, farming/gardening, organization…

Give you students the worksheet entitled "What Are Your Talents?" Have them read what is written in the balloons and draw or stick a star on the everyday things that they know they do well or that they enjoy doing. After they have finished, ask a few volunteers to share what they like to do with the class.

Explain that just like they have special talents and abilities, God used people with special talents and abilities to do something very special.

Developing the Bible Story

Ask: "Have you ever tried to help build something? How did you feel when you finished?" (Let them relate their experiences.) Ask them to pay attention while you read the Bible story:

"Bezalel! Bezalel!" called Oholiab, "Where are you off to so fast?"

"I'm going to Moses' tent," responded Bezalel. "He wants to talk with me."

"He asked me to come as well," said Oholiab.

"I wonder what he wants to tell us? I'm sure it has something to do with building the tabernacle," said Bezalel, while they hurried to meet Moses.

They knew that God had given plans to Moses to build the tabernacle. This would be a place for the whole city to unite and praise God. Moses told Bezalel and Oholiab that God had chosen them to lead the construction of the tabernacle. This would be a huge mobile tent, since the Israelites traveled so much. Therefore, the tabernacle would look like a tent on the outside, but would be amazingly beautiful on the inside.

When Bezalel and Oholiab got to Moses' tent, he greeted them. "Welcome! I've asked you to come so I can tell you what God told me when I was on Mount Sinai," Moses said. "The Lord said to me, '*Tell the Israelites to bring me an offering. You are to receive the offering for me from everyone whose heart prompts them to give. Then have them make a sanctuary for me, and I'll dwell among them. Make this tabernacle and all its furnishings exactly like the pattern I'll show you.*' God has promised that if we do everything exactly as He has instructed us that His presence will descend upon the tabernacle and He will dwell there," continued Moses.

"The city has brought many offerings," said Bezalel.

"Yes," agreed Moses, "We have all the materials that we need. The city was very happy to give what they had for the construction of the tabernacle."

"They've brought, gold, silver, wood, and fine linen," said Oholiab.

"Now we are ready to get started on building the Tabernacle just like God showed us," continued Moses.

"What would you like us to do?" Bezalel asked.

"When I was on Mount Sinai," responded Moses, "the Lord also told me, 'See, I have chosen Bezalel son of Uri, the son of Hur, of the tribe of Judah, and I have filled him with the Spirit of God, with wisdom, with understanding, with knowledge and with all kinds of skills—to make artistic designs for work in gold, silver and bronze, to cut and set stones, to work in wood, and to engage in all kinds of crafts. Moreover, I have appointed Oholiab son of Ahisamak, of the tribe of Dan, to help him.'"

Bezalel and Oholiab were happy to have been chosen by God for this job but they were scared. When he noticed this, Moses said, "Don't be afraid, God has chosen you for this construction and he's given you the talents and ability to do so."

"This is such a huge job," said Oholiab, "can we really do it?"

"Yes," replied Moses, "God and the people will help you so you know what to do."

Some artists worked on the wood. Others made decorations out of gold and silver for the inside of the tabernacle. Some sewed animal skins together for the outside of the sanctuary. Others made curtains and still others made clothes for the priests.

At the end of the narration ask:

• What decisions did Bezalel and Oholiab make when God told them what to do?
• What abilities or talents did they use to serve God?
• Who helped Bezalel and Oholiab to build the tabernacle?
• What happened when Moses, Bezalel and Oholiab obeyed God?

Life Application
Activity: I'll Do It For God

Tell your students that just like Bezalel and Oholiab, we also can serve God. Have them write on their worksheets the abilities and talents that they have that they have decided to use for God's purpose.

IV. ACTIVITIES
Learning Activity

Have the students share what they wrote on their worksheets and help them make plans to use their talents in church. (Emphasis what 1 Peter 4:10 says.)

Memory Verse
Verse of the Month Club

Ask who remembers the memory verse. If they can say it, make them part of the Verse of the Month Club. Give everyone an opportunity to say the verse. Bring it written on a piece of cardboard and cut it up, word by word; give each student a piece of cardboard and have them organize themselves so the verse is in the correct order. Have them repeat it out loud together and then let them say it from memory. Relate it to today's lesson.

Ask them to give thanks for the abilities and talents that God has given them. End class by praying for your students, that the Lord allows them to use their abilities to honor Him and bring Him glory.

21

LESSON 6

STOP!!! BEWARE OF BAD DECISIONS

I. OVERVIEW

Biblical Base: 2 Samuel 15:1-37, 16:15, 18:33, Proverbs 8:10-11.

Memory Verse: *"So whether you eat or drink or whatever you do, do it all for the glory of God."* (1 Cor. 10:31)

Biblical Truth: Bad decisions destroy us and make those around us suffer.

Lesson Objective: To help students understand that if they makes decisions that don't please God, it will bring them terrible consequences.

II. TEACHER PREPARATION

The two oldest sons of David and possible successors to the throne of Israel, Amnon and Absalom, turned into irreconcilable enemies when Amnon dishonored his half-sister, Tamar, sister of Absalom. Absalom takes his revenge on his older brother (Amnon) by killing him. In both instances, the dishonoring of Tamar and the murder of Amnon, King David looked like a weak father lacking moral authority to correct his children.

After three years of voluntary exile, Absalom returned to Jerusalem, but his intentions weren't good. He knew that he was next in line for the throne of Israel, he made the decision to conquer the people and take control of the army and not wait until his father died to become the new king.

Absalom was ambitious and calculating, beside being very vain because he knew he was good looking. Nowhere in the Bible does it say that he is a man who feared God. On the contrary, the Bible says he was very proud, self-confident and ruthless; killing people to get what he wanted wasn't beneath him.

With the support of Ahitophel, one of King David's chief advisors, Absalom proclaimed himself king of Israel in Hebron, the place where Samuel had anointed his father, David, at the command of God. With this act, Absalom was not only acting against his father, who had not chosen him to be king, he proclaimed himself to be king, basically just taking control without any authority.

Because of Absalom's rebellion, David had to flee from Jerusalem so his own son wouldn't murder him. God allowed Hushai, another one of King David's counselors, to give plans to Absalom and then had those same plans given to David so that David would be saved. In the end, the two armies fought each other and David, acting like a father and not a general, asks his army to be gentle on Absalom and asked that they not kill him.

The experience of David's army helped them overtake Absalom; however over 20,000 men died in battle.

While Absalom was fleeing, his hair got caught on an oak branch and Joab, one of David's generals, killed him. Absalom's choices had tragic consequences for him and for Israel.

III. LESSON DEVELOPMENT
Introduction

Start the lesson by asking the students what important decisions they make during the week, and what would have happened if they had chosen differently. Say: "Did you make a decision that seemed fantastic and then it had a bad consequence?" (Let a few students tell their stories.)

Organize your students into 3 teams and give them the worksheet entitled "What Are The Consequences Of . . . ?" Have each team choose a picture. Then have the teams think about the consequences that they might experience if they chose one decision over the other. After they've had time to talk about it in their groups, have each group share what they came up with.

Developing the Bible Story

Say: "Today we're going to study the life of a young man who made some very wrong decisions that brought about fatal consequences. First, let's read the story and then we'll study it."

"If only I were king," thought Absalom, son of King David. Absalom was very proud of his good looks.

He wanted to take his father's place as king. He got up in the morning and stood on the side of the road, next to the palace door and asked everyone who came to appear before the king *"What town are you from?"* And they would respond, *"Your servant is from one of the tribes of Israel."* Absalom would then respond, *" 'Look, your claims are valid and proper, but there is no representative of the king to hear you.' And Absalom would add, 'If only I were appointed judge in the land! Then everyone who has a complaint or case could come to me and I would see that they received justice.'"*

One day, Absalom asked David's permission to go to Hebron to worship the Lord and David let him go. But in reality, Absalom didn't want to go worship, he wanted to build a palace there, because then he would be king of Israel in place of his father.

As soon as he left, secret messengers were sent throughout the tribes of Israel to say, *"As soon as you hear the sound of the trumpets, say, 'Absalom is king in Hebron.'"*

Absalom asked Ahithophel, one of David's counselors, to help him take the throne from his father. One day, a messenger came to David and told him, *"The hearts of the people of Israel are with Absalom."* So David said to all his officials who were with him in Jerusalem, *"Come! We must flee, or none of us will escape from Absalom. We must leave immediately, or he will move quickly to overtake us and bring ruin on us and put the city to the sword."* But David continued up the Mount of Olives, weeping as he went. David had been told that Ahithophel was among the conspirators, so he prayed, *"Lord, turn Ahithophel's counsel into foolishness."*

Hushai was one of David's loyal counselors. David told Hushai to return to Jerusalem and pretend that he was with Absalom. At first, Absalom was suspicious of him but Hushai said, *"Your Majesty, I'll be your servant; I was your father's servant in the past, but now I'll be your servant."*

Absalom wanted to make sure that his father couldn't conquer his kingdom again, so he asked for advice from Ahithophel. Ahithophel told him, *"I would choose 12,000 men and set out tonight in pursuit of David. I would attack him while he is weary and weak."*

Absalom also asked Hushai what he should do. Hushai knew that Ahithophel's advice would bring bad results for David, and that David and his men needed time to rest and plan their next move. Hushai told Absalom that he should wait until he could get together more men for his army.

So Absalom, and all of Israel. said: *"The advice of Hushai the Arkite is better than that of Ahithophel."*

When Absalom's army finally set out to fight David, David and his men were rested and ready for battle. *"King David commanded Joab, Abishai and Ittai, 'Be gentle with the young man Absalom for my sake.' David's army marched out of the city to fight Israel, the battle took place in the forest of Ephraim."*

"Now Absalom happened to meet David's men. He was riding his mule, and as the mule went under the thick branches of a large oak, Absalom's hair got caught in the tree. He was left hanging in midair, while the mule he was riding kept on going."

"When one of the men saw what had happened, he told Joab, 'I just saw Absalom hanging in an oak tree.'"

Then Joab, David's commander, took three javelins in his hand and plunged them into Absalom's heart while Absalom was still alive in the oak tree. When David heard of his son's death, he wept and said, *"O my son Absalom! My son, my son Absalom!"* David returned to his throne in Jerusalem very saddened.

(The italicized words are from 2 Samuel 15:2-4, 10, 13-14, 31, 34; 17:1-2, 14, 18:5-6, 9-10, 33.)

Review Questions:

1. What decisions did Absalom make?
2. What were the consequences in his own life because of his choices?
3. What were the consequences in the lives of his family and the city of Israel?

Life Application

Today, many people make decisions without first talking with God. The man who thinks he is wise makes decisions without thinking of the consequences until it's too late, much like Absalom. Many times, parents, want to make decisions for their children because they don't know what will happen if their children make the wrong decision, but this doesn't show their children how to make the right kinds of decisions either. In this story, it seems that David, like many fathers, didn't teach his children to make good decisions, and because of this, there were awful consequences.

IV. ACTIVITIES

Learning Activity

Activity: How Do I Make Good Decisions?

This activity will help your students understand some Biblical principles that will help them in making decisions that honor God. Read Proverbs 8:10-11 and have your students fill in the blanks on the worksheet and think more about what they've learned.

Memory Verse

Have the students repeat the memory verse for the unit out loud (1 Corinthians 10:31). Afterwards, ask each student to write one word of the verse on the board until it's complete. Explain how the verse relates to us in today's world. If Absalom had known this verse and had been obedient to God, maybe he would have ended up being king of Israel, and he would have had God's approval.

Ask one of your students to pray that God would help all of the class make wise decisions and that they would honor Him. Invite them to try to make good decisions this week and to come next time with a list of their experiences to share with the class.

DO THE RIGHT THING & YOU WILL BE DIFFERENT

I. OVERVIEW

Biblical Base: Daniel 1:1-20.

Memory Verse: *"So whether you eat or drink or whatever you do, do it all for the glory of God."* (1 Corinthians 10:31)

Biblical Truth: We can be confident that God will help us make wise decisions that will honor Him.

Lesson Objective: To help students stand firm in making the right choices, even if those decisions make them different from others.

II. TEACHER PREPARATION

The Babylonians were geniuses in administration. They ruled their huge empire with the help of the young people from the nations they had defeated, and trained in their culture. Daniel and his friends were chosen to be a part of their leadership training program.

As a part of their change to life in Babylon, Daniel and his friends were given new names. And both their old and new names had religious significance. However, changing their names didn't change their faith.

They were served the food and drink of the royal table as a sign of their future leadership. But Daniel and his friends refused to eat what they were given because it would defile them (make them unclean). The Bible doesn't say exactly why the food would make the unclean, but perhaps it was because the food was offered to the Babylonian gods as an offering, and if Daniel and his friends ate it, they would have been considered unclean according to Hebrew law.

This food represented a challenge to their faith, and God honored them because of their decision. King Nebuchadnezzar recognized that these young men were "different" from the other young men, and that's why he gave them positions of authority in his kingdom.

III. LESSON DEVELOPMENT

Introduction

Decisions That Honor God

Ask your students how they honored God with the decisions that they made this last week and what negative consequences they avoided.

Ask, "Who knows the story of Daniel and his friends and their decision about the King's food?" (If someone knows it, let them tell the class.)

Developing the Bible Story

We won't eat that!

Ask some of your students to participate by reading the dialogue of Daniel and his friends from their worksheet. (Assign one student for each character):

Narrator 1: Nebuchadnezzar, king of Babylon, declared war against Judah. Babylon won and took many of the Israelites prisoners. And the king told Ashpenaz, chief of his court officials, to bring into the kings service some of the Israelites of the royal family and the nobility. They were to be young men without any physical defect, handsome, talented and fast learners.

Narrator 2: King Nebuchadnezzar arranged for the young Hebrews to be educated for three years, and then to appear before him. Among the young prisoners were Daniel and his three friends, Hananiah (**Shadrach**), Mishael (**Meshach**) and Azariah (**Abednego**).

Ashpenaz: (speaking to Daniel and his friends): King Nebuchadnezzar has ordered that you all be educated in the language and literature of Babylon. You've also earned the privilege to eat and drink from the king's table.

Daniel: We are Israelites. Our God has demanded that we not eat this food. Please, serve us something else.

Ashpenaz: I would love to do what you've asked me, but I fear my master, the king, who assigned your food; and when he sees that you have become paler and fainter than the other men, he will condemn me to death. Plus, everyone else loves eating what he serves.

(Ashpenaz leaves and Daniel and his friends talk.)

Shadrach: Daniel, what should we do? We can't eat the food or drink of the king!

Meshach: No! If we do, we would be disobeying God.

Abednego: But, what will happen if we don't accept the food that has been offered?

Daniel: I don't know, but it doesn't matter what happens, I'll never eat or drink from the king's table!

Shadrach, Meshach and Abednego: Then neither will we!

Guard: It's almost time for dinner. Aren't you all excited! They are serving you food and drink from the king's table!

Daniel: Please, sir, can't you serve us vegetables and water?

Guard: But, why do you want to eat only vegetables

and drink only water when you can eat all of that?

Daniel: Because, this food will defile us.

Guard: Look, I just follow orders. Look at the others! They are enjoying the food. Just give it a try!

Daniel: Please test us for 10 days: give us nothing but vegetables to eat and water to drink. Then compare us to the other young men who eat the royal food.

Guard: (whispering) We'll try this, but only for 10 days. After that you'll have to eat the royal food. I'm going to go find you some vegetables and water.

Narrator 1: After 10 days Daniel and his friends had only eaten vegetables and had water to drink.

Shadrach: How do you feel Meshach?

Meshach: Fantastic!

Abednego: I agree! I'm imagining the face the guard will make when he sees us.

(The guard enters.)

Guard: The 10 days of trial have finished. Let's see how you guys look. Move closer to the window.

Daniel: What do you think?

Guard: Incredible! I wouldn't believe it if I wasn't seeing it with my own eyes!

Abednego: What is that supposed to mean?

Guard: That you guys look healthier and stronger than all of the other young men who have eaten the king's food!

Daniel: So, can we continue to eat our vegetables, sir?

Guard: Well of course! I'll order some more for all of you now.

Narrator 2: God blessed Daniel and his friends because they had the courage to remain steadfast in what they knew was right. God gave them knowledge and intelligence in reading and science.

Narrator 1: Three years later, the time had come for Daniel and his friends to be examined by King Nebuchadnezzar.

King Nebuchadnezzar: Ashpenaz! Have the four young men that you told me about come to me!

Ashpenaz: Yes, your majesty. At once!

Narrator 2: Ashpenaz brought Daniel and his friends before the king. The king talked to them and couldn't find anyone else in the group of prisoners quite like Daniel, Shadrach, Meshach, and Abednego; so, they remained in the service of the king. In any matter of wisdom or intelligence that the king consulted them on, he found them ten times better than all the magicians and astrologers that served in his kingdom.

Have the kids who didn't participate in the reading answer some questions related to the story:

1. *Why did Daniel and his friends not want to eat the king's food?*
2. *What tragic consequences could have happened to them if they had chosen to eat the royal food?*
3. *Why was the king's food defiled (unclean)?*
4. *Who helped Daniel and his friends to be able to be different and not defile themselves by eating the king's food?*
5. *If you had been in Daniel's place, would you have disobeyed a king's order?*

Activity

Put some fruit and vegetables on a plate, and some potato chips, sodas, candies and chocolate on another. Ask your students: "Which one would you choose to eat?"

Life Application

The example of these young men in Babylon makes us think about the situation that many kids, teens and young adults live in today. Daily they are seeking to feel accepted by their classmates and friends, and this pressures them to do or say things which sometimes don't agree with the will of God.

The church must be a strong support to our students so that they remain firm in their convictions and decide to keep themselves clean from sin, regardless of pressures from their friends. Their Christian values will be more valuable than what their friends may offer. Your students must have the ability to decide to obey God, even if it makes them different from those around them.

IV. ACTIVITIES

Activity: Follow The Leader

Have your students start at the letter "E" and follow the path, writing down each letter on the lines below the maze. They will soon discover the secret phrase: "Everybody's Doing It." Have them continue until they figure out the phrase. When they've figured it out, have them put an X at that point.

Encourage them to stay firm in their convictions and beliefs and not to get carried away by what others say and/or do.

Activity: Dare To Be Different

This is a certificate of commitment that each student, if they choose to, can fill in with their name. Those that do promise God to remain firm in their faith and won't participate with others in actions that don't please God. Ask a volunteer to read it with their name inserted: "I, (students name) have decided to stay firm in what I believe is good, even when others don't agree with me."

Memory Verse

This is the second to last class of the unit. Remind the students to memorize the Bible verse, and if they can say it during the next class, you'll give them a prize. (Prepare a small gift for the students who know the memory verse.)

Pray for all the students, that God gives them the ability to remain firm in their faith.

DECIDE TO MOVE FORWARD!

I. OVERVIEW

Biblical Base: Nehemiah 2:17, 4:21.

Memory Verse: *"So whether you eat or drink or whatever you do, do it all for the glory of God."* (1 Cor. 10:31)

Biblical Truth: The decision we make to follow and obey God should be so firm that we can resist any opposition.

Lesson Objective: To help students understand that in everyday life we must decide to continue to follow God, even when we face opposition.

II. TEACHER PREPARATION

Nehemiah was king Artaxerxes' cup bearer. One day Nehemiah heard that his hometown, Jerusalem, was in ruins; he was very sad and made the decision to help his people. He asked for the king's support to go to the city and authorization to rebuild the walls. Upon arriving in Jerusalem, first he saw the needs of the people, then he gathered them to motivate them to do the work together.

The people were encouraged and they organized themselves so they could get to work. In order to complete this huge project, men of all socioeconomic levels and of all ages participated. Bible commentators say that the walls were so wide that a horse-drawn carriage could be driven on top of them.

They also needed to reconstruct the gates of the wall, which was not an easy task. But the people decided to obey God and they continued following Nehemiah's instructions.

As Nehemiah and the people worked, three enemies arrived: Sanballat, governor of Samaria, Tobiah, the Ammonite official and Geshem the Arab. They came together to attempt to stop the construction of the wall because they were afraid that Jerusalem would rise up and be the most powerful nation.

Those three men challenged and threatened not only Nehemiah and the people but they also mocked God. They pressured the workers to the point that they thought that they could not complete the work, and they wanted to stop working on the wall. That would mean that they wouldn't fulfill the will of God.

But the people of Israel succeeded in rebuilding the walls of Jerusalem because they were obedient to God's commands and they worked together with Nehemiah, their leader. Then they ccould live safely, united to worship God, as a people chosen by Him.

III. LESSON DEVELOPMENT

Introduction

Ask your students if any of them made a decision that honored God during the week. Then ask them to tell the class their about their experience.

Activity: Giving into Pressure

In this activity, your students will see that they need to learn to make good decisions, even when they feel pressure from others around them not to. Say, "Will you give into peer pressure if your friends laugh at you? What about when they say they don't want to be your friend anymore?" (At the bottom of their worksheet, have your students circle the number they think is how they would respond to peer pressure.) Encourage them to talk about a time when someone pressured them to do something that wasn't right.

Developing the Bible Story

Let's Rebuild The Wall!

Read the Bible story to your students and have them follow along on their worksheets.

"Nehemiah, why are you so sad?" asked King Artaxerxes.

Nehemiah replied, *"Why should my face not look sad when the city where my ancestors are buried lies in ruins, and its gates have been destroyed by fire?"*

This city was Jerusalem. After king Nebuchadnezzar won the war against Judah, he burned God's temple and the doors into the city and tore down the walls.

The king asked Nehemiah, *"What is it you want?"*

Nehemiah prayed to God before he answered. He knew he had to be careful and say exactly what God wanted him to. *"If it pleases the king and if your servant has found favor in his sight, let him send me to the city in Judah where my ancestors are buried so that I can rebuild it."*

The king didn't want Nehemiah to leave because he was his cup bearer and he liked Nehemiah. But he gave permission for Nehemiah to go. When Nehemiah arrived in Jerusalem, no one was told what he had come to do. And one night when the moon was shining brilliantly, Nehemiah went out to inspect the wall and saw that is was in total ruins: there were no doors for its inhabitants to defend themselves against enemies.

The next day, Nehemiah got the whole city together and told them, *"You see the trouble we are in: Jerusalem is* in ruins, and its gates have been burned with fire. Come, let us rebuild the wall of Jerusalem, and we'll no longer be in disgrace."

The people replied, *"Let us start rebuilding."* And they began their work. Soon, some leaders of neighboring kingdoms heard what was happening. They didn't want Jerusalem to regain their strength and be a secured city again, so they went and tried to stop the construction.

They said, *"What is this you are doing? Are you rebelling against the king?"*

Nehemiah answered, *"The God of heaven will give us success."*

When Sanballat heard that they were re-building, he got angry. He made fun of Nehemiah and the people working with him. He asked, *"What are these feeble Jews doing?"*

Tobiah was at his side and said, *"What they are building – if even a fox climbed up on it, it would break down their wall of stones."*

Nehemiah and the city prayed and asked God to help them. So, they *rebuilt the wall until all of it reached half its height, for the people worked with all their heart.*

But when Sanballat, Tobiah, the Arabs, the Ammonites and the people of Ashdod heard that the repairs to Jerusalem's walls had gone ahead and that the gaps were being closed, they were very angry. They all plotted together to come and fight against Jerusalem and stir up trouble against it.

But Nehemiah and the people *prayed to our God and posted a guard day and night to meet this threat.*

Nehemiah said, *"Don't be afraid of them. Remember the Lord, who is great and awesome, and fight for your families, your sons and your daughters, your wives and your homes."*

Afterwards, a few people from the city stayed on guard while others built the rest of the wall. Those who carried material did their work with one hand and held a weapon in the other. They worked every day until the stars came out.

They finished the wall in 52 days. When word came to Sanballat, Tobiah, Geshem the Arab and the rest of their enemies that Nehemiah had rebuilt the wall and not a gap was left in it, the other nations were humiliated and recognized that God had helped them in their work.

SKIT

Ask your students what they liked the most about the story. Ask them to act it out, some can be the townspeople, others can be Nehemiah, Artaxerxes, Tobiah, Sanballat and Geshem. Once they're done, comment on the decision that the Jews took to reconstruct the walls of their city to protect themselves from their enemies.

Life Application

In reality, many Christians want to do good and honor God, but sometimes peer pressure can get the best of us. Our pact with God is tested daily; as long as we love Him with all our heart and want to honor Him with our decisions, we'll always have opposition, whether it's our family, friends, at school or at work.

The children are very pressured at school by their companions to conduct themselves in a way that is not worthy of God. This passage shows us how Nehemiah and the Jewish people, even though they were pressured by their enemies, stayed strong and completed the will of God

IV. ACTIVITIES
Learning Activity
Activity: Let's Build A Wall Of Protection

Tell your students: "Just like the people of Jerusalem built the wall to protect themselves from their enemies, you need to prepare yourselves spiritually to protect yourselves from any pressure or opposition you may feel from others. Do you want to be strong to stay firm in what you know is good? Then, "build a wall" now to protect yourselves!"

Look up these Bible verses and match the verses with the phrases:

1. Read and Study the Bible (C) James 1:22
2. Develop friendships and fellowship with other Christians (B) 1 Corinthians 15:33.
3. Pray Every Day (A) 1 Thessalonians 5:17

Ask a volunteer to read Nehemiah 6:15.

Remind them that Nehemiah had to pray and seek help from God to confront their enemies.

Now, tell the students to write on the board what oppositions they face when they obey God. Emphasize that God won't leave us if we depend on him all the time; obviously, we must do our part also.

Memory Verse

It's the last day for the students to memorize the verse for this unit. Ask some of them to say it out loud from memory. Remind them that this verse can help them when they have a decision to make, so they should not forget it. Remember to give each student who memorized the verse a small present for being in the Verse of the Month club.

Give an opportunity for several kids to give a testimony of how this unit has helped them make better decisions in their life. Encourage them to always stand firm in their convictions with respect to God, and never let anything make them give in to the temptation to disobey God or do something He doesn't like.

In your final prayer, mention each child by name and pray specifically for the needs of each one. Ask God to help the children follow Him and do what is good, even when they are confronted with opposition.

Prepare the following for a skit in the next lesson: Tunics/cloaks, a trashcan and bags to simulate suitcases or old suitcases. Ask your students if they have any of these items that they can bring to the next class.

WHO ARE THE PEOPLE OF GOD?

BIBLICAL TRUTH: God invites us to be part of his people and helps us to know their purpose.

UNIT OBJECTIVE

- That students learn the significance of a covenant with God.
- That students can identify some of their responsibilities as a member of God's covenant.
- That students believe that God is faithful to his covenant.
- That students rejoice in learning that Jesus made a new covenant, a covenant of love and forgiveness.

UNIT LESSONS

- » **Lesson 9** - The Covenant Family
- » **Lesson 10** - God's Covenant with His People
- » **Lesson 11** - The New Covenant

UNIT VERSE: *"'Though the mountains be shaken and the hills be removed, yet my unfailing love for you won't be shaken nor my covenant of peace be removed,' says the Lord, who has compassion on you."* (Isaiah 54:10)

Today we start a new unit, and like the previous ones, encourage your students to memorize this verse. Each lesson will provide ideas on how to help them memorize it. Give them incentives that will make them eager to learn it. Tell them that the first ones to memorize it will win a prize at the end of the unit.

At the end of the unit, you can have a special time with them celebrating a covenant between you and them.

Suggestions:

1. Lesson 9 is the start of the unit, bring the memory verse written out on a piece of poster board and put it in a place where everyone can see it in your classroom.

2. Bring in a robe or a cloak, something like a tunic, trees made of paper and bags or something to represent a suitcase for Developing The Bible Story.

3. For lesson 10, prepare 8 x 13 cm cards of two different colors for the Lesson Development. Also, draw a big picture of Mount Sinai at the time of the covenant, as well as one of the two tablets of the Law. Invite an adult to come and represent Moses and read the Bible story. Also, write the 10 Commandments on a large piece of paper.

4. For lesson 11, bring some herbs, grape juice in a cup or glass, bread or crackers, a piece of meat or a picture of all these things, a sheet or tunic/robe for Jesus and the figure of a lamb.

THE FAMILY OF THE COVENANT

I. OVERVIEW

Biblical Base: Genesis 12, 15, 17:1-21.

Memory Verse: " *'Though the mountains be shaken and the hills be removed, yet my unfailing love for you won't be shaken nor my covenant of peace be removed,' says the Lord, who has compassion on you."* (Isaiah 54:10)

Biblical Truth: People who make a covenant with God can be confident that he will be faithful to His promises.

Lesson Objective: To help students understand that God is faithful to fulfill His covenants; even if we don't see how He does it.

II. TEACHER PREPARATION

Genesis 12 and 15 cover a period of several years in which God revealed himself to Abraham many times and promised to bless him. God established a covenant with Abraham and his descendants to show that he intended to keep his promises.

In chapter 12, God tells Abraham to leave his land and go to a new land where he would be a foreigner and his descendants would inherit it forever.

In chapter 15, God formalizes his wish and makes a covenant with Abraham (this covenant is the first that would affect the people of Israel). God tells Abraham that they wouldn't possess the land immediately.

The covenant with God wasn't just with Abraham, but with all his descendants, who would have a unique identity. The Lord symbolized his participation and sealed the covenant by showing himself in a distinct way. He walked through the sacrificed animals with a flaming torch. This fire signified the presence of God.

We should remember that during this time in history in the valley of Mesopotamia, it was very common for covenants to be made between men and between nations. God used this form of personal relationship to make his promises relevant to Abraham and his descendants. Abraham relied on God's integrity.

III. LESSON DEVELOPMENT

Introduction

Write the Bible verse on the board or on a piece of poster board and hang it in your classroom. Designate two students to read Genesis 12:3 and 15:5. Then form groups of three of four students and have each team write on a piece of paper the promises that God made to Abraham. Hang these promises on the wall. Emphasize that God's promises are sure.

Activity: What Would You Do If God Told You...?

Give your students the worksheet for this lesson. Read Genesis 12:1 *"...go from your country, your people and your*

father's household to the land I'll show you." Ask, "How would you feel if God asked you to leave your home?" (Scared, nervous, unsure) "What questions would you ask him?" (Where are we going? What should I bring?) Have them write their responses and attach them to the "suitcase" or whatever you have to represent a suitcase. "What would you have to leave behind?" Have them write their answers and put them in or on a trashcan. "What do you think you'd miss the most?" (Accept the reasonable answers.)

Developing the Bible Story

You can act out this lesson. Designate students to read the part of each character. In the previous lesson, you were given instructions on what you would need for this.

Characters: Narrator (preferably the teacher since you are able to read it with enough enthusiasm to keep your students engaged.) The other characters are: Abraham, Servant 1, Servant 2, Sarai, Voice of God, Lot and Lot's wife. Start in one corner of the room. First, present the characters to the class and then start the dialogue:

Abram: Sarai, Lot, it's time for us to leave.

Servant 1: Where are we going? Why are we leaving? We like it here.

Abram: (in a strong voice directed toward his servants): Gather all of the sheep and cattle together. Guard everything we own. Lot and his family will also come with us. We are going to a new land that God will show us.

Servant 2: Let's hope God shows you a good land, my lord.

Narrator: Abram, Sarai, his wife, and Lot took their families with them and went to the new land (walk together towards the other side of the room, which would be Canaan).

Narrator: (Abram is walking): One day the Lord appeared to Abram and said,

Voice of God: "I'll give this land to your descendants."

Abram (with a happy face): I'll build an altar to

you, Jehovah! Because you have not only given me this wonderful land, but you will give me a son.

Narrator: Many years passed. Abram waited patiently for God to fulfill the promise to give him a son; but he and his wife were getting older and they had no children.

Sarai: Abram, we are getting older every day. I don't think it's possible for us to have children anymore.

Abram: (embraces Sarai): Don't worry, Sarai, we must trust in God!

Narrator: Abram walks away from Sarai, and God speaks to Abram.

Voice of God: "Don't be afraid, Abram, I am your Creator and your reward will be great!"

Abram: Lord, how will you keep your promises if you have not given me any children? You said that this land would belong to my children, but I don't have any children.

Narrator: God answered Abram.

Voice of God: "Look up at the heavens and count the stars; can you count them all? That's how numerous your descendants will be.

Narrator: Abram and Sarai waited for a long time and still didn't have children. One day, Abram walked alone and God told him:

Voice of God: "I'll make a covenant with you and multiply you greatly. You will no longer call yourself Abram, your name will be Abraham, because I have made you the father of many nations. And your wife, Sarai, will now be called Sarah. Many nations and races will come from you. I'll establish a covenant with you forever and I'll be your God."

Abraham: (bowing down with his face to the ground): Lord, I am one hundred years old. How can I have a child at this age? My wife is ninety years old, how can she have a child?

(Thank your students for their participation.)

Life Application

If we put ourselves in Abraham's place for a moment, maybe we can understand what he was going through. If your pastor or church leader asked you to leave your home to go live in a city where you didn't know anyone, it would be a very difficult decision.

Abraham's attitude was one of obedience; we need to obey the Lord's command like Abraham. We don't need to go very far from our homes or to another city; we all have people around us that don't know Christ, and that is where our task is (neighbors, peers at school, work, friends, parents, relatives, etc.).

IV. ACTIVITIES

Activity: What is a Covenant?

Give your students the worksheet entitled "What is a Covenant?" Have them unscramble the words to discover the definition of the word "Covenant."

A covenant is an (agreement). God (offers) the covenant to His people. God's covenant makes it possible to have a (good) (relationship) with Him. The covenant of God (affects) (many) people. God's covenant shows us his (love) and (faithfulness).

Clarify each key term and have the students explain it in their own words. Ask them about an agreement or covenant that they've made with someone. It's suggested that the following exercise be done to continue the class:

Activity: The Formation Of A Great Nation

Divide the class into several small groups and name a representative for each group. Then write the following sentences on the board. Ask your students to read the sentences in their groups and then discuss them to decide if they are true or false. Have them note their answers on a piece of paper: a 'T' if it's true and an 'F' if it's false.

Then have the representatives share their answers with the class. Discuss the sentences that are true.

- God initiated the covenant with Abraham (T)
- God chose Abraham to make the covenant with because Abraham was a good man (T)
- God told Abraham: "Don't leave your home so I can bless you." (F)
- God didn't promise anything to Abraham in the covenant that they made. (F)
- Abraham stayed calm the whole time that he waited for the son that God promised him (F)

Activity: God Keeps His Promises

Help your students with this worksheet. Have your students look up the Bible verses that are mentioned and then answer the questions.

Memory Verse

You can divide your class into 3 or 4 groups to help them learn the verse. Write the verse on a big piece of poster board and cut out each word. Then, have your students put the words in the correct order and hang it up on the board/wall.

Have a volunteer explain the verse; it's necessary for kids of this age to learn how to reflect and then give their point of view.

1. It's good for each student to participate in class so they can develop and be active.
2. Sing a song of thanksgiving to God.

To finish the class, pray with the children. Ask each of them privately to make a covenant with God (i.e. don't tell lies, be obedient, don't fight, etc …).

GOD'S COVENANT WITH HIS PEOPLE

I. OVERVIEW

Biblical Base: Exodus 19, 20, 23:20-33 and 24.

Memory Verse: " *'Though the mountains be shaken and the hills be removed, yet my unfailing love for you won't be shaken nor my covenant of peace be removed,' says the Lord, who has compassion on you.*" Isaiah 54:10.

Biblical Truth: Being a part of the covenant people of God brings its own responsibilities.

Lesson Objective: To help students identify some responsibilities that are established in a covenant with God.

II. TEACHER PREPARATION

Three months after they had left Egypt, the people of Israel came to Mount Sinai, where God called Moses to be the deliverer of his people (Exodus 3:12).

Israel knew God because of the miracles He performed, but they didn't have any rules to govern their life as a community. Every community needs laws that govern them so that they can live successfully.

For the Israelites, Moses was like a prophet and priest; God spoke to him and he made God's divine will known to the people. But the people themselves had no personal experience of being in God's presence.

The encounter between God and Moses was an extraordinary event, accented by thunder and lightning storms. The people had to purify themselves because they were going to be in the presence of the holy God.

Until now, Israel had practiced a life much like the other pagan people they had lived among; but now God was preparing them to be His chosen people, a people who would follow Him. This was the starting point for the difference between the people of God and the gentile people.

Israel needed rules to guide their relationship with God, as well as rules to govern their relationships with others. This covenant that God made with his people fulfilled those two great needs.

The church, formed by Christians, is God's people, and they have a mission to demonstrate to everyone outside the church the kind of life that is possible if they have a relationship with Him.

The rules that were given to Moses on Mount Sinai continue to be valid today and should be obeyed.

III. LESSON DEVELOPMENT

Introduction

Remind your students that we are studying the covenant that God made with mankind in order to include us in a holy relationship with him.

Prepare 8 x 13 cm cards in two different colors. On the cards of one color, have your students finish the phrase: "If you _____" (Example: If you clean the classroom…") On the cards of the other color, they will complete the phrase: "Then I'll _____." (Example: "I'll invite you out for an ice cream.") Then, pick up the cards and redistribute them. It will be fun to read what someone else has written on the cards.

At the end of this activity, discuss with your students what a covenant is and help them understand that there is always a promise and a condition, and to be able to fulfill that covenant, you must be responsible.

Activity: Responsibility?

Give your students the worksheet for this lesson and have them answer the questions.

- What is a responsibility? (An obligation or duty that we need to complete.)
- What responsibilities do you have? (Study, help around the house, read the Bible, be a good friend.)
- What responsibilities do children your age have? (Feed your pet, clean your room, do your homework.)

Developing the Bible Story

Prepare pictures of Mount Sinai at the time of the covenant, including the two stone tablets of the law. Ask your students if they've seen lightning and heard thunder before. Also, refer to agreements that are made when you celebrate an important event: like a wedding, a birthday, graduation party, etc. (How much does it cost to rent a location, buy the food, the refreshments, etc…)

Moses and all the Israelites set up their tents at the base of Mount Sinai. And Moses went up the mountain to meet God. Jehovah called to Moses from the mountain and said: *"This is what you are to say to the descendants of Jacob and what you are to tell the people of Israel: 'You yourselves have seen what I did to Egypt, and how I carried you on eagles' wings and brought you to myself. Now if you obey me fully and keep my covenant, then out of all nations you will be my treasured possession. Although the whole earth is mine, you will be for me a kingdom of priests and a holy nation.' These are the words you are to speak to the Israelites."*

Then Moses went back to the people and summoned the elders and he told them what God had said. And they, in turn, spoke to the people and told them what God had said. The people all responded together, *"We'll do everything the Lord has said."*

"On the morning of the third day, there was thunder and lightning, with a thick cloud over the mountain, and a very loud trumpet blast. Everyone in the camp trembled. Then Moses led the people out of the camp to meet with God, and they stood at the foot of the mountain."

"And God spoke all these words: 'I am the Lord your God, who brought you out of Egypt, out of the land of slavery. You shall have no other gods before me.'"

Moses told the people all that God had told him while he was on the mountain. God gave them the Ten Commandments and warned them about what they should and shouldn't do in order to be a holy people.

To narrate the story, invite an adult to dress up like Moses; present him to the class and then have him leave the classroom. Tell the students he went to Mount Sinai to talk to God. Then have him return and say, "God wants you to remember everything He did to free you from your enslavement in Egypt; now He wants to make a covenant with you all, so that you will be His people, among all the people the world. You will be my consecrated people and you will have many blessings if you fulfill the covenant."

Have your students answer, "We'll do what God commands."

Write on a large piece of paper the Ten Commandments. Point out the commandments that regulate man's relationship with God and those that regulate man's relationship with each other.

Commandments that regulate man's relationship with God:

1. You shall have no other gods before me.
2. You shall not make for yourself an idol. You shall not bow down to them or worship them.
3. You shall not misuse the name of the Lord your God.
4. Remember the Sabbath day by keeping it holy.

Commandments that regulate man's relationship with each other:

5. Honor your father and your mother so that you may live long in the land the Lord your God is giving you.
6. You shall not murder.
7. You shall not commit adultery.
8. You shall not steal

9. You shall not give false testimony against your neighbor.
10. You shall not covet . . . anything that belongs to your neighbor.

This was God's covenant with His people.

Activity: A Formal Covenant

Help your students find Exodus 19:4-8 in their Bibles and complete the scripture passage by writing in the missing words in the blanks.

" 'You yourselves have (seen) what I did to Egypt, and how I (carried) you on (eagles') wings and brought you to (myself). Now if you (obey) me fully and keep my (covenant), then out of all nations you will be my (treasured possession). Although the whole earth is (mine), you will be for me a (kingdom) of (priests) and a (holy) nation.' The people all responded together, '(We will) do everything the (Lord) has said.'"

The shepherd gives the sheep a place of honor on the right. Tell them that this covenant indicates responsibility from both parties, God and the Israelites.

Life Application

In a promise between two people, there are responsibilities that both people need to adhere to. God held up His end and fulfilled his promise to His people; but when Israel didn't do the same, God told them that they had just invalidated the entire covenant, and with it, they lost their blessings as well. Israel went into a downward spiral; their enemies defeated them because God stopped helping them win their wars.

Sometimes, because children have disobeyed their parents, they encounter difficulties. If we stop attending church on Sundays, we stop praising and worshiping God.

Not telling the truth also brings serious consequences, as well as when you take things that aren't yours, or you speak badly about another person.

IV. ACTIVITIES

Activity: Responsibilities of the People of God

Give each student the worksheet entitled "Responsibilities of the People of God." Ask them to make a list of responsibilities based on the commandment listed.

a. Second Commandment: The responsibility is to not worship idols.
b. Fourth Commandment: The responsibility is to attend church on Sundays.
c. Fifth Commandment: The responsibility is to obey your parents.
d. Eighth Commandment: The responsibility is to not take things that belong to someone else.
e. Ninth Commandment: The responsibility is to not speak badly of others (rumors, gossip).

Activity: A Class Covenant

As a learning activity to reinforce what they have learned in this lesson, make a covenant with your students so they can fully understand the concept of a covenant or pact. It could be:

A Covenant to Make Our Class Better:

- Come to class on time.
- Always bring your Bible.
- Always come looking your best.
- Complete your worksheets in a timely manner.
- Respect each other.

Memory Verse

Write the memory verse on poster board and cut out each word, like a puzzle. Mix up the pieces and then give each student a piece. Now have them come up to the board and put the puzzle pieces together so they can see the verse – use tape on the back of each piece so they will stick to the board.

To finish the class, have everyone hold hands and pray for your students out loud. Let them hear you ask God to help them to obey the covenant that they have made with each other.

NOTES:

A NEW COVENANT

I. OVERVIEW

Biblical Base: Luke 22:14-20.

Memory Verse: " *'Though the mountains be shaken and the hills be removed, yet my unfailing love for you won't be shaken nor my covenant of peace be removed,' says the Lord, who has compassion on you.*" Isaiah 54:10

Biblical Truth: Christ made a new covenant of love and grace.

Lesson Objective: To help students understand the blessings of the new covenant of grace, love, and forgiveness accomplished through Christ's death, and that they can be a part of it (conversion).

II. TEACHER PREPARATION

In this passage, Jesus and his disciples were about to celebrate the Passover. This was most important for the Jews, for they remembered the departure of the people of Israel from Egypt after four hundred years of slavery. On that day, the angel of death killed the firstborn of Egypt. The Israelites sacrificed a lamb without blemish, and with it's blood they marked the threshold of their doors so that the angel would not destroy them.

The passover feast consisted of bitter herbs, unleavened bread, and the roasted meat of a male lamb without blemish (Exodus 12:8).

This feast was celebrated on the 14th day of the first month, and was to be celebrated annually by all generations to teach their descendants how the people of Israel were liberated. (It's recommended to read Exodus 12: 1-36.)

This is the last lesson of this unit. Students have developed the concept of what a "covenant" is through the lessons of Abraham and Moses. But this lesson is about a different covenant, not with the people of Israel, but with us. It doesn't affect the condition in which we find ourselves, it turns out to be a covenant of forgiveness and love that gives us the freedom to approach God without hindrance. This is for everyone, without distinction of persons.

Christ represents the slain Lamb, establishing a new covenant with His blood shed on the cross for us. It cost him his body being broken and his blood being shed. Anyone who needs forgiveness no longer has to do anything, just accept Jesus as Savior and Lord of his life. When this happens, sinners receive forgiveness and begin a new relationship with God ... a new covenant.

III. LESSON DEVELOPMENT

Introduction

Review the previous lessons with the following questions:

- With whom did God make a covenant? (Abraham and Moses)
- What is a covenant? (Listen to your students' answers.)
- What event do we remember on December 25th?
- How do you celebrate this date at home?
- How do you celebrate your birthday?

Say: "Today we'll learn how the Jews celebrated a special feast, and how Jesus made that feast special for us."

Developing the Bible Story

For this lesson, as already stated, you will use the following: some herbs, grape juice in a glass or cup, bread or crackers, a piece of meat (or a picture of these), a picture of a lamb, a sheet or tunic for Jesus. (It's recommended to prepare these things during the week.)

Begin the lesson by showing the objects one by one to your students and tell them what they are. Then read the following:

When the people of Israel were enslaved in Egypt, God promised to deliver them, and in order to do that he sent the ten plagues. (Ask your students which plagues they remember: the river becoming blood, flies, lice, boils, etc.) The last of the plagues was the death of the firstborn, that is, the first born child. (Ask them to raise their hands if they are the oldest child in their family and tell them that they are the firstborn.)

In order for the firstborn of each Israelite family to survive, they were instructed to kill a lamb without blemish, the best of the flock, and with the blood of this animal paint the threshold (the edges) of the doors of their houses (show the picture of the lamb). They were to prepare a meal using bitter herbs (show them the herbs) and unleavened bread (show them the bread or crackers). This became a yearly celebration called the Passover, which was to remind the Israelites of how God freed them from Egypt.

When Jesus came to earth, he also celebrated the Passover with his disciples, but in a different way. Let's read Luke 22:7-23. (Act out this scene. You will represent Jesus by putting on the sheet or robe, and the children will be the disciples.)

Jesus said:

"*I have eagerly desired to eat this Passover with you before I suffer.*" (Take the cup, lift it and give thanks to God and then say): "*Take this and divide it among you.*" (Take the bread, say a prayer of thanks, break it and give pieces to your students and say):

"*This is my body given for you; do this in remembrance of me.*" (Have the children eat the bread. Then take the cup again and say):

"*This cup is the new covenant in my blood, which is poured out for you.*"

Explain that the disciples didn't understand what Jesus had said, they thought it was a different way to celebrate the Passover; But at that moment, Jesus made a new covenant - not with Moses or with Abraham, but with his disciples-and the cost of this new covenant was his blood shed on the cross for us.

IV. ACTIVITIES

Activity: Complete The Verse

Give each student a worksheet for this lesson and have them use their Bibles to complete the verses below. This is found in Luke 22:14-20.

"When the (hour) came, Jesus and his (apostles) reclined at the (table). And he said to them, 'I have eagerly desired to (eat) this (Passover) with you before I suffer.' . . . And he took (bread), gave thanks and broke it, and gave it to them, saying, 'This is my (body) given for you; do this in remembrance of me.' In the same way, after the supper he took the (cup), saying, 'This cup is the new (covenant) in my (blood), which is (poured out) for you.'"

Activity: What is the New Covenant?

Give your students the worksheet with the section entitled "What is the New Covenant?" Review with them the meaning of the work "Covenant." Ask a volunteer to look up Hebrews 8:13 and read it out loud. Then have them fill in the answers to the questions.

1. What is a covenant? A covenant is an agreement with God. A relationship with him.
2. What was the "Old Covenant"? Covenants that God made with Abraham and Moses for the people of Israel. They contained laws and rules for the people to live by that would make their lives better, and God's promise to protect them.
3. Look up Hebrews 8:13 and fill in the missing words in the following verse.

"By calling this covenant ("new,") he [Christ] has made the (first) one (obsolete); and what is obsolete and (outdated) will soon (disappear)."

Children of this age like to know about other countries; explain that no matter what country we are from, we can be part of God's people.

Activity: Add a Branch

Give each student the worksheet entitled "New People in the Old Covenant Made by God." In Romans 11:11-24, it says that the people who were not part of the people of Israel have been grafted onto the tree of the chosen family. Ask a student to read Matthew 28:19 and Acts 1:8. Ask: "Who is the new covenant for?" (For the whole world.) Make sure your students understand that they can be part of the new covenant. Have them cut out the branch, put their name on it and stick it on the tree.

Life Application

This lesson gives you a great opportunity to tell your students that Jesus shed his blood on the cross for every bad deed (sin) we have done (lying, stealing, disobeying, etc.). Show your students a needle and ask them if it would hurt if you put it into your hand. Then show them a nail and ask them to imagine what it would be like to have their hands and feet nailed to a board. Remind them that Jesus endured this because of his love for us. That was the covenant he was talking about, but he didn't do it only for his disciples, he wanted us all to have a covenant with him (point to each of your students and yourself), and he's waiting for you with open arms, YOU are very important to him.

Ask those who wish to be part of this new covenant with Jesus to raise their hands. Tell them that Jesus wants to enter into their hearts and forgive all that they have done wrong. He will always be with them to guide them to do good, and will reserve a place in heaven for each of them.

Lead those who raised their hands in a prayer to receive Christ as their savior.

Memory Verse

Since the verse has already been reviewed in previous lessons, you can write it on the board and read it out loud a couple of times; then erase a word and continue to read it, even though the word is not there: continue to erase more words (one by one) and say it as if the words were there. Continue until the whole verse is erased and your students can say it without seeing any of the words.

If you don't have a blackboard, you can write each word on a piece of paper and stick it on the wall, so that the students can read it. Take off one word at a time until all of the words have been removed.

JESUS, OUR KING

BIBLE TRUTH: Jesus is our living king.

UNIT OBJECTIVE:
Lessons from this unit will help students:
- Understand how the events of Jesus' last days on earth show that he is our Living King.
- Allow Jesus to be King of their lives.
- Understand that Jesus offers forgiveness when we fall into sin.
- Understand that someday Jesus will return to earth.

UNIT LESSONS
- » **Lesson 12** - Jesus, A Different King
- » **Lesson 13** - Jesus, The Risen King
- » **Lesson 14** - Jesus, A Forgiving King
- » **Lesson 15** - Jesus, The Living King
- » **Lesson 16** - Jesus, The King of kings
- » **Lesson 17** - Jesus, A Returning King

UNIT VERSE: *"At the name of Jesus every knee should bow, in heaven and on earth and under the earth."* (Philippians 2:10)
- At the end of the unit, have your students draw a picture of what this verse means to them.
- Offer small prizes as an incentive to the first children who memorize the verse.

Suggestions:
1. While studying this unit, encourage your students to prepare articles and make a newspaper mural. At the end of the unit, present the mural to your church family.
2. Cutout six crowns in yellow or gold paper. Write one lesson title on each of the crowns.
3. Let the Holy Spirit guide you and invite your students to accept Christ as their personal Savior.
4. At the end of each lesson, pray with your students. And on some occasions, ask one of your students to lead the class in prayer.

JESUS, A DIFFERENT KING

I. OVERVIEW

Biblical Base: John 12:12-19, Zechariah 9:9.

Memory Verse: *"At the name of Jesus every knee should bow, in heaven and on earth and under the earth"* (Phil. 2:10).

Biblical Truth: Christ came to become King of our lives.

Lesson Objective: To help students understand that the Jews didn't understand what kind of King Jesus was and the reason for his coming.

II. TEACHER PREPARATION

The idea of the kingdom is an important part of the Christian and Jewish faith. And Christ is the fulfillment of the covenant that God made with David.

The crowd that received Jesus in his "triumphal entry" to Jerusalem didn't understand the kind of king that Jesus was to be, nor did they understand his mission to save the world from sin.

In this context, the news about the ministry of Jesus increased the hatred and resentment of the Jewish Pharisees and leaders. The crowd followed him from Bethany to meet him. There was no way for Jesus to speak to them, because each time the crowd was bigger. However, he gave a signal about the kind of king he had come to be. He entered Jerusalem on a colt, the baby of a donkey.

In the time of Jesus, the donkey was an animal used by the nobility. A king who entered a city riding on a donkey, did so as a sign that he was coming in peace. The people cried without ceasing: "Hosanna! Hosanna!" Which means "Save us now!" With this cry of joy, the crowd recognized Jesus as the Expected Messiah. But they had a misconception of thee promise and prophecy. Instead of wanting Christ to save them from sin, they wanted to be liberated from the dominion and power of the Roman Empire, which had dominated them for years.

While the people rejoiced in acclaiming their conquering Messiah, some Jews were not so happy. The Jewish leaders owed their power and prosperity to the tolerance of Rome; they knew that the Romans would not stand for a rebellion, and Jesus, acclaimed by the multitude that emerged as the hope of freedom, could ruin everything. That is why the Sanhedrin ordered his arrest and plotted to kill him.

Even today, God has promised us freedom from the slavery of sin. He is the King of the heavens and is preparing his kingdom where we'll live if we are faithful to him. Jesus, the Son of God, wants to be the king of our life. Perhaps man doesn't understand the message of salvation or the gift of eternal life because of the sinful condition in which he finds himself, and he is crying out, like the Jewish people: "Hosanna! Hosanna!" But he doesn't want to accept Christ because he fears he will lose the privileges and comforts he has. We must accept him as the king and liberator of our lives. He is a mighty king who will reign for all eternity, and invites us to be part of his kingdom.

III. LESSON DEVELOPMENT

Introduction

Begin the lesson by talking with your students in a fun and enjoyable way. Ask the children if they have ever received the news that someone very important would be coming to their town. What do people do when someone famous or important is coming to town? (They fix the streets, clean, decorate, plan a fancy reception and publicly recognize the important person.) Have your students try to imagine how they would behave or what they would do if this was happening to them. (Let each child give their ideas.)

On the first page of this lesson's worksheet, you will find a dialogue between a child and a Pharisee. Invite two students to read it before reading the Bible story.

Developing the Bible Story

The King is Coming

"Is he coming?" asked a man.

"Yes!" said another. "He's not far from the city."

There were a lot of people in Jerusalem. Large crowds who had come to Jerusalem to celebrate the Passover Feast. Upon hearing that Jesus was coming to Jerusalem, they took palm branches and went out to meet him.

"Look! Jesus is riding on a donkey. It's exactly how the prophet Zechariah said that it would happen: 'Fear not, daughter of Zion; Your King comes, seated on a donkey's colt. Jesus is the Messiah!' Hosanna!"

"Blessed is he who comes in the name of the Lord, the King of Israel!" cried the crowd.

People cut palm branches and waved them. Some put them on the ground and made a path for Jesus.

"Is this the man who raised Lazarus?" a woman asked her friend.

"Yes!" her friend answered. "I was visiting Martha, Lazarus' sister, and I saw it! Jesus commanded Lazarus to come out of the tomb, and he had been dead for days."

"Anyone who resurrects someone is greater than the Romans and their armies," said another woman. "Surely Jesus will become king. He will defeat the Romans."

"I heard that his father, Joseph, is from the house of David. Perhaps this is how God will fulfill his promise to David. If Jesus becomes King, one of the descendants of David will have the throne! Is this not exactly what God promised David so many years ago?"

"Jesus must be the king that God promised us."

The crowd shouted again and again: "Hosanna! Hosanna!"

The Pharisees and other religious leaders were angry.

"This is all out of control. If Herod or the Romans find out, they will punish us all." So the Pharisees plotted to kill Jesus.

Life Application

Discuss with your students what happened when Jesus entered Jerusalem. Many people received the news that he was coming, and they told others, and they all prepared to receive him as king of the Jewish people.

Have your students read John 12:12-13 and discuss the passage by answering the following questions:

- Who went to the Passover Feast? (Large crowds)
- What did they have in their hands? (Palm branches)
- What did they say? (Hosanna! Blessed is he who comes in the name of the Lord!)

If you know a song with these lyrics, you can teach it to your students and sing it together.

Continue with the reading of John 12:14-16 and ask:

- How did Jesus come into the city? (Sitting on the colt of a donkey)
- Do you know what a donkey is? (Wait for answers)

At this time in history, kings usually rode into a city sitting on their horses because it signified power. But Jesus entered riding a donkey because it represented peace.

However, the people didn't care. Read John 12:17-19.

- Why did this not interest the people? (Because they remembered that he had resurrected Lazarus.)

The people were interested in seeing the works of Jesus. However, there were people who were not happy about all this.

- Who were they? (The Pharisees)

IV. ACTIVITIES

Activity: The King of kings

When Jesus entered Jerusalem, the Jews thought that he would be their earthly king. But the cross revealed that they had the wrong ideas about Jesus.

Have your students each draw a symbol that represents what Jesus really suffered. If they need clues, they can read John 19:2. For example, they could draw a "golden crown", put an X over it and draw a crown of thorns; or they could draw a "royal throne," with an X over it; or draw a "royal robe" with tears in it with a whip next to it.

Guide the children to think about the kind of king that Jesus is in their life. Ask: "How do you demonstrate in your daily life that Jesus Christ is your King and Lord?" "What do you do when things don't happen the way you want them to?"

Activity: What Should A King Do?

Give your students the worksheet entitled "What Should A King Do?" Have your students read the phrases that appear on the leaves of the palm branch. Then have them draw a heart next to the things Jesus did and an X next to the things Jesus didn't come to do.

Description of the work of the Messiah

- Lead the armies of Israel
- Deliver the Jews from the Roman Empire
- Take care of the poor
- Save God's people from their sin
- Restore the glory of King David
- Be forever King of the people of God
- Ensure that justice is carried out
- Punish the bad guys
- Become the High Priest in order to bring his people back to God
- Heal all the sick

When your students have finished their worksheets, encourage them to answer the following questions, which will help them understand why the Jewish people didn't understand the message of the Son of God, and the kind of king that Jesus came to earth to be.

- *What kind of king did the crowd expect Jesus to be?* (Explain to your students that the Jews, instead of wanting Christ to save them from sin, wanted a king to free them from the power and rule of Rome.)

- *Why did the crowd want a warrior king?* (They wanted someone to defeat the Romans and make Israel a free and independent nation.)
- *Why did the religious leaders fear Jesus?* (Because they were afraid that Jesus would try to be a military leader, and that a war would destroy everything, and they didn't believe that Jesus could win the war.)
- *Why did the crowd want a king who was a descendant of David?* (Because the Jews believed that God would fulfill the promise he made to David: That his descendants would reign.)

The Jewish people wanted the Romans to leave their country, and so they were frustrated when they discovered that Jesus wasn't what they expected.

At this point, draw your students attention to think about our **Biblical Truth:** Christ came to become King of our lives, and the **Lesson Objective:** To help students understand that the Jews didn't understand what kind of King Jesus was and the reason for his coming.

Say: "Many years ago, the prophet Zechariah made a prophecy (Zechariah 9: 9), and Jesus knew the prophecy and that he was the one to fulfill the prophecy. When he entered Jerusalem on a donkey, it was a way to show the people that he was the promised Messiah. But they didn't recognize him as the Messiah. When they realized that they were wrong and Jesus was not going to be the earthly king they had hoped for, they felt frustrated. They despised the King of kings and Lord of lords.

NOTES:

JESUS, THE RISEN KING

I. OVERVIEW

Biblical Base: John 20: 1-18

Memory Verse: *"At the name of Jesus every knee should bow, in heaven and on earth and under the earth."* (Phil. 2:10)

Biblical Truth: Christ is our Risen King.

Lesson Objective: To help students rejoice in knowing that Christ is our risen king.

II. TEACHER PREPARATION

In John 10:1-18, we find the precious story of the news of the resurrection of Jesus Christ. The Law of the Jews indicated that on the Sabbath, all Jews should remain in their homes remembering the law of Moses. Jesus' followers were very sad because they were remembering what happened to Jesus (his crucifixion).

At that time, it was very common for the tombs to have huge round stones at their entrance. The authorities wanted to make sure that no one would take the body of Jesus, so they sealed the tomb with a stone, and declared that opening it would be a crime. Mary Magdalene was very surprised when she arrived at the tomb and saw that it was open. She thought someone had stolen the body of Jesus, so she ran to warn the disciples.

As soon as she broke the news to Peter and "to the other disciple" (who is believed to be John), they ran to the tomb to see what was happening; they could not understand the resurrection of Christ.

The resurrection of Christ is not a fairy tale, nor is it a simple "happy ending" after the crucifixion. Because Christ is risen, we have the hope of eternal life. Your students should learn the significance of the resurrection. He is alive and active in our world; He is with us.

III. LESSON DEVELOPMENT

Introduction

Start with some review questions from the previous class. Remember that the central idea of this unit is to present Jesus as the Risen King.

Say: "What did we study last week about Jesus?" (The triumphal entry) "What kind of king did the Jews expect?" (A warrior king) "What kind of King was Jesus?" (A King of peace)

Continue the dialogue of what happened in Jerusalem in those last days before the crucifixion. Ask: "What happened next? (They crucified Jesus.) "What was so special about Saturday?" (It was the Sabbath and the Jews were to rest from their work.)

"The disciples were very anxious and wanted to go to the tomb. How do you thing they felt when they went to the tomb?" (Sad)

Activity: Walking to the Tomb

Give each of your students the worksheet for this activity. Ask them to draw an expression on the face describing how they would feel and to write in the bubble what they imagine they would think about on the way to the tomb.

Developing the Bible Story

This lesson can be narrated by your students, with everyone reading a section. Encourage your students to read it with the correct emphasis. As it's read, explain little by little what is happening.

He Lives!

Jesus' disciples and their friends were very sad because they had seen him die on the cross. Let's see how they felt on Sunday morning when they made a discovery that changed history.

"They have stolen the body of Jesus, it's no longer in the tomb!" cried Mary Magdalene, hurrying out. She went to meet Simon Peter and the other disciple and said to them, *"They have taken the Lord out of the tomb, and we don't know where they have put him!"*

"Calm down, Mary, tell us, what has happened?" Peter said.

"I went to the tomb early this morning and when I arrived I saw that the huge stone which sealed the tomb had been moved and the tomb was open. I looked inside and the Master's body was not there; someone must have taken it.

- Ask: "How do you think Mary Magdalene felt?" (Scared)

Peter and the other disciple left and went to the tomb. They ran together, but the other disciple ran faster than Peter and reached the first tomb. Then, Simon Peter came behind him, entered the tomb, and saw strips of linen lying there along with the shroud which had covered Jesus' head.

The two men were stunned, what had happened to the body of Christ? They had to decide what they were going to do. And the disciples returned to their homes.

- Ask: How do you think the disciples felt? (Frightened and angry)
- Read verses 5-8 out loud and ask: "Do you think they understood what was happening?" (No, they did not.)
- Ask a student to read verses 11-14 and ask: "What did Mary think?" (That someone had stolen Jesus' body.)

- Before explaining verses 15-18, ask your students to show the expressions they drew on the faces on their worksheets and have them tell how they think they would have reacted. Ask: "What would the disciples have thought if, when arriving at the tomb, they had found the body of Jesus?" (Accept multiple answers.)
- Continue with the Bible story:

"Now Mary stood outside the tomb crying. As she wept, she bent over to look into the tomb and saw two angels in white, seated where Jesus' body had been, one at the head and the other at the foot. They asked her,"

"Woman, why are you crying?"

She replied: *"They have taken my Lord away, and I don't know where they have put him."*

Having said this, she turned and saw Jesus standing there; but she didn't know it was Jesus.

Then Jesus said to her, *"Woman, why are you crying? Who is it you are looking for?"*

Mary didn't yet recognize Jesus, she thought he was the gardener, and she said to him: *"Sir, if you have carried him away, tell me where you have put him, and I'll get him."*

"Jesus said to her: 'Mary!'"

"Is it true?" Mary wondered when she heard his name. "Yes it's him! He is alive!" "Teacher!" Mary cried

Jesus said: "Go to my disciples and tell them that I live. Tell them, 'I am ascending to my Father and your Father, to my God and your God.'"

Again Mary ran to go and get the disciples.

"Jesus lives!" she said to herself. "They'll all be happy when they hear the news. Jesus really lives!"

Then Mary Magdalene went to give the disciples the news that she had seen the Lord.

Ask a volunteer to read verses 15-16 and ask: "How do you think Mary Magdalene felt when she recognized Jesus and realized that he was alive?" (Very happy and glad) (Italicized quotes from John 20.)

Life Application

Many people knew Jesus. Some were very sad because of his death, others less sad because they didn't believe he was the Messiah. Ask:
- "Who was sad when Jesus died?" (His mother, the disciples, his friends)
- "Who rejoiced when he died?" (Soldiers, Romans, Pharisees)

Put your students in groups of four, and give each group a sheet of paper and something to write with. Assign each of them one of the Bible characters below to represent. Have each group draw a face that expresses how their character felt when they found out that Jesus was resurrected. Give them the corresponding verses to help them:
- Mary, the mother of Jesus (John 19: 25-26)
- The Disciples (John 20:20)
- Roman Soldier (Matthew 27:54)
- The Pharisees (Luke 19:47)

IV. ACTIVITIES

Activity: A Reason To Rejoice

Give each student a worksheet entitled "A Reason to Rejoice." Have them draw a face representing their response to the good news of Jesus' resurrection and then write in the balloon what they would have thought. Then ask:
- "If you had been in Jerusalem and had found out that Jesus was alive, how would you have felt?"

Encourage your students to rejoice over the resurrection of Jesus Christ. Sing a song related to the subject. Continue the lesson by asking:
- "Do you remember another character in the Bible who was resurrected?" (Lazarus)
- "What happened to Lazarus years later? (He died again.)
- What is the difference between the resurrection of Jesus and that of Lazarus? (Jesus was resurrected on the third day and is still alive today.)

Although many people try to hide the fact that Christ has risen, we believe that he lives and his resurrection has changed history for all people, everywhere.

Activity: Our Risen King

Help your students complete the bottom of their worksheet. Make a list of how the disciples felt and what they believed about Jesus before the resurrection and after the resurrection of Jesus.

Before the resurrection, how did the disciples feel?
- *They were sad.*
- *They felt alone.*
- *They believed that Jesus was like any man.*

After the resurrection, how did the disciples feel?
- *The disciples felt happy.*
- *They and other people believed that Jesus is the son of God.*

Explain that the most important thing is that the resurrection of Jesus is the proof of our salvation; and that we'll have eternal life with him.

Read John 14:19 and find the promise that Jesus gave to those who believe in him: *"Before long, the world won't see me anymore, but you will see me. Because I live, you also will live."*

Memory Verse

Do an activity with your students to help them memorize the memory verse.

Before finishing the class, ask your students to give reasons why the resurrection of Jesus makes us happy.

1. It gives us the opportunity to receive salvation.
2. We can have eternal life.
3. We have the promise that we'll someday be resurrected with Christ.

Explain that these promises are for everyone who accepts that Jesus died in their place and receives him as their personal Savior.

Ask if any of your students want to accept Jesus as their Savior and lead them in prayer. End the class by praying for each of your students.

JESUS, A FORGIVING KING

I. OVERVIEW

Biblical Base: John 13: 36-38; 18:15-18, 25-27; 21:15-17.

Memory Verse: *"At the name of Jesus every knee should bow, in heaven and on earth and under the earth."* (Phil. 2:10)

Biblical Truth: Christ offers forgiveness to all who sin.

Lesson Objective: To help students understand that Christ always offers forgiveness to those who sin, and he invites them to follow him.

II. TEACHER PREPARATION

Peter was always an impulsive and violent disciple. He seemed to always be willing to obey and follow Jesus. Before being arrested, Jesus talked with him. Peter was so sure of his love and dedication for his Master that he wanted to follow him, and thought that he was capable of even giving his life for Jesus.

Jesus, confronting Peter's confidence, announced that Peter would deny him three times. What did that mean in Peter's life? Was he not always the tenacious and courageous disciple who stood beside Jesus? The other Gospels tell us that Peter was offended by this question, and immediately responded that he would gladly die for Jesus, but he would never deny him. Peter was sure of his faith in Jesus! But the Lord knows beyond our thoughts.

Luke shines a little more light on this situation (Luke 22:31-34). Jesus said that Peter's faith would be tested, but that he himself would help strengthen Peter's faith and that Peter should then help the other disciples. How great is the love of God for our feeble humanity!

But now, when Jesus had been taken prisoner and Peter's courage was not enough, he stayed far away from his Master. When confronted by a maid standing near the door of the high priest's residence, he lied, saying: "I don't know this Jesus." A second and third time Peter was asked the same thing: "Do you know Jesus?" And each time he lied. When he gave the same answer for the third time, the rooster crowed and Peter remembered the words of his Master. What a difficult situation for him! When his own life was threatened, fear seized him and his faith was diminished. When Jesus was resurrected, the disciples again regained their composure. But shortly before his ascension, Jesus had a personal conversation with Peter. There, Jesus showed him his forgiveness and asked him to continue being his disciple.

In the conversation between Jesus and Peter, we find the excitement of having reconciliation with Jesus. Some of His followers had already accepted Jesus as their Savior and learned to follow Him. But when they failed, they felt guilty and perhaps were tempted not to continue. This lesson helps us understand that God is generous and offers forgiveness, even when we fail.

III. LESSON DEVELOPMENT

Introduction

Begin the class by asking your students to share the name of one of their friends who lives close to their homes (friends at school and at church).

Ask them if their friends have ever offended them and for what reason. You can be specific and use the names that the students have shared. (i.e. "Johnny, has your friend Sam ever offended you?")

Give them the worksheet entitled "How Could You?" Ask: "What do you think happened to this girl to make her feel rejected by her friend? What kinds of things can happen between good friends that can harm their friendship? How do you feel when a friend does something that offends you?" Encourage your students to answer honestly and accept all answers.

Developing the Bible Story

You can ask a young man to dress up as Peter and read Peter's part, and you can be the narrator. To get your students' attention, act out the parts indicted and use the tone of voice indicated in the lesson.

Narrator: Peter took a stone, threw it hard and saw it fall into the sea.

Peter: Ah, the sea of Tiberias! *(Use crumpled paper wadded up to be the stone and do what's indicated.)* What beautiful memories I have of the times I came to fish on these beaches! So many things have happened lately! The arrest of Jesus, his crucifixion . . . final, terrible things.

I'll never forget what happened. Jesus appeared to us a third time in this same place. He even served us breakfast.

Then he said to me, "Simon, son of John, do you love

me more than these?" *(Use a soft tone of voice.)* I was surprised by the question, but I said: "Yes Lord, you know that I love you!" *(Use a tone of voice that represents security.)*

Jesus said to me, "Feed my lambs."

I miss the company of Jesus a lot. But you know? Again he asked me, "Do you love me?" I could not understand why he asked me again, but I replied firmly: "Yes Lord, you know that I love you!" Jesus said to me, "Take care of my sheep." However, after the second question I began to remember things that had happened recently, when suddenly Jesus fixed his eyes on me and asked me again: "Simon, son of John, do you love me?" I could not answer, I remembered that I had not been a loyal friend to him, I had denied him! *(Now the tone of voice should reflect despair.)* I didn't deny him once, but three times. In the most difficult moments I was not with him. I got up quickly and stretched out my arms for his forgiveness and said: "Lord, you know everything, you know that I love you." But this time, I said it with great humility, recognizing that Jesus' love for me was much greater than what I felt for him. Jesus said to me: "Feed my sheep."

Narrator: Peter always remembered this scene, but not with sadness, but with deep gratitude to the Lord for his mercy. He became one of the disciples who worked hard to spread the gospel.

Activity: Quiz Time?

Make sure each students has a worksheet with today's story on it. At the bottom, read the questions and have your students underline the correct answer for each question.

1. When did Jesus and Peter have this conversation?
   a. Before the crucifixion.
   b. After the resurrection. (Correct)
2. What did Jesus mean when he asked Peter, "Do you love me more than these?".
   a. That Peter loved Jesus more than he loved anyone else. (Correct)
   b. That Peter was the best disciple.
3. What was Jesus asking of Peter when he said, "Feed my sheep?"
   a. To guide his followers. (Correct)
   b. To represent Christ on earth.
4. How many times did Jesus ask Peter a question?
   a. six
   b. three (Correct)

Life Application

Gather your students together and reflect on the following questions:

- Why do you think Peter denied Jesus? (Because of fear, shame.)
- Do you think Jesus forgave Peter? Why? (Yes, he forgave him because he loved him.)
- Do you think that we Christians today also fail Jesus? (Accept all answers.)

IV. ACTIVITIES
Activity: Lets Talk With God

To begin this activity, tell your students to think about a time when they have done something wrong (taking something that was not theirs, telling a lie, disobeying their parents, etc.). Then, give them each the worksheet entitled "Let's Talk With God." Have each student write in the section below the words "Dear God" a prayer to the Lord asking for forgiveness for the sin they mentioned.

Teach them that, as Christians, we should not fail Christ, but if we do, we can immediately ask for His forgiveness, and trust that He will forgive us.

Talk to your students about how they can experience God's forgiveness through Christ, the Forgiving King. Explain that they must first recognize that they have disobeyed God (sinned) and that they need to be forgiven.

We should approach God in prayer with a sincere heart and ask Him to help us to be obedient.

Lead your students in a time of prayer. Some may wish to accept Jesus as their Savior, or perhaps those who have already accepted Him need to ask for forgiveness.

Encourage them to ask Jesus for forgiveness and to ask Him for help to not sin again. Close the class by thanking God for His love and forgiveness, even when we have strayed from His path.

Memory Verse:

It's very important that your students are memorizing the verse. Ask them to repeat it a couple of times before leaving class.

JESUS, THE LIVING KING

I. OVERVIEW

Biblical Base: Luke 24:36-49.

Memory Verse: *"At the name of Jesus every knee should bow, in heaven and on earth and under the earth."* (Phil. 2:10)

Biblical Truth: Jesus is our King.

Lesson Objective: To help students know that Jesus is our King and the Son of God.

II. TEACHER PREPARATION

After Jesus' death, the disciples were very frightened. The hope that they had in Jesus had disappeared. They had expected the salvation of Israel, and what they got instead was the death of their Teacher.

However, there were rumors that Jesus was alive and had appeared to Mary Magdalene, and two disciples on the road to Emmaus said the same thing.

Jesus appeared to his disciples suddenly in their midst, surpassing the laws of nature. He greeted them saying: "Peace to you!" indicating that he came to bring them comfort, courage and hope.

At that moment, Jesus invited the disciples to look at the scars of the wounds in his hands and in his feet and his sweet voice said to them: "I am myself! Touch and see." This removed the fear that, for a moment, had occupied a place in the heart of each of the disciples. That is why Jesus ate; to show them that he was not a spirit, but that he had risen after defeating death and the grave; thus showing his infinite power.

He also reminded them of what he had taught them, and now the disciples understood the Scriptures.

Children at this age don't quite understand what death means. So it's important for them to know that death is not the end of a person, but a step that we'll all take.

The plan of salvation is God reconciling the world to himself because the world is separated from him because of sin. But to achieve this plan, Jesus, God's Son, had to suffer the cross of Calvary, the contempt of others, the cruel suffering, and the confrontation with death itself. The forces of evil thought that they would destroy Jesus, but scripture says that Christ would suffer and rise from the dead on the third day.

God the Father resurrected Jesus, his Son, and he will never die again. He lives today and will live triumphantly for eternity.

III. LESSON DEVELOPMENT

Introduction

Talk with your students and remind them about some of the important things Jesus did while he lived with his disciples during his ministry on earth. For example, feeding the five thousand, calming the storm, etc. Highlight the power of God through His Son Jesus. (If possible, have or draw pictures of these miracles.)

Explain that Jesus also announced his death and resurrection. Choose one of your students and place a blindfold over their eyes so they cannot see. Then have their classmates try to explain a classroom object to them without saying what it is. Have them describe it's characteristics. When they are done with their description, ask the blindfolded child if they understood what the class was describing. Most likely, their answer will be no. They could not understand when their eyes were blindfolded.

Take advantage of this moment to explain to your students that this is like how the disciples were understanding Christ. They were not prepared to fully understand or comprehend the mission of the Son of God.

Developing the Bible Story

Ask for volunteers to read the parts of Jesus, James, Andrew, Peter, and John. You will be the narrator.

It's a Spirit!

Narrator: It's the third day since the crucifixion of Jesus. Ten of his disciples are talking in a room. The doors are closed and locked because they are afraid of the authorities.

James: All this is so confusing. We saw Jesus die. We saw him buried.

Andrew: Yes, and a large stone covered the entrance of the tomb. They sealed it and put soldiers there to guard it.

James: But Mary Magdalene says she saw Jesus, and that he spoke to her early this morning.

Andrew: Peter and John went to the tomb. They saw that the stone to the entrance of the tomb was rolled to one side and that the tomb was empty.

Peter: Yes! The tomb was empty and the grave clothes were left there!

John (thoughtfully): The shroud covering the face of Jesus was perfectly folded and separated from the rest of the cloth.

44

Peter: Exactly!

Andrew: And now Cleopas and his friend, who were going to Emmaus, say that they saw Jesus on the road.

James: And not only that! They invited him to dinner with them! And when He blessed the bread, they recognized Him.

Andrew: What does all of this mean?

Narrator: At that very moment, Jesus appears among them and speaks to them.

Jesus: Peace to you!

James: It's a spirit!

Andrew: Yes, it's a ghost!

Jesus: Why are you troubled and why do doubts rise to your mind? Look at my hands and my feet, I am myself. Touch me and see, a spirit or ghost doesn't have flesh and bones, as you see I have.

Andrew: Look! There are the scars of the nails with which they crucified Him!

Peter: It looks so real! Maybe we're all dreaming.

James: It's too good to be true!

Jesus: Do you have something to eat?

John: Yes, here is some fish left-overs from dinner.

Peter: Look, he's eating! A spirit cannot eat!

James: Jesus is alive!

John: Yes, he has risen!

Jesus: This is what I told you while I was still with you: Everything must be fulfilled that is written about me in the Law of Moses, the Prophets and the Psalms.

Andrew: It's Jesus, there's no doubt about it!

Narrator: Then Jesus opened their minds so they could understand the Scriptures.

Jesus: "This is what is written: The Messiah will suffer and rise from the dead on the third day, and repentance for the forgiveness of sins will be preached in his name to all nations, beginning at Jerusalem."

All Together: We'll do everything you say, Lord!

Continue to talk with your students about the role play. Ask them the following questions and listen to their answers. Encourage all your students to participate Ask them:

- "What happened after Jesus died?" (Jesus was buried in a tomb by Joseph of Arimathea.)
- "To whom did Jesus appear?" (First to Mary Magdalene, then to the disciples on the road to Emmaus, and finally to the eleven disciples who were meeting together.)
- "What did Jesus show his disciples and why?" (He showed them the scars on his hands and feet so that they would be convinced that he was not a spirit.)
- "What did Jesus command his disciples to do?" (To stay in the city of Jerusalem until they were

filled with the power of the Holy Spirit.)

Life Application

Now, reflect on what it means to us that Jesus has risen. Emphasis that this is the basis of our faith. We should always be joyful in this knowledge and tell others about our faith in Jesus.

ACTIVITIES

Activity: They Saw Him!

The disciples had trouble believing that Jesus was alive. But after they all saw him, they wanted to announce the good news. Give each student the worksheet entitled "They Saw Him" and have them choose a character from the sheet. Instruct them to read the Bible verses for their character and then write down what that person supposedly told others about Jesus' resurrection.

The characters are:

1. A Roman soldier sent to guard the tomb of Jesus. [Matthew 27:65 and 28:2-4] (There was a great earthquake, the tomb was opened and an angel appeared.)

2. Mary Magdalene. [John 20: 11-16] (The body of Jesus was gone. I asked him, when I thought he was the gardener, where they had put Jesus, but that man was Jesus! He lives!)

3. Cleopas on the Road to Emmaus [Luke 24:13-16, 28:31] (This man joined us on the road as we were walking. We invited him to dinner with us and when he prayed for the meal, we realized it was Jesus.)

4. Simon Peter [John 20:1-7] (I went to the tomb and saw that Jesus' body had disappeared. Later, he appeared to us while we ate. Jesus was sad because we didn't believe he was alive.)

IV. ACTIVITIES

Activity: Jesus Lives Today!

Give each of your students the worksheet "Jesus Lives Today!" Have three students read the verses out loud. Then have each student write on their postcard what they think Jesus is doing for all of humanity today.

Memory Verse

Divide the class into 2 groups and have each group form a circle. Each group will say one word of the Bible verse, taking turns until they say the whole verse. For Example:

- Group 1: will start - they will say "At"
- Group 2: "the"
- Group 1: "name"
- Group 2: "of"

When they're done, do it again, but now let group 2 start. To end the class, pray aloud, thanking God for the resurrection of our Lord, Jesus Christ.

JESUS, THE KING OF KINGS

I. OVERVIEW

Biblical Base: John 14:1-4, Acts 1:1-11.

Memory Verse: *"At the name of Jesus every knee should bow, in heaven and on earth and under the earth ."* (Phil. 2:10)

Biblical Truth: Jesus is King.

Lesson Objective: To help students accept Jesus as the King of their lives.

II. TEACHER PREPARATION

After His resurrection, Jesus appeared to His disciples over a period of forty days. He reminded them of his teachings about the kingdom of God. However, they still didn't understand the spiritual nature of this kingdom. They hoped that Jesus would restore the kingdom to the Jews and destroy Roman power. With these ideas in mind, they asked him, "Lord, are you at this time going to restore the kingdom to Israel?"

This shows us what kind of king they thought Jesus would be. They didn't understand that the earthly ministry of Jesus was over, and now a new period was beginning, not only for them, but for all of mankind.

Jesus left heaven and came into the world to be the sacrifice for our sins. He is now the only one worthy to intercede for us before the Father. His work, as the second person of the Trinity, continues today. Jesus promised to return to earth one day, to bring those who know Him to be with Him forever.

Jesus also promised the disciples that after he returned to heaven, he would ask the Father to send them the Comforter who would be with them forever (John 14:16-18). The disciples obeyed Jesus and returned to Jerusalem to wait for this Comforter. He had shown his disciples that He was the expected Messiah, the King of kings who had conquered death and went to the throne of God with power and glory.

The most important decision in the life of a human being is to recognize that Jesus must be the king of their lives. Your students are already at an appropriate age to understand what Christ's salvation means, and accept or reject it.

III. LESSON DEVELOPMENT

Introduction

Remind your students of some of the aspects of Jesus' resurrection. What day did he rise from the dead? (The first day of the week, Sunday.) How was the tomb left after Jesus' body was placed in it? (Sealed) Who announced his resurrection? (The Angels) Emphasize how wonderful and amazing Jesus' resurrection is.

Ask: "What does the resurrection of Jesus mean to you?" (Accept all answers.)

Emphasize the idea that Jesus demonstrated his power and glory when he was resurrected, and that is the proof to Christians that he is the King of kings.

Developing the Bible Story

Have the worksheets with the story on them for your students. Ask them to follow along as you tell the story.

It was late, Peter and Andrew could not sleep.

"These last forty days have been incredible," Peter said. "So many things have happened! I can't help but wonder what could be waiting for us next."

"I know what you mean, Peter," Andrew said.

"When we believed that Jesus would be crowned king, great problems began. I'll never forget the fear I felt when the soldiers took Jesus away. Nor can I stop thinking about how he suffered."

"We were very afraid of the Romans, too!" said Peter.

"Yes, and now we're more afraid of them. The news of Jesus' resurrection is spreading throughout Jerusalem. The city officials find themselves increasingly angry, trying to hide the truth of the resurrection. They say that one of us stole his body. But let them say what they want. Jesus is alive! We have seen Him and so have many people in different places. How can they deny that he is the Messiah?"

"I'm still very afraid of what the Romans will do to us if we don't keep quiet," Andrew said.

Peter asked, "Do you remember the words of Jesus before he was crucified? He said: *'Don't let your hearts be troubled. You believe in God; believe also in me.'*"

Andrew relaxed, sighed and said, "I remember something else that Jesus told us; He said that he was going to his Father's house. Peter, do you remember his words? *I am going there to prepare a place for you . . . I'll come back and take you to be with me that you also may be where I am.'*"

"I've thought about that a lot," Peter said. "And I also remember what he told us when he ate with us: " *'Don't leave Jerusalem, but wait for the gift my Father promised ... but in a few days you will be baptized with the Holy Spirit.'*"

Andrew looked confused. "Yes, I know," he said. "I'm not sure what he meant, but did you hear how he talked about his kingdom?"

Then those who were gathered around him asked, *"Lord, are you at this time going to restore the kingdom to Israel?"*

"It is not for you to know the times or dates the Father has set

by his own authority. But you will receive power when the Holy Spirit comes on you; and you will be my witnesses in Jerusalem, and in all Judea and Samaria, and to the ends of the earth.'"

"After he said this, he was taken up before their very eyes, and a cloud hid him from their sight. They were looking intently up into the sky as he was going, when suddenly two men dressed in white stood beside them. "Men of Galilee," they said, "why do you stand here looking into the sky? This same Jesus, who has been taken from you into heaven, will come back in the same way you have seen him go into heaven."

Life Application
Activity: The Kings That People Follow
A king is a person or a thing that people put first in their lives. Give your students the worksheet for this activity and tell them to look at the banners each child is holding in their hands - Who is their king?

Figure 1 - Money
Figure 2 - Friends
Figure 3 - Celebrities

Ask your students to draw on the blank flag a person or something that is very important to children their age that they try to follow like a king. Remind them of the triumphal entrance to Jerusalem.

Ask:
- "What kind of king did the people think Jesus was?" (A warrior king)
- "What did people do when Jesus entered the city?" (They praised him and left their robes on the ground for him to walk on.)
- "What did the people shout?" (Hosanna to the son of David!)

However, after his arrest, they were disappointed when He was crucified. Even his disciples were frightened. Do you remember what Peter did? (He denied Jesus three times.) Only John was at the foot of the cross. But after three days, Jesus rose from the dead and appeared to His disciples. They regained their confidence in him!

IV. ACTIVITIES
Activity: Jesus Is King
Have your students refer to the worksheet that has the story on it. Find the section entitled "Jesus is King." Read the sentences out loud. Have your students draw a happy face in the circle next to the sentences that are correct and a sad face next to the incorrect sentences.
- The disciples understood all that Jesus said. (Incorrect)
- Christ returned to heaven as our King. (Correct)
- Christ promised to send the Holy Spirit to help the disciples tell others that He is the King. (Correct)
- The kingdom of Christ is a kingdom of love. (Correct)
- Christ came to earth to be a king. (Incorrect)
- Our King Jesus will come again. (Correct)

Now lead your students in a time of reflecting on their relationship with Jesus as King. Ask them:
- "How can Jesus become our King?" (If we ask him

into our hearts.)
- "How will we know what Christ wants from us?" (By reading the Bible, His Word.)
- "Will we be different from other people?" (Yes, in our behavior and attitude.)
- "Do you want Jesus to be the King in your life?"

This is a special time - let the Holy Spirit guide you. Invite the children to accept Christ as King of their life; he is inviting them. Ask:
- "Have you already invited Jesus to be your King?"
- "Do you want to ask Him right now? (If some children say yes, tell them to come forward.)

You can ask another adult to stay with the rest of the class to maintain order. Ask the children who said "yes" the following questions:
- "Do you recognize that you have disobeyed God and done evil?"
- "Do you feel sorry for the bad things you have done?"
- "Have you asked God to forgive you?"
- "Do you believe that God can forgive you?"
- "Have you asked Jesus to be in control of your life and to be your King?"

Once they have answered these questions, pray with them to accept Christ as their savior.

Activity: Let's Review
Give your students the worksheet for this activity. Let them work in groups. Read Acts 1:1-11 out loud with them and let them answer the questions.
- How many days was Jesus with his disciples after his resurrection? (Forty)
- How do you think the disciples felt to have Jesus with them? (Happy)
- Did Jesus demonstrate great power when he rose from the dead? (Yes)
- What did Jesus promise? (That the disciples would receive power to be his witnesses.)
- What did the disciples ask Jesus? (Verse 6 -- Will you restore the kingdom of Israel?)
- What kind of kingdom were the disciples thinking about? (An earthly kingdom)
- In what kind of kingdom does Jesus reign? (The kingdom of our hearts.)
- What happened next? (Jesus ascended into heaven.)
- What did the angels promise? (That he will return the same way that he left.)

Let the groups compare their answers and determine a single answer for each question. Let the children pray in their own words. Then ask them to repeat a prayer that you lead. Mention each child's name during your prayer. If any of them accepted Christ, tell the pastor of the church and his parents so they can follow up.

Memory Verse
This is the second to last lesson of the unit and students should have the verse memorized. Encourage those who don't know it to come with it memorized next week.

JESUS, THE RETURNING KING

I. OVERVIEW

Biblical Base: Matthew 25:31-48; 1 Thessalonians 4:13-18.

Memory Verse: *"At the name of Jesus every knee should bow, in heaven and on earth and under the earth."* (Phil. 2:10)

Biblical Truth: Those who faithfully follow Jesus will always be joyfully awaiting his return to this world.

Lesson Objective: To help students know that they can joyfully wait for the return of Christ.

II. TEACHER PREPARATION

The second coming of Christ is described in language that reveals the greatness of the event. Jesus will come in great glory, surrounded by angels, acting as our righteous Judge, and will face all the people. *"He will separate the people one from another as a shepherd separates the sheep from the goats."* (Matthew 25:32)

The shepherd gives the sheep a place of honor on the right, and the rest are put to the left, and they won't receive the reward of the righteous. The Bible points out to us the glorious invitation of Christ: "Come, you who are blessed by my Father; take your inheritance, the kingdom prepared for you since the creation of the world" (Matthew 25:34).

After this invitation from Jesus, he points out the reasons why men are rewarded: "Truly I tell you, whatever you did for one of the least of these brothers and sisters of mine, you did for me." (Matthew 25:40)

In regards to this, Professor Ralph Eade says the following:

"It seems better to maintain that, in the incarnation and in his compassionate love for all men, Christ is referring to suffering humanity as my brothers. Works of mercy are not the basis of eternal reward and punishment. But can any man read these words of Jesus and believe that a Christian would dare to be indifferent and inactive when his neighbor is in need?"

It's clear that good works come from the heart of a person who has a good relationship with God.

As we have seen in previous lessons, the resurrection of Christ is the basis for our resurrection. Paul, in 1 Thessalonians 4:13-18, encourages the members of the church of Thessalonica. They were waiting for the announced return of Christ, and wanted to be alive at the time of His second coming. However, when some of their members died, they lamented that they would not see the glory of Christ's return. That is why Paul reminds the believers that those who had already died in Christ would also be resurrected. We too have the same hope of a final resurrection through Jesus Christ.

III. LESSON DEVELOPMENT

Introduction

Take time to review this units "Unit Objectives." Invite volunteers to tell the class what the different lessons were about. You can bring some objects to represent each lesson that will help your students remember the lessons.

Emphasize the idea that Jesus is King of kings now; he was not only a king at the time that this part of the Bible was written, but He also is king today.

Ask your students if they have family members who have traveled to another country or city, and say: "How did you communicate with them?" (By telephone, letters, postcards, etc.) "Did they return from their trip?" "How did you feel when they said they would come back?" (Discuss these questions for a few moments with your students. Then explain how Jesus promised to return and give us a special gift.)

Developing the Bible Story

Call five volunteers to the front; give each one a number. As you read the following descriptions, have the student act out what you read (like a mime). At the end of the performance, congratulate them with applause.

Student 1. The disciples loved Jesus as an intimate friend. They recognized Him as the Messiah and were filled with fear and confusion when He was arrested.

Student 2. After being arrested, he was subjected to interrogation, different punishments, and finally crucified.

Student 3. On Friday afternoon, Jesus died on the cross and was buried. The disciples were very sad and scared because they didn't know what would happen.

Student 4. On the third day after Jesus died, they discovered that the tomb was empty. And they were filled with excitement and joy.

Student 5. Then, Jesus appeared to the disciples several times; He helped them understand who he was and what would happen in the future.

Activity: Time Line

Give your students the worksheets that contain the story and the time line. They will need to cut out the boxes on the right that represent the important events in the lives of Jesus and his disciples. Then they need to glue or tape them in the correct order, according to what happened before the resurrection.

1. A period of three years: Jesus' ministry
2. A sad night: the arrest of Jesus
3. A dark day: the crucifixion

Continue the Bible story. The resurrection of Christ begins a new stage. Find Acts 1:3 in your Bible and read it to the class. Have your students get into groups and give them the worksheet "Forever With Jesus." Then ask the following questions, (these are the questions on the worksheet). The group that answers the most questions correctly wins:

- **How many days was Jesus with his disciples after his resurrection?** (Forty days)
- **What did Jesus do during those forty days?** (He told them about the Kingdom.)
- **What did Jesus tell them before he left?** (To wait for the gift that the Father had promised.)
- **What was that promise?** (That He would send the Holy Spirit: Acts 1:8.)
- **What would the Holy Spirit give?** (Power to be Christ's witnesses.)
- **Where would they be witnesses?** (In Jerusalem, in Judea, in Samaria, and to the ends of the earth.)
- **When Jesus ascended to heaven, what did the angels say?** (*"Why do you stand here looking into the sky? This same Jesus, who has been taken from you into heaven, will come back in the same way you have seen him go into heaven."* Acts 1:11)
- **How do you think the disciples felt?** (Joyful to know that Jesus would return.)

Continue with the Time line activity. Have your students glue the remaining 3 boxes in the correct place on the time line according to what happened after the resurrection:

1. About forty days after the crucifixion: Jesus' ascension.
2. The promised gift: the coming of the Holy Spirit.
3. A future event: Jesus' return.

There may have been many questions about Jesus Christ's return to earth. Remember what he taught about his return. Look in your Bible at Matthew 25:31-35. Explain that the Son of man is Jesus. Continue by asking

the following questions to the groups:

- **What will the Son of Man do?** (He will separate the sheep from the goats.)
- **Where will each go?** (The sheep on the right, goats on the left.)
- **Why reward those on the right?** (Because they loved those who were in need; they fed the hungry, gave water to the thirsty, etc.)

Ask: "What group would you like to be in - the sheep or the goats?" (Wait for the children's answers and see if they understood the meaning.) In this passage, Jesus shows us that by doing good to those who are in need, we reflect our love for Him. However, this is not the only requirement to get the reward he has offered.

Life Application

Reflect with your students about the importance of Christ's return to earth.

Ask: "Why do you think it's important for Christ to return?" (To be able to live with him for eternity.)

Tell the students that no one except the Father knows the day and time that Jesus will return to Earth. That is why we must be prepared all the time by obeying his commands.

Give you students a sheet of paper and colored pencils and have them draw a picture of what they imagine the second coming of Christ will be like. Tell them that you will display their drawings in an important place in the classroom, as a way to encourage everyone with the good news of Christ's return.

IV. ACTIVITIES

Activity: A Close Inspection

Give your students the worksheet called "A Close Inspection." Ask them to examine the city scene for a moment. Then ask them the following questions:

Would you like to live in this world forever? (List your students answers on the board, both positive and negative.)

Read aloud Acts 1:4-8 and ask: "What did Jesus promise his disciples? How would the Holy Spirit help them after Christ returned to the Father in heaven? In Acts 1:9-11, what promise did the angels give to the disciples as they watched Jesus ascend to heaven? How do you think the disciples felt about the words of the angels? To conclude, have a time of prayer with your students, asking the Lord for help so that you all can live properly while awaiting his return.

Memory Verse:

This is the last lesson of the unit, ask the students if they know Philippians 2:10. You can encourage them by having a small gift for the students that have the verse memorized.

UNIT 5 GUIDE

THE BIRTH OF THE CHURCH

BIBLE TRUTH: The growth of the church is a work of the Holy Spirit.

UNIT OBJECTIVE:

- That students know that the source of a Christian's power comes from the Holy Spirit, giving them the desire to testify to others about Christ.
- That students understand that the early church gives us an example of Christian love and fellowship.
- That students understand that it's necessary to obey God rather than men.
- That students understand that a church filled with the Holy Spirit is a powerful influence in the world.

UNIT LESSONS

- » **Lesson 18** - The Birth of the Church
- » **Lesson 19** - The Love of God and the Church
- » **Lesson 20** - We Obey God
- » **Lesson 21** - Nothing Stops the Church!

UNIT VERSE: *"Now you are the body of Christ, and each one of you is a part of it."* (1 Corinthians 12:27)

For students of this age, the concept they have of what "power" means is different from what the Bible teaches us. For many of them, it's about exerting the strength to do something and achieving victory this way. They think that the one who has the most strength is the one with the greatest power.

Through these lessons, we'll learn that the Christian can acquire power, but only through the Spirit. This is not acquired through physical strength, but through a heart that is surrendered to God.

The power of the Holy Spirit will help us love and obey God, as well as love and care for our neighbor, just as Christ takes care of his people.

Let's help students understand how the Christian church grew and how it's important to us today. Your students also need to know the importance of the work of the Holy Spirit in our lives.

Suggestions:

1. For lesson 19, you will need to bring some newspapers. Distribute them among the students, and let them create something with the newspaper (boats, book cover, hat, airplane, etc.).
2. For lesson 20, plan ahead of time and invite two adults to come to your class to participate in the Bible story by dressing up like Peter and John. Also invite some young people to represent other characters in the story.
3. For lesson 21, prepare a small box and put something inside it to make it heavy. Wrap it as a gift, with a pretty bow.

THE BIRTH OF THE CHURCH

I. OVERVIEW

Biblical Base: Acts 1

Memory Verse: *"Now you are the body of Christ, and each one of you is a part of it."* (1 Corinthians 12:27)

Biblical Truth: The Holy Spirit helped in the formation and growth of the early church, allowing many nations to hear the message of Christ. Today, with the Holy Spirit's help, Christians can be witnesses of Jesus, sharing the plan of salvation He has for the world.

Lesson Objective: To help students learn the role that the Holy Spirit played in the birth and development of the church.

II. TEACHER PREPARATION

Luke, the "beloved physician," wrote the book of Acts. It's a continuation of his account in the book that bears his name. After his resurrection, Jesus appeared to his disciples, and speaking to them he opened their minds so that they understood the Scripture and how they were fulfilled, for it was necessary for him to die and be resurrected on the third day, and to preach repentance and forgiveness of sins to all nations, beginning in Jerusalem (Luke 24:46-47).

The disciples witnessed these events, for they walked with Jesus, received his teaching, observed the wonders he did; they saw the resurrection of the dead and also witnessed Jesus' ascension. The command not to leave Jerusalem suggests that the disciples were planning to return to Galilee. The religious leaders of Jerusalem had instigated Jesus' death, and it was believed that they would persecute his followers.

But Jesus had other plans. He commanded them to wait in the city for the promise of the Holy Spirit: *"But you will receive power when the Holy Spirit comes on you; and you will be my witnesses in Jerusalem, and in all Judea and Samaria, and to the ends of the earth."* (Acts 1: 8)

This describes the power and work that the church of Jesus Christ has to do, the evangelization of the world. Power comes with the Holy Spirit. Every person filled with the power and presence of the Holy Spirit will feel the impulse to carry out God's command. The Great Commission cannot be fulfilled without this power.

And while this was happening, the disciples persevered - they prayed constantly. They clung to prayer until the answer came (Acts 1:14; Luke 11:13).

What was the result? When the day of Pentecost came, and they were all together, a sound came from heaven like a strong wind, which filled the whole house. Those who were present saw what looked like tongues of fire rest on each one of them. And they were all filled with the Holy Spirit and began to speak in different tongues (languages), which were recognized by the Jews who were in Jerusalem from every nation under heaven.

Fire, like the wind, symbolized the divine presence of the Holy Spirit that purifies and sanctifies (Exodus 3: 2; Malachi 3: 2-3). When the Holy Spirit fills the heart of the believer, it gives him power and purity. No one can have one without the other. What does this mean? That supernatural power was available to transform lives and equip the church to obey the Great Commission.

Their hearts had been purified so that they could be filled with the Holy Spirit, and thus bring the knowledge of the gospel to every nation. Today this truth continues to be fulfilled. When the believer seeks the power of the Holy Spirit in his life, the Holy Spirit fill them and helps them to be witnesses of Jesus.

III. LESSON DEVELOPMENT
Introduction

The book of Acts begins with the appearance of Jesus after his resurrection to his disciples, and his instructions to them during that 40 day period. Jesus reaffirms the promise of the Holy Spirit so that the disciples will be filled with the power of God to preach and make known the message of salvation. How do we present the concept of the Holy Spirit to students?

Write the following Bible verses that describe the Holy Spirit on the board or a poster:

John 14:16 - Remains with us forever

John 14:26 - Teaches us and reminds us of the words of Christ

John 15:26 - Testifies about Christ

John 16:8 - Convinces the world about sin

John 16:13 - Guides us in truth

Romans 8:26 - Intercedes for us

Talk to your students about these verses.

DEVELOPING THE BIBLE STORY

Give your students the worksheet with the Bible Story on it so they can follow along as you tell the story. They will also need it for an activity later in the lesson.

Like A Strong Wind

Jesus' disciples were sitting together, talking about what they would do now that Jesus had ascended to heaven.

"I want to get out of Jerusalem," one of them said. "I'm tired of waiting for something to happen. If the Romans decide to come after us, they will easily find us!"

"We can't go," said another. "Jesus said to us, 'Don't leave Jerusalem, but wait for the promise of the Father.'"

"But how long do we have to wait?"

"I thought Jesus would be back soon! And it's been a week since we saw him go to heaven; And those men dressed in white told us that he would come again, in the same way that he left. I think we should go to the place where we saw him ascend. What do you think?"

"Jesus told us to wait in Jerusalem, and that's where I'm going to stay!" said Peter, standing among the crowd of 120, encouraging them to continue praying. He said to them, "Jesus promised us that after the Holy Spirit comes, we'll be witnesses for him. Please have patience."

As the group prayed, suddenly a sound came from the sky, like a strong wind blowing, and it filled the whole house.

"What is that?" they wanted to know.

Then tongues like fire appeared, resting on each one of them. And they were all filled with the Holy Spirit. Outside were Jews from all the nations under heaven visiting Jerusalem. When they heard the noise many went to where the disciples were to see what was happening.

They were astonished and amazed, saying, *"Aren't all these who are speaking Galileans? Then how is it that each of us hears them in our native language?"*

"This is incredible!" said another.

Others mocked the disciples and said, "They must be drunk."

Then Peter proudly stood up and with a loud voice began to preach to them.

"Fellow Jews and all of you who live in Jerusalem, let me explain this to you; listen carefully to what I say. These people are not drunk. If you had listened to what the prophets said, you would know that God promised to send His Spirit to all people, and this is what is happening here today. *Therefore let all Israel be assured of this: God has made this Jesus, whom you crucified, both Lord and Messiah."*

"Oh no!" cried some. "We crucified the Promised One!" Then they asked the apostles, *"Brothers, what shall we do?"*

Peter said to them, *"Repent and be baptized, every one of you, in the name of Jesus Christ for the forgiveness of your sins. And you will receive the gift of the Holy Spirit."*

"Those who accepted his message were baptized, and about three thousand were added to their number that day." (Italicized words are direct quotes from the NIV Bible.)

Life Application

Ask the following questions to review the lesson:
- What do you think Peter might have thought before receiving the Holy Spirit? (I have no value, I denied Jesus three times.)
- What did he do after receiving the Holy Spirit? (He spoke without fear and preached the gospel with power and authority.)
- Can Christians today be filled with the Holy Spirit? (Yes)
- What can we do to make this happen in our lives? (Repent of our sins, Acts 2:38.)

IV. ACTIVITIES

Activity: A Human Silhouette

Give your students the worksheet with the silhouette of a human body. Explain how the church is the body of Christ (Romans 12:4-5). The body has only one head (Christ), and within it is the brain, which is responsible for sending messages to the body, telling it what to do (run, breathe, eat, sleep ...).

To get on our feet, the brain sends orders to two hundred muscles, and then they all work together. Christ is the head of the church. And since the Father (God), the Son (Jesus Christ) and the Holy Spirit are one, they will guide us (the body of Christ) in truth and tell us what we should do (Colossians 1:18).

When you're done with the explanation, let the children color in the body however they'd like to.

Memory Verse

Review the verse (1 Corinthians 12:27). Write it on the board/poster and repeat it with the students. Then cover a word and repeat the entire verse, including the missing word. Continue covering words until they can say it by heart.

Activity: If I Was Peter

On the worksheet that has the Bible Story, have your students find the section titled "A Big Change" and have them write in the speech bubbles what Peter said in each situation. Ask them, "How could Peter's reactions be so different? What caused the big change?" (Have them share their responses with the class.)

Activity: He Makes The Difference

Give your students the worksheet that says "He Makes The Difference." The church uses many names and symbols to refer to the Holy Spirit. Say: "How do these symbols represent the Holy Spirit?"

Dove: peace and love
Fire: purification, cleanliness
Wind: power
He is also comforter, guide, and defender.

Activity: The Birth of the Early Church

On the same worksheet, have your students find and circle the words hidden in the word search. The words are listed below the word search.

GOD'S LOVE WITHIN THE CHURCH

I. OVERVIEW

Biblical Base: Acts 2:42-47, 4:32-37

Memory Verse: *"Now you are the body of Christ, and each one of you is a part of it."* (1 Corinthians 12:27)

Biblical Truth: The first Christians were characterized by their unity; having everything in common, they shared their possessions to meet the needs of others.

Lesson Objective: To help students understand that a true Christian will look out for his neighbor. We are part of the body of Christ and therefore we have a responsibility to others.

II. TEACHER PREPARATION

After Pentecost, the apostle Peter was transformed by the power of the Holy Spirit and spoke powerfully to the Jews who there, giving them his testimony and exhorting them to repent of their sins (Acts 2:38). Those who accepted what he said were baptized, and that day about three thousand people were added to the church.

This was a great demonstration of the power of the Holy Spirit. The new converts persevered in the teachings of the apostles. All of them were of the same mind, they loved each other in a brotherly way and shared with one another what they had (1 Peter 3: 8). The Holy Spirit united these people in community. They lived as if everything belonged to the Lord. When there was a need, the Christians sold their possessions and gave the money to the church to be used to meet that need.

Today, as Christians, we have a duty to our neighbors. As part of the body of Christ, we have a responsibility. Christ is the head of the church and we, his believers, can be his hands to give to and help the needy, his feet to go preach the Word, or his ears to listen and console.

Can anyone understand the message of Christ if he is hungry or cold? No. But if we meet their need, they not only understand, but will see the love of God reflected in our actions.

III. LESSON DEVELOPMENT
Introduction

Using the illustration of the human body, ask your students what part they would like to be and why. Explain that each part of the body has a specific purpose (1 Cor. 12: 11-18), and each part is important because of it's specific purpose. The body alone doesn't work - it needs the coordination of all of it's parts/members.

Tell the following story:

Juan's family had just arrived in the neighborhood; He was sad because he had to leave his friends, his school and his beautiful home to move there.

Since they had arrived at this new place, he had continually heard his parents arguing.

His father was unemployed, so the family had many needs. At his new school, Juan could not concentrate on his classes. All he could do was think about the problems his parents were going through and wondered why they argued so much. "When Dad had a good job, they had hardly argued and they loved each other. I try to do my best to help in the house, but everything stays the same."

One day after school, a new friend named Miguel invited him to play. Juan turned down the invitation, but Miguel insisted, because in Sunday school he had learned that God loves us and wants us to love one others. In Sunday School, the teacher had encouraged them to think about how they could show God's love to another person. Miguel prayed and thought about Juan, who was always sad and lonely, so Miguel decided to become his friend.

Juan told him that he could not play because he had to help his family with the chores at home. "Don't worry, I'll help you with that and then we can do our homework together," Miguel proposed.

While they were working, Miguel found out about the situation that Juan's family was facing. When Miguel went home, he told his parents what had happened to his friend. "I feel very sad, they have almost nothing. Is there anything we can do?"

"Yes, do you remember the story of the child who shared his food of five loaves and two fish with Jesus?" asked his father.

"Yes, I remember," Miguel agreed. "The child gave his lunch to Jesus and Jesus blessed it. Many people were fed because God multiplied the food."

"How about we start there," his dad said.

"What a good idea," said his mother. "I'll prepare a basket of fruit and vegetables from our garden. I also have some food already prepared that you can share. Why don't you go with your dad to Juan's house and take it all with you?"

Miguel was so excited! It felt good to share with others!

Juan's family was amazed at the gift and thanked

53

Miguel and his father. With the help of Miguel's dad, Juan's dad got a new job. They also began attending church. There, in communion with the other believers, they learned about the love of God because they saw it in the lives of the Christians at Miguel's church.

Activity: The Power of Friendship

Give each student a worksheet entitled: The Power of Friendship. Ask the following questions regarding the story. Have your students write the answers on their worksheets.

1. Why was Juan sad? *(He had to leave his friends and his school, and his parents argued a lot.)*
2. Why did Miguel want to help Juan? *(Because he is a Christian and had learned that God loves us and we should love one another.)*
3. How did Miguel help Juan? *(He helped with his chores, and when he learned about Juan's situation, he asked his parents how they could help. Miguel and his parents took food to Juan's family and helped them.)*
4. What was the result of this action? *(Juan's family learned about the love of God and how he cares for us through the testimony of Miguel's family.)*
5. How does this story relate to the life of the early Christians as recorded in Acts 2:43-47? *(The first Christians shared all they had with each other; they ate together with glad and sincere hearts, and meet together every day in the temple courts to praise God.)*

Before moving on to the Bible story, give your students the first page of the Christian Friendship Club. Tell your students to think about whether they would like to start a group like this, and write down the rules they would like for their group, so the rules can be used in an advertisement.

Developing the Bible Story

Christ's Best Friends

Ask students to follow the reading in their worksheet as you read the lesson.

"Peter, can you come to my house today?" a new convert asked. "My friends and I would like to speak with you about Jesus. You know so much about him and his teachings."

After Peter's first sermon, 3,000 new Christians needed a place to grow stronger in their faith. They devoted themselves to the apostles' teachings, to fellowship with one another, and to the breaking of bread and to prayer. They were filled with awe at the many signs and wonders performed by the apostles.

People gathered in the temple to worship. Some small groups met in houses. Sometimes people meet in a place outside the temple called "The Porch of Solomon" to tell each other their problems, and to enjoy time together.

"Hello Joseph!" said Matthew. "Is there anything I can do for you?"

"I'm fine, thank you," replied Joseph. "I just came to give you something; I sold some of my property and would like to give the money to someone who needs it."

"Thank you, Joseph," said the apostle, "we will call you Barnabas instead of Joseph, because Barnabas means 'Son of Encouragement', and it's a perfect name for a man as generous as you are."

Joseph smiled.

The multitude who believed what Peter shared were of one heart and one soul. None of them said that they had anything of their own, but they shared everything with each other.

Then Joseph said, "I am not the only one who has sold their property to help those in need. We all must love and help each other, just as Jesus commanded."

Life Application

Ask the following questions from the Bible Story and ask students to think about what they can do to have better fellowship with other children.

1. What made it possible for there to be fellowship among these people? *(The Holy Spirit had filled them and they had faith in Christ.)*
2. How can we become friends and have fellowship with others? *(By showing them love, lending them our toys, sharing our food, etc.)*
3. What do we need for there to be true Christian fellowship? *(To have Jesus Christ in our hearts and to ask the Holy Spirit to help us.)*
4. What else do you need to have true Christian fellowship? *(A faith united in Christ and the desire to have the Holy Spirit direct our lives.)*

IV. ACTIVITIES

Activity: Discover the Bible Verse!

Explain to your students how they can discover the Bible verse by using the code.

Activity: What Can I Do?

Give each student a piece of newspaper and ask them what they can do with it. Allow them to use their imagination (ex. paper boats, hat, book cover, towel, etc.). Explain that just as we have the opportunity to use a newspaper to make different things, God can use us to accomplish different things. In what ways can we be useful to God? (We can tell about him by giving, helping the needy, visiting the sick, etc.) Let them draw pictures of things we can do to be useful to God. Make a mural with all the drawings.

Memory Verse

Divide the class into two groups: boys and girls. Let the girls start by saying the first word of the memory verse and then the boys the second. Continue until they say the entire verse.

WE OBEY GOD

I. OVERVIEW

Biblical Base: Acts 4

Memory Verse: *"Now you are the body of Christ, and each one of you is a part of it."* (1 Corinthians 12:27)

Biblical Truth: No one can stop the Gospel message.

Lesson Objective: To help students understand that although the first Christians were persecuted, they continued to preach the gospel of Christ, and the church continued to grow.

II. TEACHER PREPARATION

In his first sermon on the day of Pentecost, Peter accused the Jews of having killed Jesus, and declared that he had risen (2:23-24). Miraculously, the result of this was the conversion of 3,000 people. Peter escaped persecution.

But after he had healed a well-known paralytic man and then in his second sermon condemned the Jews for the murder of the Messiah and announced to them that in Jesus there is resurrection from the dead, and then approximately 5,000 men heard the word and believed (4:4), the Sadducees decided that it was too much. This provoked the first persecution. The result was the imprisonment of Peter and John.

The Sadducees were one of the most important religious groups in Israel during the time of Jesus. They believed neither in resurrection nor in eternal life. They were more concerned about appearing good than with obeying God. When Peter and John were asked about this act of healing, Peter made the most significant statement found in the book of Acts (4:12): "Salvation is found only in Jesus Christ." Religious leaders marveled at the freedom and authority with which Peter and John spoke without any theological training. They could not deny the authority and power of the Holy Spirit in the apostles' lives, for the crippled man had been healed.

After warning them to not speak about Jesus again, Peter and John were released. But the apostles ignored this command saying, "Judge whether it's right before God to obey you rather than to obey God; Because we can't stop talking what we have seen and heard."

After being released, they met with the brothers of the church and told them what had happened. Together they prayed to God, but they didn't ask for protection, but rather for courage to go and preach. When they prayed, the place where they were gathered trembled; And they were all filled with the Holy Spirit and spoke the Word of God without fear.

When believers pray, they receive a response from God. Even in the face of the persecution towards those who obey God's commands, the work of salvation will continue to be made known, because that is the will of God. That is why we should not fear.

III. LESSON DEVELOPMENT

Introduction

Ask the students if they remember what was talked about in the previous class, and what they might have done to help others and what the result was. Say: "How did it feel to help someone in need?" (If anyone was disillusioned because they were not thanked for what they did, tell them that it's more important to obey God and fulfill his commands than to receive recognition from people.)

That's what Peter and John did. They decided to obey God and the result was that many people heard the message of salvation and believed; although there were also many who didn't want to accept it. But for the apostles, the most important thing was to obey God and not men.

Activity: Prison Bars

Give each of your students the worksheet titled "Prison Bars" and ask: "Why do people get locked up in a prison?" (Because they disobey the laws.)

"Do you think those people deserve to be there? Why? Why not?" (Most children will say "yes" and explain that when people don't obey the law, they deserve to be imprisoned.) "Do you think that someone has ever been imprisoned for doing something good?" (Listen to their opinions.)

Developing the Bible Story

Students of this age like to hear stories of real-life heroes. Use pictures or drawings to add interest to the story. You can also ask two adults (in advance) to help with your class by dressing up as Peter and John, and reading their part in the story. Ask some of your students to volunteer as the other characters.

Narrator: Peter and John walked towards the temple.

Peter: Hey, John, what time is it?

John: Almost three. We must go to the temple to pray.

Narrator: Peter and John walked towards the temple. As they arrived, they saw a lame man sitting next to the gate that was called "Beautiful".

John: Why are you sitting here?

Lame man: I can't walk, I was born like this. I can't work to earn money, so I sit here and ask those who come to the temple to help me. Do you have money to give me?

John: I'm sorry, but I don't have any money, do you, Peter?

Peter: Silver or gold I don't have, but what I do have I give you. In the name of Jesus Christ of Nazareth, walk.

Narrator: (with enthusiasm): Then he took him by the right hand and lifted him up. Immediately his feet and ankles straightened, jumping up, he stood and walked. He went with them into the temple, walking, leaping, and praising God. All the people were astonished at what had happened.

Peter: Israelites, why do you marvel at this? Why do you set your eyes on us, as if by our power we have made him walk?

Narrator: However, not everyone was happy that the lame man was healed. The rulers of the temple were very angry.

Temple leader: What are you doing here? Who gave you permission to teach? We don't like what you say about Jesus. We all know he was crucified. We don't want you to tell more stories about him being resurrected! Either you stop talking, or we'll put you in jail!

Narrator: Then the soldiers took Peter and John and threw them into prison. But many of those who had heard their message, believed, and their number grew to about 5,000 men. The next day, they brought Peter and John to the Council. The man who was healed was standing there too. The priests began to question the apostles.

Temple leader: By what power or in what name have you done this?

Peter: In the name of Jesus Christ of Nazareth, whom you crucified and whom God raised from the dead, through him this man stands before you, healed.

Narrator: Then, seeing the courage of Peter and John they recognized that they had been with Jesus.

Temple leader: Gentlemen, we give you your freedom on the condition that you refrain from preaching and teaching about Jesus. Do you understand this?

Peter and John: Which is right in God's eyes: to listen to you, or to him? You be the judges! As for us, we cannot help speaking about what we have seen and heard.

Narrator: After that, the rulers of the temple could not think of anything to say or do. They could not decide how to punish them, because all the people were praising God for what had happened. So, after threatening them, they let them go free. Peter and John went to their fellow believers and told them all that had happened to them.

Life Application

Using the human body as an example, ask students what the body does when part of it gets hurt. For example, if we touch an iron with our hand, what happens? Immediately, the head receives stimulus and sends a message to the rest of the body, indicating that there is an injured area. In addition, the affected party receives another stimulus, reacting quickly to remove our hand from the iron.

The other parts react to this stimulus. The other hand touches the sore part; The eyes look at the injured area; Feet move quickly away from danger, etc.

So it's with the body of Christ. *"If one part suffers, every part suffers with it; if one part is honored, every part rejoices with it."* (1 Corinthians 12:26)

When Peter and John were persecuted and imprisoned, the other Christians prayed to God, interceding and asking for help from him to be able to continue the work of preaching the gospel.

IV. ACTIVITIES

Activity: Persecuted Christian's Hall of Fame

In the history of the Christian Church we know that many people have been persecuted because of their faith. Give your students the worksheet with the "Persecuted Christian's Hall of Fame" and have them look up the Bible verses and write down how these heroes of the Bible were persecuted.

Jesus (John 19:1-6). He was whipped, they made him wear a crown of thorns, he was beat and crucified.

Stephen (Acts 7:56-60). They threw him out of the city and stoned him.

Paul (2 Corinthians 11:23-27). He was beaten, he was imprisoned many times, stoned.

Whose place is this? (2 Timothy 3:12)

(Those who want to live with Christ Jesus in their hearts will suffer persecution.)

Activity: How Do We Survive Persecution?

Give your students the worksheet entitled "How Do We Survive Persecution?" Have them fill in the columns as you discuss this as a class. Ask them: "What would you do if you were persecuted for believing in Christ?" Explain that this may happen to them, but they can be prepared to face this situation. Say: "This exercise will help you to be prepared."

1. Don't be taken by surprise! Make a list of situations in which you could be persecuted for what you believe. (People could make fun of you for not wanting to sin, like lying, stealing, or hurting someone.)
2. What was the secret of the courage of Jesus, Peter, John, Stephen and Paul? (The Holy Spirit gave them strength to continue and face persecution, because God was with them.)
3. How can the Christian community help make persecution more bearable? (The Christian community can encourage us to do the right thing. They can pray and take care of us.)
4. What can you do to protect yourself? Ephesians 6:10-18 (The Armor of God)
5. Why must we face persecution with honor? Matthew 5:11-12. (Because we'll be rewarded if we do. There are people who will lie and don't want to hear the message of God. They will try to make us doubt our faith, but we know that we are not alone.)

Memory Verse

Ask if they have already memorized the verse; If most of them already know it, repeat it out loud. To review, play this simple game. You say the first word; have the girls say the next, and the boys the next; and so on until you have said the whole verse. You can do it several times, this way those who don't know it yet will learn it.

End the class by praying with the students, thanking God for today's lesson and asking for his help to be good Christians.

NOTES:

LESSON 21
NOTHING CAN STOP THE CHURCH!
I. OVERVIEW

Biblical Base: Acts 5:12-42

Memory Verse: *"Now you are the body of Christ, and each one of you is a part of it."* (1 Corinthians 12:27)

Biblical Truth: As Christians, we have a duty to teach and preach about Jesus Christ. Although many may oppose our message and there are enemies who will try to destroy the church, we must continue because God is working through us.

Lesson Objective: To help students understand that nothing can stop the work Christ gave his church; and to know the power of the Holy Spirit that is in the lives of believers.

II. TEACHER PREPARATION

Review the memory verse to encourage your students to memorize it, and ask the students how the verse relates to the lives of believers. Every function of the body of Christ is directed toward teaching and preaching about Jesus Christ, sharing the gift of salvation with the world.

"So Christ himself gave the apostles, the prophets, the evangelists, the pastors and teachers, to equip his people for works of service, so that the body of Christ may be built up." (Ephesians 4:11-12) 1 Peter 2:9 says, *"But you are a chosen people, a royal priesthood, a holy nation, God's special possession, that you may declare the praises of him who called you out of darkness into his wonderful light."*

Although they encountered opposition, the apostles continued to preach the gospel. Their authority and power, given them by Christ, gave them the ability to heal the sick and cast out demons (Matthew 10: 1).

The church grew rapidly. The believers went to the temple, and the apostles continued preaching and working wonders. People brought them the sick and God healed them. Jealous of the signs and wonders that the Apostles did in the name of Jesus, members of the Sadducees placed Peter and John in jail. But their plan didn't work, because that night, an angel of the Lord freed Peter and John from prison. Then the angel told them to stand in the temple courts and tell the people all about this new life. The next morning they entered the temple and taught.

The commission given to the apostles required courage. But because they were filled with the Holy Spirit, they did it. The members of the Sanhedrin were furious and once again threatened the apostles. Peter and the apostles reminded them that "We must obey God rather than man." This further infuriated the religious leaders, who wanted to kill them. But a respected Pharisee told the opposition to leave the apostles alone, reminding them that if their work was man-made, it would fade away, but if it was of God, they would not be able to stop it.

III. LESSON DEVELOPMENT
Introduction

Even after being persecuted by the religious leaders, the apostles continued to preach the gospel, and every day the church continued to grow. People continued to go to the temple to worship and learn with each other; and brought the proceeds of what was sold to the apostles so that it would be spread among people, according to each person's needs. People even came from the neighboring cities of Jerusalem, bringing the sick to seek healing. Peter taught us that this was done by the power of Jesus, the Son of God; that if we ask in his name, he will do wonders. Peter and the apostles taught people about the forgiveness of sins, and that only through Jesus Christ can our sins be forgiven (Luke 19:10, Romans 5: 8).

Ask your students: "What is sin?" (It's disobeying God and not believing in him. [James 4:17].) "What sins have you committed?" (Stealing, lying, disobeying) "Is there anyone who has never sinned?" (No, we all have sinned! We are born with a sinful nature. The Bible says; *"for all have sinned and fall short of the glory of God"* [Romans 3:23] and *"...there is no one who does good, not even one..."* [Romans 3:12]) Nothing sinful can remain in the presence of God, for he is holy. But the Lord's love for sinners is so great that He gave us something valuable: His Son, Jesus Christ (John 3: 16-18). God didn't send his Son Jesus into the world to condemn the world, but that the world would be saved through him.

It's through Jesus that we can approach the Father (John 14: 6). If we repent of our sins, He will forgive us (Romans 10: 9-10). The Holy Spirit will help us to live a holy life that is pleasing to God. This was the message of Peter and the apostles. Peter told the people to repent of their sins and believe in the Lord Jesus Christ. The last thing Jesus told his disciples before ascending into heaven was: *"But you will receive power when the Holy Spirit comes on you; and you will be my witnesses in Jerusalem, and in all Judea and Samaria, and to the ends of the earth."* (Acts 1: 8) Peter, John and the other apostles continued teaching and proclaiming the message of Jesus Christ, even though they were persecuted and imprisoned. And believers in the Lord were increasing every day. God took care of his servants then, just as He takes care of us today.

Developing the Bible Story
You Can't Stop Them!

Give each student the worksheet entitled "You Can't Stop Them!" Read this Bible story to your students and ask them to follow along:

"Please step aside to hear what Peter is saying!" someone in the crowd cried out.

The people of Jerusalem gathered around to hear what the apostles were preaching. Those who believed in the Lord increased. Large numbers of men and women came to Jerusalem with the sick and those afflicted with unclean spirits, and they were all healed. After a while, the high priest and some of his associates, called "Sadducees," became very jealous of the apostles. They complained, "All these people are in the temple to hear Peter preach about Jesus? Those followers of Jesus are ignorant men, and have never studied the books of the Law like I have!"

"But nobody can deny that something has happened to these men," said one of the Sadducees. "Have you seen the miracles done in the name of Jesus?"

"Yes, it's amazing!" said another in the group. "They speak with authority, and we have seen how they have healed people in the name of Jesus Christ."

"It seems to me that you have started to believe all of this" shouted the High priest. "I don't care what good these men have done, but I'm furious that they keep saying that Jesus rose from the dead! If they continue with that, they will convince everyone that Jesus is the Messiah."

Then they arrested the apostles and put them in the public jail. But that night, an angel of the Lord opened the prison doors and set them free, saying, "Go, stand in the temple courts and tell all the people about this new life."

The next day, when the high priest and his associates arrived at the temple, they summoned all of the Elders of Israel and ordered the guards, "Bring the prisoners for interrogation!" When the guards found the prison cells securely locked and no one inside, they reported back to the assembly, "We found the jail securely locked, with the guards standing at the doors; but when we opened them, we found no one inside."

Then someone came and told them that the men who were put in jail were standing in the temple court teaching the people.

The high priest was furious. He said to the apostles, "You were warned to stop teaching about Jesus and have not obeyed our orders!" In response, the apostles said, "We must obey God rather than men."

The members of the court were so angry that they wanted to kill the apostles. But Gamaliel, a beloved leader of the group, stood and said, "Leave these men alone! Let them go! For if their purpose or activity is of human origin, it will fail. But if it's from God, you won't be able to stop these men; you will only find yourselves fighting against God."

Life Application

Find a box and put an object in it to add a little weight. Wrap it with gift wrap and a pretty bow. Ask a student to leave the room so they cannot hear what you say. This student will be the "seller." When the student leaves, tell the other students what's inside the box; they are the "buyers."

Ask the seller to enter the room, give the seller the box and explain that they need to sell the product to the buyers (don't tell them what's inside). The buyers will ask questions to the seller to try to discover what the product is, and the seller will answer according to what they think is inside. After a short time, let the seller open the box to see the product that he/she was trying to sell.

After this demonstration, explain that God wants to give us the gift of salvation, a gift for which Christ already paid the price (Hebrews 9:22). Only those who know God and repent of their sins and receive Christ as their Savior have received this gift and can tell others about Christ. But those who don't know him will be like the seller wanting to offer something unknown to them.

IV. ACTIVITIES
Activity: Find The Way Out

Give your students the worksheet titled "Find The Way Out." Students need to figure out which path the apostles must take to be free from prison.

Activity: Discover The Secret

Make sure your students have the worksheet with the Bible story on it. Help them find the "Discover the Secret" section. Your students get to discover what Gamaliel told Peter's accusers that caused them to let Peter go and allowed the church to continue to grow. They will need to unscramble the words and write them on the blank lines. "Leave these men alone! Let them go! For if their sproupe (purpose) or activity is of amuhn (human) origin, it will laif (fail). But if it's from God, you won't be able to ostp (stop) these men; you will only find yourselves ghgitnif (fighting) nstaiga (against) God." (Acts 5: 38- 39)

Activity: From Where Did Peter Get His Courage?

Give your students that worksheet with "From Where Did Peter Get His Courage" at the top. Give your students time to complete this activity. Students must write down the Bible verses that gave Peter the courage to face those who opposed him.

Activity: I Need Courage To…

Ask your students to think about times when they will need courage to do something. Then have them complete the following sentences on the worksheet:

I need courage to… (Examples: Talk to my friends about Christ; to love the person who did something bad to me; to not tell lies; to be obedient to my parents and teachers, etc.)

I have courage knowing that . . . (God is with me; that Christ is my Savior; that his angels take care of me; that my parents love me, etc.)

Don't forget to pray with your students at the end of this lesson, and ask them not to forget what they learned.

Remind them that they are not alone; if during the week they need courage to do something difficult, don't doubt that God will help them and give them courage.

Memory Verse

Tell the children: "According to the memory verse, who forms the body of Christ?" After they have answered, have them say the verse and repeat it two or three times so they won't forget it. During the next class, we'll start learning a new verse.

NOTES:

OUR MISSION: REACHING OTHERS

BIBLE TRUTH: God uses Christians to tell everyone that he loves them and wants to forgive their sins and be part of His big family.

UNIT OBJECTIVE
- That the students will know that it's important to obey God.
- That the students will realize that we all need to know Jesus Christ as our Savior.
- That the students will understand that our actions and attitudes say more about our relationship with God than our words.

UNIT LESSONS

» **Lesson 22** - A Christian's Duty

» **Lesson 23** - Changing Paths

» **Lesson 24** - God Makes No Exceptions

» **Lesson 25** - Everyone Can Testify!

UNIT VERSE: *"Then he said to his disciples, 'The harvest is plentiful but the workers are few. Ask the Lord of the harvest, therefore, to send out workers into his harvest field.'"* (Matthew 9:37-38)

It's important when teaching this verse that your students understand what all of the words mean. Besides preaching and healing, Jesus also taught by using whatever was around him, like things in nature, so that people could understand his message.

The harvest is when a planted field is mature and ready to be harvested/picked. The worker is a person who follows Jesus and obeys his command to share the Gospel. Jesus, with compassionate eyes, saw the crowd as a great harvest field, ready for harvest (to hear the gospel). But he acknowledges that there is a lot of work and few workers (followers) willing to do the work.

Suggestions:

1. For Lesson 23, plan ahead to bring flowers to class, preferably one per student. You will need them after you read the Bible story.

2. Bring a map with the route of Paul's missionary journey on it to help with the development of Lesson 24. You will also need a Wordless Book. This is made with a sheet of paper of each of the following colors: black, red, white, yellow and green.

A CHRISTIAN'S DUTY

I. OVERVIEW

Biblical Base: Acts 13:1-12

Memory Verse: *"Then he said to his disciples, 'The harvest is plentiful but the workers are few. Ask the Lord of the harvest, therefore, to send out workers into his harvest field.'"* (Matthew 9:37-38)

Biblical Truth: The Holy Spirit guides us when we present the gospel to others.

Lesson Objective: To help the students understand that we are used by God to spread the gospel and win souls for Christ.

II. TEACHER PREPARATION

After the death of Stephen, there was great persecution against the church in Jerusalem, and Christians scattered throughout the regions of Judea and Samaria. The apostles remained in Jerusalem, while those who were scattered went everywhere preaching the gospel.

When the apostles who were at Jerusalem heard that Samaria had received the gospel, they sent Peter and John who went and prayed for them that they might receive the Holy Spirit. Among the transformed was Saul of Tarsus, a persecutor of the Christian church who had an encounter with God, thereby becoming a Christian. His name was changed to Paul, which means "small."

In chapter 13, the brothers pray, fast and minister. Now God, by means of the Holy Spirit, wanted to set apart Barnabas and Paul for the work to which he had called them. Barnabas preached and oversaw the congregations in Antioch and Paul helped him. The Lord always prepares us and teaches us before he calls us. Barnabas and Paul were obedient to God's call and began the first missionary journey. They prayed and fasted, searching for the Lord's guidance.

They went to Antioch, and from there sailed to the island of Cyprus, to the city of Salamis, where John Mark, the cousin of Barnabas, joined them. They were preaching in the synagogues where the people gathered to pray, read and study the Word of God.

After crossing the island of Cyprus, they came to Paphos, where an intelligent man named Sergius Paulus sent for Barnabas and Paul because he wished to hear the gospel. While in Paphos, the first person to try to prevent the sharing of the gospel appeared. His name was Bar-Jesus (Elymas in Greek), a Jewish sorcerer and false prophet. We know that these things are forbidden by God; his Word says that any lie is sin (Matthew 5:19-21; Revelation 21:7-8).

This man accompanied the governor of the Roman city of Paphos. Elymas tried to make Paul look like a liar, because the governor was convinced that what Paul preached was the truth about God; if Sergius Paulus knew the truth, then the magician Elymas could not deceive him with lies (see John 8:32). The governor was converted to Christ.

When we talk to others about Christ, wonderful things happen, and God is always victorious. We can always trust him. Elymas was a Jew, and although he knew God, he didn't do the Lord's will and opposed God's word. Anyone who does that will be punished if he doesn't repent. Elymas' punishment for his attitude was that he became temporarily blind.

Whoever doesn't seek God is spiritually blind. God wants us to come into his presence with a repentant heart, confessing our sins so he can make us his children; that is God's justice for us. Elymas didn't want the governor to believe, because if he didn't believe, God could not do give him justice. Elymas was an enemy of justice.

From this lesson we've learn that:
1. God calls his children to tell others about him, whether in their home, community or another country;
2. The Word of God will be preached and people will accept Jesus as Lord and Savior, even when there is opposition from others, and
3. Those who preach the message of salvation are protected by the Holy Spirit. Let's become followers of Jesus, like Barnabas and Paul.

III. LESSON DEVELOPMENT

Introduction

Explain to your students that in the life of a Christian, there are difficult times when we feel that others will reject us because we love Jesus. Ask your students, "How would you feel if someone hated the fact that you love

Jesus?" "What could you do?" (Allow them to express their views.) Explain that the Bible speaks of two men, Barnabas and Paul, who had to face this situation. Let them listen to this interview of the Biblical account and see what happened.

Developing the Bible Story

Assign students to be the characters. Let them set up the room to look like a studio to simulate an interview (a table, four chairs and two microphones; made with a cardboard tube and a ball of paper).

Reporter 1: Paul and Barnabas, I am so excited to meet you! Can you tell me what you did before becoming missionaries?

Paul: I'm ashamed to admit it, but my name was Saul and I hated Christians.

Reporter 2: Are you the same Saul who arrested and beat Christians?

Paul: Yes, I am….

Barnabas: Of course he is! It was very difficult for believers in Jerusalem to imagine Paul as a Christian. At first they thought it was a trick. And until I was sure he wasn't the same as before, I didn't take him to see the other Christians.

Reporter 1: How did you become missionaries?

Paul: Through God's command!

Reporter 2: What do you mean?

Paul: Let me explain: we were in Antioch worshiping with other believers when the Holy Spirit said, "Set apart for me Barnabas and Saul for the work to which I have called them."

Barnabas: There were many preachers and teachers in Antioch who laid their hands on us, prayed for us and sent us out to share the gospel.

Reporter 2: You were called "special agents"?

Paul: I guess you could say that.

Barnabas: But that doesn't mean we are more important than other believers, because God has given us all special assignments.

Reporter1: I heard that you are called "the first missionaries." How did you know what you had to do?

Paul: Actually, we didn't know exactly what we were going to do. We just trusted and followed the mandate of the Holy Spirit.

Barnabas: When we went to a new city, we proclaimed the Word of God in their synagogues. We told people that Jesus was the Messiah, the Savior of the world! Only he can forgive their sins and restore their lives.

Reporter 2: How did the people respond?

Paul (to Barnabas): Barnabas, do we talk about Elymas and Sergius Paulus?

Barnabas: Sure.

Paul: We traveled across the island of Cyprus until we came to Paphos. The Roman governor Sergius Paulus lived there; He was an intelligent man because he wanted to hear the Word of God. I told him I was no longer Saul but Paul.

Barnabas: There we also met Elymas, the magician. He didn't want Sergius Paulus to listen to us, and tried to turn him from the faith. He didn't like what we had to say.

Reporter 2: What did you do?

Barnabas: The Holy Spirit gave Paul courage. He looked directly at Elymas and said, *"You are a child of the devil and an enemy of everything that is right! You are full of all kinds of deceit and trickery. Will you never stop perverting the right ways of the Lord? Now the hand of the Lord is against you. You are going to be blind for a time, not even able to see the light of the sun."*

Reporter1: What a dreadful rebuke! What happened next?

Paul: Darkness fell upon him immediately and he went around looking for someone to lead him by the hand.

Reporter 2: Unbelievable!

Barnabas: Amazing! It's not very wise to fight against the Holy Spirit

Paul: That gave us the opportunity to teach Sergius Paulus about Jesus.

Reporter 1. What did the Governor think of all this?

Barnabas: *"When the proconsul saw what had happened, he believed, for he was amazed at the teaching about the Lord."*

Reporter 2: Imagine! The Roman Governor became a believer!

Reporter 1: What an exciting experience you had on your first missionary trip! I'm sure you have a lot more that you could tell us.

Paul and Barnabas: We sure do. But let's save that for another time. Thank you for allowing us to testify to you about what God did on our first missionary trip.

Life Application

What Kind Of A Witness Are You?

Tell your students that they may never be missionaries like Paul and Barnabas, but they will always be witnesses. People look at how we respond when they opposed our faith. Give each student the worksheet with the activity entitled "What Kind of a Witness Are You?" Read the responses and tell in what situations a Christian could react in these ways.

Anger: Do you react violently when someone attacks you for what you believe?

Denial: Do you pretend, for the moment, NOT to be a Christian?

Courage: With a lot of courage, do you tell others that you love Jesus?

IV. ACTIVITIES

Find Your Partner

Write down the following words or phrases on a piece of paper. Each student will have to find who their partner is by matching the name to the phrase that goes with that name. For example: "Saul Paul" goes with "Barnabas: Paul's companion on the first missionary journey." When your students have found their partner, ask them to pray for each other, that God will give them the courage to be true witnesses of Christ.

Saul Paul - Barnabas: Paul's companion on the first missionary journey.

Sergius Paulus - Wanted to hear the gospel and then became a Christian.

Elymas - Magician who didn't want Paul and Barnabas to preach the gospel.

Holy Spirit - Directs us and gives us courage to obey God's command.

Memory Verse
Verse of the Month Club

In this lesson, there is a certificate for the Verse of the Month Club. Encourage children to join this club, and to learn the Bible verses for this quarter. Put a star on the certificate when they have memorized each month's verse. During the last class of the quarter, if they have learned all three verses, they will receive their certificate, and you can put it up it in the classroom.

Activity: The Lord's Workers

Give your students the worksheet with the section titled "The Lord's Workers". They need to put vowels in the blanks to complete the Bible verse - Matthew 9:37-38.

"The harvest is plentiful but the workers are few. Ask the Lord of the harvest, therefore, to send out workers into his harvest field." (Matthew 9:37-38)

Activity: Great Missionaries!

On the same worksheet, have your students find the section called "Great Missionaries" and have them mark the path of Barnabas and Paul's first missionary journey. It's found in Acts 13:1-6.

NOTES:

CHANGING PATHS

I. OVERVIEW

Biblical Base: Acts 16:6-15

Memory Verse: *"Then he said to his disciples, 'The harvest is plentiful but the workers are few. Ask the Lord of the harvest, therefore, to send out workers into his harvest field.'"* (Matthew 9:37-38)

Biblical Truth: God guides and shows his will to those who obey and follow him.

Lesson Objective: To help students understand the importance of obeying God's command and to know that we are instruments in his hands.

II. TEACHER PREPARATION

Have you ever been told to do something that you thought was strange? Maybe you didn't understand why you received that request, but if it was God who made the request, it's important to obey him.

This is what happened to Paul, he didn't understand why the Holy Spirit forbade him to share the gospel in Asia, where he wanted to continue preaching. He left Galatia to Bithynia but again the Holy Spirit forbade him to speak.

He continued his journey to Troas. Once there, he had a vision during the night: A man from Macedonian was standing there begging him, saying, "Come over to Macedonia and help us." Macedonia was in Europe. Now Paul understood why the Holy Spirit had not allowed him to speak in Asia; God needed him urgently in this city.

In Philippi (the first city in the province of Macedonia) there were no synagogues. People gathered on the river bank to pray (Acts 16:13). To establish a synagogue, according to rabbinic law, there had to be at least ten men. Paul and his friends spoke to women who believed in God. Among them was a woman named Lydia. She sold purple cloth. In the ancient world, purple cloth was highly valued. The Bible says that Lydia worshiped God. She received the Lord as her Savior and was baptized. She begged Paul and his companion to stay at her home while they were in Philippi.

What can we learn from the direction of the Holy Spirit in the life of Paul? He was a man who sought to obey and please God. Through prayer and studying God's Word, we can know the Lord's will for our lives so we can obey him. It's beautiful to see how God takes care of us when we obey.

III. LESSON DEVELOPMENT

Introduction

What would you think if God commanded you to build an ark that you would enter with only your family and two of every kind of animal? (Genesis 6) Or if you had a vision in which God told you to kill and eat animals that were unclean? (Acts 11) These men of God received a mandate from God, and obeyed even though they didn't understand the purpose. The result of their obedience was that the gospel was proclaimed and many people received salvation.

Noah and Peter were instruments in God's hands. Do you know someone who has been an instrument in the hands of the Lord? Could you be an instrument of God? (Yes) What should you do to be an instrument of God? (Obey God.)

It was Saturday afternoon; Mary was looking forward to going shopping with her friends. She wanted to have fun, but her mother asked her to go to her grandfather's house to take him some food.

"But Mom! Why do I have to go to grandpa's house? I want to go with my friends to have fun!"

"I need you to go," her mom said. "Maybe you can be helpful to your grandpa."

Mary thought, "I'll go to grandpa's house early and then I'll have time to meet up with my friends. I love my mom and I learned from the Bible that we must obey our parents like we must obey God."

Upon arriving at her grandpa's house, Mary called out, but no one answered the door. She walked into the house and found her grandpa lying on the floor. He had fainted. With Mary's help, the old man recovered quickly.

Ask the students: "How do you think Mary felt when her mother asked her to go to her Grandpa's house?" (Angry) "What did Mary want to do?" (Go have fun with her friends.) "Why did she decide to obey her mother?" (Because she loved her and had learned that we must obey God and our parents.) "What was the result of her obedience?" (She was there to help her grandpa.) "How do you think Mary felt after seeing what had happened?" (Happy to know the result of her obedience.)

Developing the Bible Story

Narrate the following story. Some words are hard to pronounce. Help your students learn how to say each of the names using the pronunciation key. List the names several times. Then, ask the children to look in the story until they find the names, draw a circle around them and then repeat the pronunciation of them. Do this with each name to help them feel confident that they can read the story. Let volunteers read aloud, or you can read to them.

Bithynia - bih-**thin**-ee-*uh*
Macedonia - mas-i-**doh**-nee-*uh*
Mysia - **mish**-ee-*uh*
Troas - **Troh**-as
Philippi - **fil**-*uh*-pie

"I wish I knew why the Holy Spirit didn't allow us to preach in Asia," said Paul.

"Maybe we should go anyway," said one of his companions. That seemed like a good idea to everyone and they began to make their way to that city. They tried to enter Bithynia, but the Spirit didn't allow it. Then, they passed Mysia, and continued down to Troas. Paul told Silas, "I'm tired, we should rest when we reach Troas." "I'll be ready to rest then too." Silas agreed.

When they arrived at Troas, Silas, Timothy and Luke laid down to sleep.

That night, Paul had a vision: a man was standing, begging him saying, "Come over to Macedonia and help us."

"Silas! Luke! Wake up!" Paul exclaimed. "I know where God wants us to go."

While the others woke up, Paul explained his vision: "God wants us to go to Macedonia."

"Macedonia? But it's so far away!" someone said.

"Yes, Macedonia! In my vision I saw a man there. The man said, 'Come over to Macedonia and help us.'"

Paul and his friends packed up their things and went down to the port and arranged for their trip. When they arrived in Macedonia, the missionaries continued on to Philippi.

"Why did we come to Philippi?" It was the main city in that part of Macedonia. But there was no synagogue. "Why did the Holy Spirit bring us here?"

"How are we going to find people to talk to about Jesus if there isn't a synagogue?"

"We must start one!" Paul suggested, "Why don't we go outside the city? Many times when there is no synagogue, people meet at the river to pray. We should go to the river and see if anyone is there." The missionaries didn't have to look for long; they quickly found a group of women who gathered there every Saturday to pray and encourage one another. Along the river, Paul, Silas, Timothy and Luke sat down and began to talk to the women about Jesus. One of the women was named Lydia. She sold purple cloth. God had opened her heart so that she was attentive to Paul's message. "I believe. I want to be Christian!" Lydia said. Paul baptized Lydia and all of her household. Lydia was very happy because these missionaries had come to Macedonia. She invited them to her home. She said to them, "If you consider me a believer in the Lord, come and stay at my house."

Life Application.

If possible, give each student a flower. Explain that when flowers die, they produce seeds which travel through the air by the power of the wind. If these seeds fall on fertile ground, they reproduce. So it is with the power of the Holy Spirit.

God leads us to different places to preach. If the Gospel falls onto a heart that receives it, it will bear fruit.

IV. ACTIVITIES

Give each student the worksheet "When, Where, How". Have the children help James find the shortest route to Lake Beautiful. Challenge students to see who makes it to the finish line first.

Memory Verse

Remind students they must learn the memory verse so they can receive a star on their certificate.

Activity: Whom Did God Call?

Tell the students to match the Bible character with the calling they received from God.

A. *"Have seven priests carry trumpets of rams' horns in front of the ark. On the seventh day, march around the city seven times, ... then the wall of the city will collapse."* (Joshua) (Joshua 6:4-5)

B. *"Get up, Peter, kill and eat ... Don't call anything impure that God has made clean."* (Peter) (Acts 11: 4-15)

C. *"...make yourself an ark of cypress wood ... you will enter the ark—you and your sons and your wife and your sons' wives ... bring into the ark two of all living creatures, male and female,..."* (Noah) (Genesis 6:13-22)

D. *"Raise your staff and stretch out your hand over the sea to divide the water so that the Israelites can go through the sea on dry ground."* (Moses) (Exodus 14:16)

E. *"Come over to Macedonia and help us."* (Paul) (Acts 16:6-10)

Activity: Lesson Review

Give each student the work sheet entitled "Lesson Review". Students need to cross out the words in bold that should not be part of the following sentences:

1. We were allowed - ~~forbidden~~ by the Holy Spirit to speak the gospel in Asia.

2. A man of Macedonia standing and begging Paul to go to Macedonia and ~~not help us~~ - help us.

3. After Paul had the vision, we got ready at once to leave for Macedonia, concluding that God had - ~~had not~~ called us to proclaim the gospel there.

Activity: Does It Please God?

Have your students write YES or NO to indicate what does or doesn't please God.

a. _____ I tell a lie
b. _____ I obey my parents
c. _____ I read the Bible
d. _____ I take what doesn't belong to me
e. _____ I help the needy
f. _____ I talk to others about Christ
g. _____ I make fun of the elderly
h. _____ I pray to God every day
i. _____ I obey the law
j. _____ I destroy other people's property

GOD ACCEPTS US ALL

I. OVERVIEW

Biblical Base: Acts 17:13-34

Memory Verse: *"Then he said to his disciples, 'The harvest is plentiful but the workers are few. Ask the Lord of the harvest, therefore, to send out workers into his harvest field.'"* (Matthew 9:37-38)

Biblical Truth: God doesn't make any exceptions - salvation is available to those who seek him and also for those who don't know him, no matter what. That is why God sends us to share the Gospel.

Lesson Objective: To help the students understand that you cannot judge a person's relationship with God simply by their appearance or religion, and we all need to know God and accept Him as our Savior.

II. TEACHER PREPARATION

Who will know a country better: the person who has read or seen pictures of it, or the person who has visited it, learned the customs, tasted the food and has walked in its streets? The answer is that the person who has had a personal experience knows it better than th one who has only heard and imagined things about that country.

So it's with our relationship with God. It's different to know about God, and to know God - this implies a personal experience.

In his second missionary journey, Paul arrived in Berea. The people who lived in Berea received his preaching with willingness, examining the Scriptures daily to see if what he said was true.

The result of this honest examination of the Scriptures day after day was that they realized that what Paul was saying was in fact true. Many Jews and Gentiles accepted Christ.

Again, persecution rose against the Christians, trying to hinder the work of God. But Paul went from place to place, preaching the message of salvation, and many came to believe. Arriving in Athens, Paul encountered an idolatrous city. God helped Paul adapt to the conditions of each city in which he ministered.

The preferred method of teaching in Athens was "free discussion," so Paul adopted this technique; He had a double ministry in that city. Firstly with the Jews in the synagogues, and secondly among the Gentiles in the square. Paul could take the word revealed by God and the wisdom of the Greek philosophers and establish a relationship with Gentiles and Jews.

A few days after Paul arrived in Athens and he saw which gods they worshiped, he realized they didn't know Jehovah God and his Son Jesus Christ.

He began to speak to them of the "unknown God." His preaching attracted so much attention that the people invited him to the Areopagus, where the famous speakers and philosophers gathered to discuss their beliefs. Now, Paul was in the most prominent place in Athens to preach about the true God. The result was that, although some mocked him, others heard the message of salvation and believed, because God accepts everyone.

III. LESSON DEVELOPMENT

Introduction

Point out on a map the route that Paul took on his missionary journeys (Acts 13-17). Comment on their outcome. Although there was bound to be opposition wherever he proclaimed the Gospel, Paul was able to preach, and many heard the message of salvation, repenting of their sins and receiving Jesus Christ as their Lord and Savior.

Write on a piece of paper the name of each place Paul visited, stick it along with the map on the wall or draw it on a blackboard, and highlight some of the important events that occurred in each place. For example: Berea -- People searched the scriptures. You can use this to review previous lessons as you narrate this lesson.

Ask: "What should we know to be able to tell others about Christ?"

1. Recognize Christ as our Lord and Savior.

2. Know His Word, the Bible.

3. Know the people around us.

4. Develop the ability to teach.

Jesus knew God the Father (John 14:24). He knew the Scriptures (Luke 2:46-47). He knew the people (John 2:24-25) and he knew good methods to teach, because he used what he had at his disposal (parables, questions, nature, etc.). Paul, like Jesus Christ, knew the same things.

Developing the Bible Story

"Paul, are you sure you'll be fine here alone in Athens?" asked one of the men who accompanied him in Berea.

"I'll be fine, thanks," Paul replied. "Silas and Timothy will soon be here anyways."

And so the men left. Paul began to observe the streets of Athens and the beautiful buildings. And as he looked around, his spirit became heavy seeing the city given over to idolatry. Every day he went to the synagogue and to the market to speak to the Jews and the Greeks.

In Athens, people were proud of their skills and knowledge. They were well-educated people who enjoyed going to public places and having conversations with well-prepared people.

Paul had a good education; he began teaching about Jesus and his resurrection. People from different groups gathered to listen. Some said, "What does he talk about?" and to others he seemed to being talking about a new god.

Soon, Paul's words caused a lot of curiosity among people and they said, "We want you to attend a meeting with our religious leaders, the most prepared. We'll meet at one of our temples." This meeting was called "the meeting of Aerópago." Paul was asked by the people, "Can we know about this new doctrine of which you speak? For you bring some strange things to our ears. We want to know what these things mean."

Paul stood and said, *"People of Athens! I see that in every way you are very religious. For as I walked around and looked carefully at your objects of worship, I even found an altar with this inscription: to an unknown god. So you are ignorant of the very thing you worship—and this is what I am going to proclaim to you".*

Then he told them, *"The God who made the world and everything in it is the Lord of heaven and earth and doesn't live in temples built by human hands. And he is not served by human hands, as if he needed anything. Rather, he himself gives everyone life and breath and everything else. From one man he made all the nations, that they should inhabit the whole earth; and he marked out their appointed times in history and the boundaries of their lands. God did this so that they would seek him and perhaps reach out for him and find him, though he is not far from any one of us."*

"Therefore since we are God's offspring, we should not think that the divine being is like gold or silver or stone—an image made by human design and skill. In the past God overlooked such ignorance, but now he commands all people everywhere to repent."

Then he told them the good news: that God sent Jesus to earth to be our savior. Jesus was crucified, but God raised him from death. This proves and asserts that Jesus is the Son of God. After Paul preached about Jesus' resurrection, some mocked his words. Others said, *"We want to hear you again on this subject."* Some believed and became followers of Jesus.

Life Application

Prepare a wordless book with sheets of black, red, white, yellow and green paper. Fold each sheet in half and place them in the following order: yellow, black, red, white and green. Glue the yellow half to the black half, the black to the red half, the red half to the white half and the white half to the green half. Explain to your students what each color represents:

- Yellow: the holiness of God (Revelation 21:18-21; John 14:1-3).
- Black: sin (Romans 3:23; Romans 6:23, John 8:21).
- Red: the blood of Jesus (1 John 1:7; 1 Corinthians 15:3-4).
- White: purity. Christ blood makes us clean. (Psalm 51:7; John 1:12; 1 John 1:9).
- Green: the new life in Christ; spiritual growth (2 Peter 3:18; 2 Timothy 2:15).

Memory Verse

Tell the students that it's very important for them to be learning their memory verses. Ask for one or two volunteers to say the verse from memory.

IV. ACTIVITIES

Activity: Who Needs to Know Jesus?

Give your students the worksheet entitled "Who Needs to Know Jesus." Have them study the pictures, then ask them who needs to know Jesus? Discuss their answers together.

Beatriz (good); Isabel (smart); Ramon (religious); Mark (church member); and Elena (an employee).

Activity: Yes, Paul, We Hear You!

Have your students find Acts 17:32-34 in their Bibles. There are three different reactions that people who heard Paul's sermons in Athens had. Give your students the worksheet with the activity "Yes, Paul, We Hear You." Have your students write the three different reactions in the blank circles below each drawing.

Activity: Paul's Announcement!

Give your students the worksheet entitled "Paul's Announcement." Your students must write the letters that are not X's on the blank lines to discover what Paul announced to the people in Athens.

Don't forget after class to pray to thank God for having allowed them to be present.

EVERYONE CAN TESTIFY!

I. OVERVIEW

Biblical Base: 1 Timothy 1:4

Memory Verse: *"Then he said to his disciples, 'The harvest is plentiful but the workers are few. Ask the Lord of the harvest, therefore, to send out workers into his harvest field.'"* (Matthew 9:37-38)

Biblical Truth: As part of the body of Christ, we have a responsibility to fulfill. We are vessels that carry the good news of salvation to the world.

Lesson Objective: To help the students understand that we have a responsibility to testify to others about Christ, knowing He will help us accomplish this. We can do this by living a holy and pleasing life.

II. TEACHER PREPARATION

Because Paul was persecuted constantly, he had to leave each place he went to. However, he was the founder of the church at Ephesus. There a group of people forced him to leave. In addition, he had a vision in which he was asked to go to Macedonia. It was for these reasons that Paul left Timothy in Ephesus.

It's unknown when he wrote this letter to Timothy, but it's believed he did so from Macedonia. In this letter, Paul gives some advice to Timothy. He starts explaining why he asked him to stay in Ephesus. Paul realized that some believed in doctrines contrary to Christianity. They didn't recognize Jesus as the Son of God and as their Savior. These people brought false doctrines that kept many from the truth, but we know that the Gospel teaches the truth (John 8:32). That is why Paul left Timothy; so that the people in Ephesus would learn the truth.

Paul testified to others about Jesus and His salvation by showing love. When faith is sincere (not fake), the spirit of love prevails in the church of God.

Paul exhorts the church to pray (Acts 2) and be in thanksgiving for all men (including those who are in leadership positions), and asks that all be saved and to come to the knowledge of the truth.

Then, Paul advised the young Pastor Timothy to spend the time and energy in the task of exercising spiritually. He recommended that Timothy not let anyone look down on him for being young, but to act in a way that wins the love, respect and confidence of the people. How could he accomplish this? By being an example to the believers in speech, conduct, love, faith, and in purity.

Through Christ-like behavior and through his ability to serve effectively, he was able to overcome obstacles in his ministry.

Finally, Paul advised him to read scripture publicly, to preach and teach, without neglecting the gift he had received from God. Preaching is the proclamation of the Word of God, and teaching suggest instruction in Christian faith.

III. LESSON DEVELOPMENT

Introduction

Explain that today's story is in the form of a letter. It was written by Paul to Timothy - a young pastor in Ephesus.

Developing the Bible Story

Give your students the worksheets that contain the letter from Paul. Have them follow along as you read it to them.

A Letter from Paul

"Finally, a letter from my dear friend and teacher!" Timothy thought when he received Paul's letter. As he read it, he remembered the first time he heard Paul preach. Paul and Barnabas had come to Lystra, Timothy's birthplace.

At first, the citizens of Lystra treated Paul and Barnabas very well. But later they were angered by Paul's message. They stoned him and left him for dead. But it was through his preaching that Timothy and his mother and grandmother became Christians.

Timothy was very happy when Paul returned to Lystra for a second time. He was even happier when Paul chose him to be his assistant for the rest of his trip.

Paul and Timothy were the first Christians to go to Europe. Together they started churches in Philippi, Thessalonica and Berea. Memories flooded Timothy's mind as he thought of how they had worked in the church at Ephesus. Now he was doing what Paul had assigned him to do. He was the pastor of the church in Ephesus. Lately, some false teachers had been creating many problems. Maybe Paul had something to tell him that would help, Timothy thought as he started reading.

To Timothy, my true son in the faith: Grace, mercy and peace from God our Father and Christ Jesus our Lord.

"As I urged you when I went into Macedonia, stay there in Ephesus so that you may command certain people not to teach false doctrines . . . The goal of this command is love, which comes from a pure heart and a good conscience and a sincere faith. Some have departed from these and have turned to meaningless talk. I thank Christ Jesus our Lord, who has given me strength, that he considered me trustworthy, appointing me to his service. Even though I was once a blasphemer . . . I was shown mercy because I acted in ignorance and unbelief. The grace of our Lord was poured out on me abundantly, along with the faith and love that are in Christ Jesus."

"I am giving you this command in keeping with the prophecies once made about you, so that by recalling them you may fight the battle well, holding on to faith and a good conscience."

"Don't let anyone look down on you because you are young, but set an example for the believers in speech, in conduct, in love, in faith and in purity."

Let your life, just as your words, be an example to others. Love like Jesus commands us to love and be careful not to sin. Let your faith in Christ be known to all.

Don't neglect the gift that is in you, which was given to you by God. Timothy, you have been given gifts to build up the church. Meditate on these things; remain in them, that your progress may be seen by all. Take care of yourself and your doctrine, for in doing this you will save both yourself and those who hear you.

Paul, an apostle of Jesus Christ.

Memory Verse

This is the final week of the month; students should have the verse memorized by now. Help them say it from memory and put a star on their "Verse of the Month" certificate.

Life Application

Activity: Testify? Me? But . . .

Paul gave Timothy some important advice, such as not to let anyone think less of him for being young. Ask: "Why did Paul say this to Timothy? Do you think that being young is a disadvantage in following Jesus?"

Have them find 1 Timothy 4:12 in their Bibles. Give them each the worksheet entitled "Testify? Me? But..." Ask them: "Why do you think it's difficult to testify?" (Some will say they have to know a number of verses from the Bible or memorize a plan of evangelism. Others are embarrassed to talk about Jesus; they are afraid that the person they are witnessing to will mock them. Some will say that they never think about witnessing. Others may see it as work for adults or ministers, etc.) "What stops you from giving your testimony?" (Let your students answer honestly.)

IV. ACTIVITIES

Activity: Paul's Plan

Direct your students to the worksheet with Paul's letter on it. Have them find the activity called "Paul's Plan". Paul gave Timothy five ways of being an example to others. Find them in the Bible story and write them on the fingers of the hand.

1. Speech: means to testify. We need to tell others what God has done for us and what we believe about Him.
2. Conduct: It's doing everything well because we love God and want to please him. He wants our life to be an example of good conduct.
3. Love: show to others the care and love of God.
4. Faith: means to believe and to trust in God.
5. Purity: turn away from what is not good for us.

Activity: A Letter To A Friend

Give your students the worksheet entitled "A Letter To A Friend." Have your students write a letter to a friend telling them about Jesus. In the letter they should also invite their friend to accept Christ into their hearts as their Savior.

Activity: Dear Timothy

On the same worksheet as the letter, have your students do the word-search puzzle. Give them time to search for the words listed to the right of the puzzle and circle them.

PARABLES OF JESUS

BIBLE TRUTH: Jesus shows us how to love God and others in the same way that God loves us.

UNIT OBJECTIVE

- That the students will learn that Jesus taught us how to live.
- That the students will know that God expects us to love and care for others, as he loves us and cares for us.
- That the students will realize that God is right and just, and deals with us properly.
- That the students will recognize that a personal relationship with God is not based on material possessions.
- That the students will experience the love and forgiveness of God.
- That the students will grow spiritually.

UNIT LESSONS

- » **Lesson 26** - Who Is My Neighbor?
- » **Lesson 27** - I Am Valuable!
- » **Lesson 28** - Don't Give Up! Keep Trusting.
- » **Lesson 29** - The Parable Of The Sower
- » **Lesson 30** - Is It Bad To Be Rich?

UNIT VERSE: *"He answered, 'Love the Lord your God with all your heart and with all your soul and with all your strength and with all your mind'; and, 'Love your neighbor as yourself.'"* (Luke 10:27)

Use different memorization strategies to help students learn this verse.

1. Each lesson of this unit focuses on a different parable. You can emphasis the unit "Parables of Jesus" and then weekly, each lesson by cutting out letters placing them on a bright background and hanging them in your classroom to announce each lesson. "Who Is My Neighbor" (parable of the good Samaritan) "I Am Valuable!" (parable of the lost coin). "Don't Give Up, Keep Trusting" (the unjust judge). "Is It Bad To Be Rich?" (The "Rich Man and Lazarus") and the "Parable Of The Sower."

2. Bring a basket or box the day you teach lesson 26 for the parable of "The Good Samaritan", where the students will deposit the items that they bring to the class.

3. For the class when you teach lesson 27, before the students arrive in the classroom, hide a coin to illustrate the parable of the "lost coin." Make cards that say, "I am valuable to God, my Savior," and give them out in the course of this lesson. Also, prepare paper hearts, on which your students will write the memory verse.

4. Make plans in advance of Lesson 27, "I Am Valuable," which has an evangelistic emphasis. Pray that the Lord will help minister to the students and they will decide to accept Christ as their Savior. You can ask the pastor or children's leader to help you prepare an evangelistic invitation. Talk to them a few days before this lesson.

5. In preparation for Lesson 29, the day you teach lesson 26, bring two small pots to class, as well as some seeds - beans work the best. Hand them out to your students to see. With the help of your students, plant some of the seeds. Describe the conditions they will need in order to grow. You can use two paper containers. Fill one with soil; make two small holes in the bottom for drainage. Put the seeds one or two inches (2.5 cm to 5 cm) deep, gently add dirt and water. Place the container where it can get full sun (if using bean seeds, let them soak overnight before planting, to sprout faster). In another bowl, combine the dry seeds in the container with small pieces of wood and shells. Plant the same number of seeds, but don't add water. Place it where it won't receive much light. Don't water or care for this plant, as with the first. On the day of Lesson 29, note the two different results: the strong growth of one plant and the frustrated growth of the other. The day of the lesson of the parable of the sower use the two plants to reinforce the lesson.

WHO IS MY NEIGHBOR?

I. OVERVIEW

Biblical Base: Luke 10: 25- 37

Memory Verse: *"He answered, 'Love the Lord your God with all your heart and with all your soul and with all your strength and with all your mind'; and, 'Love your neighbor as yourself.'"* (Luke 10:27)

Biblical Truth: If we want to inherit eternal life, we must love God and our neighbor, as well as accept Jesus as our Savior.

Lesson Objective: To help students learn that we must love God and respond with love to the needs of our neighbors.

II. TEACHER PREPARATION

During the last days of his ministry, Jesus told the parable of the Good Samaritan. Back then, there was a lot of controversy surrounding him and his message. Among most of his listeners were people who loved him and listened. But within that group, there were also people who had tried to trap him into saying something that would send him to jail. Such was the case when an expert of the law (Luke 10:25) asked Jesus, *"What must I do to inherit eternal life?"*

In telling the Parable of the Good Samaritan, Jesus referred to the phrase "and love your neighbor as yourself." Although the expert of the Law asks, "Who is my neighbor?", he should have known because Leviticus 19:18, 33-34 refers to this.

In the parable, Jesus refers to the road from Jerusalem to Jericho. This road, though only 25 km long, drops about 1,000 meters into the Jordan Valley. This was a road that passed through deserted places and where there were notorious criminals. The people who were listening to the parable assumed that the person was Jewish (Luke 10:30).

Both the Levite and the priest who passed by served in the temple. Some commentators say that they didn't stop because they didn't want to become impure and thereby would not be allowed to serve in the temple.

Jesus mentioned a Samaritan who was passing by (v. 33). The Samaritans were despised by the Jews, but Christ used them as an example of one who fulfills the law.

The money mentioned in verse 35 was equivalent to two days salary. Jesus noted that the Samaritan was not interested in the nationality of the injured man, he only saw the need the man had and how he could help him.

When Jesus asked who of the these three was a neighbor, the expert demonstrated his prejudice against the Samaritans by not answering (v. 37) with the word "Samaritan," but instead by saying, "The one who had mercy on him."

Today there are many racial problems like those between Jews and Samaritans. There are problems due to different skin colors, borders, etc. (Give an example that is common in your neighborhood, city or country.)

Often times, we can act like the priests and Levites who are too busy, and we don't care for those in need! For example, at school there is a boy that nobody likes and we also make fun of him instead of helping him. Or maybe we have our group of friends and we don't let anyone else in, and so doing reject others.

III. LESSON DEVELOPMENT

Introduction

Remember the previous lesson on giving your testimony. Ask several of the students to tell what they did during the week in applying what they learned in class. Tell them that the most effective testimony sometimes is not through words, but actions. Express confidence in the students to be a positive influence as they serve Jesus.

Activity: Who Is My Neighbor?

Give your students this worksheet and read the question aloud: "Which of these is your neighbor? Why?" (Allow time for them to observe the picture and answer the questions.)

Explain that today's Bible story is a parable. Tell them that Jesus often used parables to teach the people. Ask: "Have you ever learned something difficult by doing something easy first? For example, to teach us that it's not good to tell lies, we tell the story of the boy who cried "Wolf! Wolf!" People ran to help him, but when they came to where he was, he laughed because he had lied. However, one day the wolf was real, and although he shouted, no one ran to help because they believed it was lie."

Developing the Bible Story
Who Is My Neighbor?

"Master, what must I do to inherit eternal life?"

The man who spoke to Jesus was an expert in religious law. He was testing him, trying to make him fall.

"What is written in the law?" said Jesus. "What do you read?"

This person cited the law: "Thou shalt love the Lord thy God with all your heart, with all your soul, with all your strength and with all your mind; and your neighbor as yourself."

"I already have it!" he thought. For years, people have argued about what the law means by using the word "neighbor." Some teachers would tell people to love your neighbor and hate your enemy.

He wanted to do what he thought was right, so he said to Jesus, "And who is my neighbor?"

The Lord was ready for this question and answered with a story:

"A man went down from Jerusalem to Jericho and fell among thieves, who stripped him, beat him and went away, leaving him half dead."

The expert knew the road from Jerusalem to Jericho was dangerous. Thieves lived in the hills near the road and often attacked people.

Jesus continued: "It happened that a priest came down the road, and seeing the beaten man, passed on by. Likewise a Levite, upon seeing the man passed by."

The expert continued to listen. He knew why the priest and the Levite had not stopped. The man could die while they were helping him, and the law said that the priests and Levites could not touch corpses. If they did, they were not allowed to work in the temple for some time.

Jesus continued the story: "But a Samaritan, as he journeyed, came to the place where the injured man was."

"A Samaritan!" he thought. "Everyone knows that the Samaritans are good for nothing."

Jesus continued: "When the Samaritan saw the poor man, he had compassion. He came and bound up his wounds ... put him on his donkey, took him to an inn and took care of him."

"The next day, when he departed, he took out money for the inn keeper and said: Take care of him, and whatever more you need as compensation, I'll repay you when I return."

Then Jesus looked at the expert and asked: "Who, then, of these three do you think was a neighbor to the man who was beaten and robbed?"

The expert said: "He who showed mercy on him."

Jesus said, "Go and do likewise."

Life Application

Ask the students: "Do you love yourself?" (Watch for everyone to "yes", and if someone doesn't say anything, encourage them by telling them that they are very valuable because God and you (their teacher) love them and they should love themselves.)

Tell your students that everyone is valuable. Ask again: "What are some ways you can show love and care for yourself?" (Eating, sleeping, washing, playing, being with friends, etc.) Say: "Jesus said love your neighbor as yourself, but who is your neighbor?" (Everyone, whether they need us or not, regardless of skin color, nationality or economic status.)

Say: "In what way can you show love and care to your neighbor?" (Let them tell you different ways.)

IV. ACTIVITIES

Activity: How To Love Your Neighbor

Make sure your students have the worksheet with the section "How To Love Your Neighbor" on it. Let them write on their "hearts" the different ways they can show love to their neighbor.

Ask them to close their eyes and think of someone they know who might need love and understanding during the week. Encourage them to pray silently, that God will help them serve that person through their actions of love and kindness.

Memory Verse

Write out the memory verse on the board or on a poster board where children can see it. Leave sufficient space between each word. Ask them to sit in front of the board or poster. The first child should stand and say the first word of the verse, and then sit; the student on his left will say the next word, and so on until they finish. When this is done, do it again in the opposite order.

The idea is to have them repeat the procedure until they memorize the verse.

Activity: Who Can I Share Jesus With?

Give your students this worksheet. Have them fill in the blanks to complete the word of the person they can talk to about Christ.

73

I AM VALUABLE!

I. OVERVIEW

Biblical Base: Luke 15: 1-2; 8-10

Memory Verse: "*He answered, 'Love the Lord your God with all your heart and with all your soul and with all your strength and with all your mind'; and, 'Love your neighbor as yourself.'*" (Luke 10:27)

Biblical Truth: We are valuable to God. He loves us so much that if we were to choose to fall away from His love, He would look to find us again and rejoice when we return.

Lesson Objective: To help the students learn that God loves every person and that he rejoices in those who seek Him and His forgiveness.

II. TEACHER PREPARATION

Luke chapter 15 tells us three parables that Jesus taught with a common theme: "the search for the lost, and the love of God." Jesus told these parables in response to the Pharisees and teachers of the law saying, "This man receives sinners and eats with them" (verse 2). Jesus spent a lot of time with sinners, people with whom the Pharisees and scribes didn't wish to be with. For them, it was offensive that Jesus, being recognized by the crowds as a holy man and teacher, would talk with people that were outcasts.

For this reason, Jesus used three similar parables to explain the great love that God has for all people, regardless of their state of sin. Emphasize that the Lord finds joy when someone repents and comes back to him.

The story of the "lost coin" is the second of three parables. The people who were listening to Jesus at that time could understand how difficult it could be to find a coin inside the house. The floor was a tapestry of cane stalks and reeds placed on the hard earth. The only light in the room came from a small window. The woman would have to light a lamp and sweep the floor carefully to find the precious piece of silver.

The currency in question was a drachma of silver, that is, a little more than the salary for a day's work. It was customary for a woman engaged to marry to gather ten coins in a necklace to use it on the day of the wedding. When she was married, the coins became a symbol of the couple's commitment. Nobody could take them away and they were kept in a safe place so they wouldn't be lost.

III. LESSON DEVELOPMENT

Introduction

In this story, Jesus compares the fervent search of a woman with the love of God. Just like when the women found the lost coin and rejoiced over it, God rejoices over finding us because we are valuable to Him, and he experiences joy when he finally finds those who are lost.

Jesus gave us a good model of teaching with the use of parables. He motivated those who listened to discover the truth, while there were some who were too lazy to see it (Matthew 13:10-11). He who sincerely seeks God can discover a new teaching in this parable.

In his daily life, a child may act wrongly or sin before God. You may think: "What I have done is so bad; God doesn't want me." Sometimes, adults tell children, "God won't want you because you have done this or that."

That's not true, God loves us despite all the bad things we do, think, feel or even the good we failed to do. However, it's important to understand that by acting in this way (in sin), we turn away from God.

If a child attends church faithfully, his family is Christian and knows a lot about God, but has not yet approached God, he is like the "lost coin" inside the house. Many may be lost within the Christian church.

The solution to both situations is the great love of God and his search for the lost. No matter if the child is inside the church or roams the streets, or if you have wealth or are poor, or have been abused or neglected, ALL are very precious to God.

Like the woman in the story, God makes every effort to find the lost with joy and forgiveness so they can enjoy a good relationship with him.

Provide a special welcome to each child that comes by shaking hands or even giving them a hug, and say, "You are valuable, God loves you." Ask the children if they remember last week's lesson, if anyone helped someone during the week, and what the reaction was of those they helped.

Organize a project; you can call it "Operation Good Samaritan." Arrange a box or basket and encourage your students to participate by bringing food donations to give to someone in need. Schedule a visit to a family, an elderly person or needy children to deliver your gift of love.

Developing the Bible Story

The Lost Coin

Tell the children that earlier today you saw a coin in the classroom, and ask them to look for it. (Hide it somewhere in the classroom before they come in.) When the children find it, ask: What can I buy with this money? (Allow students to think about it.)

Invite them to look in the Bible and read the Bible passage together. Explain to them things they might not understand (look at the "teacher preparation" section beforehand). You can use objects that show things about the story they are reading.

"Look at that!" said one of the Pharisees, annoyed. "See how Jesus allows these tax collectors and sinners to gather around him? This man welcomes sinners and eats with them."

"How terrible!" said a scribe angrily.

Another Pharisee said, "If he really were a prophet or the Messiah, he would have nothing to do with such despicable people."

Jesus listened. He wanted to help them understand that he doesn't reject anyone and so he shared this parable:

"Suppose a woman has ten silver coins and loses one. Doesn't she light a lamp, sweep the house and search carefully until she finds it?"

The people thought, "It would be very sad to lose a coin of that value."

"I wonder if she planned to put it in a string with ten coins before marrying," another said.

(It was customary for women to wear a chain with ten coins on their head when they got married.)

"I hope to never lose a coin like that!" thought another.

"And when she finds it," Jesus continued, *"she calls her friends and neighbors together and says, 'Rejoice with me; I have found my lost coin.'"*

People could imagine friends and neighbors happily celebrating with her.

Jesus looked at the angry scribes and Pharisees and said, *"In the same way, I tell you, there is rejoicing in the presence of the angels of God over one sinner who repents."*

Life Application

Talk to the students about actions and attitudes that can turn them away from God. Tell them that it's natural to feel sad or guilty when they do something wrong, but that doesn't mean that God has stopped loving them. Each child is extremely valuable, and so God seeks to forgive him (make reference to Luke 15:10 - There is joy in heaven when a sinner repents).

Ask them to listen while you or a guest explains the plan of salvation. Emphasize the love and grace of God. Tell them that the Lord is the One who seeks us and wants us to be with him. Help the children understand that God sent His Son Jesus to be the Savior of all, and now He is inviting them to ask for forgiveness. If they tell God they are sorry for the wrong they have done, he promises to forgive them (see 1 John 1: 9).

Bring to class some cards with the phrase: "I am valuable to God my Savior." Pray individually with each of the children who want to accept Jesus as their Savior. Then, say a final prayer with the whole group, thanking God for His love and forgiveness. Give each child a card at the end of class to take home.

IV. ACTIVITIES

Activity: Searching

Give your students the worksheet entitled "Searching." Read it with your students, let them search for Uncle Mario in the picture, and discuss the questions together.

Activity: LOST!

Give you students the worksheet entitled "Lost!" The passage for this lesson is Luke 15:1-3, 8-10. Discuss the first question and allow time for students to complete their drawing. Then talk about the sketches they made.

1. Have you ever lost something that is very important to you? Draw the lost object.
2. If it was so important or valuable to you, why did you lose it?

Encourage your students to write in the blank space what kind of reward they would offer for the lost object.

Activity: God's Response

Give your students the worksheet entitled "God's Response." Have them answer these questions according to the story and write the answers on the blank lines.

1. Who criticized Jesus?
2. Where was the coin lost?
3. What did the woman do when she realized that she had lost her coin?
4. How did the woman feel when she found the coin?

When they finish, discuss the answers together as a class. Now discuss the following questions. This will help them apply the lesson to their life.

a. Do you think that God stops loving you when you are disobedient?
b. What is sin?
c. When you sin, are you close to God?
d. Why do you think God seeks those who are sin?
e. How does God feel when we repent of our sins?
f. Why did Jesus compare the sinner with the lost coin?

Let your students draw a picture of what they believe happened in heaven when they asked God for forgiveness. Write under the picture: "I am valuable to God!"

Memory Verse

Read the verse directly from the Bible (Luke 10:27). Prepare some hearts in advance on which you will write the verse in sections, for example: "You shall love the Lord your God / with all your heart, / with all your soul, / with all your strength / and with all your mind; / and your neighbor as yourself." Stick the hearts under the chairs or benches where your students sit. You can also place them flipped over on the floor, mixed up so they cannot be read. Taking each heart, the children will try to put the verse in order. Then read it again. Mix up the hearts and let only the girls put them in order, and then let the boys do it. Each time you complete the verse, read it together aloud. Use this activity several times until the verse is in the correct order and your students have it memorized.

DON'T GIVE UP! KEEP TRUSTING

I. OVERVIEW

Biblical Base: Luke 18:1-8

Memory Verse: *"He answered, 'Love the Lord your God with all your heart and with all your soul and with all your strength and with all your mind'; and, 'Love your neighbor as yourself.'"* (Luke 10:27)

Biblical Truth: Jesus calls us to never give up. God works only for the BEST in our lives.

Lesson Objective: To help the students discover that God answers our prayers when we trust Him.

II. TEACHER PREPARATION

Children the age of your students are very good at getting what they want and getting it quickly. Children who attend church or go to Sunday school know what prayer is. However, they may have some doubts about the reasons for which we pray; also they may have misconceptions about how God answers our prayers.

This lesson will help them discover what Jesus meant when he taught us to pray without giving up. They will understand that God delights in answering prayer; and we can always trust that he wants the best for us.

Activity: Our Requests

Give your students the worksheet entitled "Our Requests." Ask them, "What kind of prayer do people pray in which they may not get the answer they want?" Have them write an example of this kind of prayer on the hand.

Then ask them, "When a person prays for something good, why do you think that sometimes God doesn't answer their prayer?" Discuss this with your class and explain that God always answers our prayers, just not always like we want Him to. He can answer with "Yes", "No", or "wait."

III. LESSON DEVELOPMENT

Introduction

Jesus' purpose in telling this parable was to show his disciples that they should always pray and not give up. However, we should not interpret this as an invitation to try to force God to answer selfish requests. On the contrary, Jesus wants to inspire our confidence in the One who can help us during any time of sadness, anxiety or concern.

Jesus prophesied his return to the Father; but the disciples wanted to know when he would return to earth to establish His Kingdom. Thus we see that prayer is described as medicine for difficult days. Remind your students about the last lesson, the "lost coin," and tell them that Jesus is our Savior and friend whom we can

approach through prayer, praise Him for His blessings, ask what we need, and thank him for what we receive.

Remind your students about the "Operation Good Samaritan" project. Ask if anyone brought donations for the needy. Tell them to deposit their items in the basket that is already prepared. Give them ideas of what items they can continue to bring.

Developing the Bible Story

Start with the following Questions and Answers:
1. Does anyone know what the inside of a courtroom is like? (Wait for answers.)
2. Have you seen a lawyer or judge on TV? (Opportunity to respond)
3. What does a judge do? (Decides what is right according to the law.)
4. What is another synonym for the word "justice"? (equality, right, fairness, etc.)

Judges have to hear both sides of a problem so they can make a fair decision. In this story, the widow has a problem with someone she calls her adversary. Who is an "adversary"? (Someone who fights against one or more enemies.)

Ask for volunteers to act out the story. Help them pronounce the difficult words and ask them to try to feel like they are their characters. You will need the following actors: two narrators, a judge and a girl to play the role of the widow.

Narrator 1: One day Jesus told his disciples a parable to showed them that they should always pray and not give up. He started by saying, *"In a certain town there was a judge who neither feared God nor cared what people thought. And there was a widow in that town who kept coming to him with* (a) *plea."*

Judge: Next case! Oh no! You again! How many times have you come here? What do you want now?

Widow: I am here today for the same reason I came last time. *"Grant me justice against my adversary!"* Please resolve this conflict so that I can live in peace.

Judge: I'm still thinking. Now go. Leave me alone.

Narrator 2: The woman left sadly. But she soon returned.

Judge: The next case. Oh no! You again. Don't tell me. Let me guess why you're here.

Widow: *"Grant me justice against my adversary!"*

Narrator 1: For many days that followed, the widow returned to the judge.

Judge: What? You? Again?

Widow: *"Grant me justice against my adversary!"*

Narrator 2: For some time, the judge refused to do what the widow asked. But after a while, he said,

Judge: *"Even though I don't fear God or care what people think, yet because this widow keeps bothering me, I'll see that she gets justice."*

Narrator 1: It was not long until the widow returned to see the judge again.

Widow: *"Grant me justice against my adversary!"*

Judge: All right, you win! Now leave me alone!

Narrator 1: Then Jesus said to his disciples, *"Listen to what the unjust judge says. And won't God bring about justice for his chosen ones, who cry out to him day and night? Will he keep putting them off? I tell you, he will see that they get justice, and quickly."*

Life Application

Tell the children that when they need something, they can ask God about it in prayer. They should not get discouraged if he doesn't answer right away; just keep praying. Tell them not to let the problem take away the peace that God has given them. Jesus is our righteous judge, and he is always attentive when we seek him. The Bible talks about God as a judge, so look in the Bible for the following passages:

2 Timothy 4:8 - God is a righteous judge.

Isaiah 33:22 - God is our judge who will save us.

Psalms 44:21 - God knows the secrets of our hearts.

1 Samuel 2:3 - God is all-knowing.

Explain that when they grow up, if they want to be lawyers or judges and they have the opportunity to help a colleague who has a problem, they must be honest and give people time to present their complaints. We all want our problems to be solved as soon as possible, and we must ask God for wisdom.

Conclude this time with a prayer; let your students present their requests, believing that God will answer them.

IV. ACTIVITIES

Activity: Judge the Judge

Give your students the worksheet "Judge the Judge." Rate the judge from the Bible story in each of the following categories. Draw an X on the line to show how he rates in each category.

1. Did the judge know the facts of the case? (A little knowledge/ a fair amount of knowledge/ full knowledge)

2. Did the judge show signs of care and concern for the widow? (No concern/ a little concern/ a lot of concern)

3. Was he a fair judge? (Not at all fair/ somewhat fair/ very fair)

What Kind of Judge is God?

Look up the following verses to find out:
- God's Knowledge: 1 Samuel 2:3; Psalm 44:21
- God's Care: 1 Peter 5:7
- God's Righteousness: 2 Timothy 4:8

Draw a star on each line to show what kind of judge God is.

Activity: What Did You Learn?

Give your students the worksheet titled "What Did You Learn" and then ask:

What have you learned from the parable Jesus told about the unjust judge?

Discuss the answers that are printed in the speech bubbles of the students on the worksheet.

The Bible teaches that God listens to us no matter how many times we go to him.

We can trust that God is fair and does the right thing.

We cannot manipulate God to give us what we want.

If even an unjust judge does good when we are persistent in asking; we don't have to worry about whether God will do good.

We can to trust that God will do the right thing, even if at times it seems that he doesn't answer our prayers.

Memory Verse

Write the memory verse on a piece of poster board:

"He answered, 'Love the Lord your God with all your heart and with all your soul and with all your strength and with all your mind'; and, 'Love your neighbor as yourself.'"

Now, draw or find pictures that represent the main words in the verse. For example:

For the words "He answered" draw a picture of Jesus and stick it above the phrase.

You can draw hearts for the word "love" and the word "heart", a child showing his muscles for the words "strength", children from different countries, making sure you can distinguish the difference, for the word "neighbor", etc. Stick each picture above the word it represents.

Have your students repeat the verse. Then cover the written words with paper, or if you can, remove or erase the words, one at a time until only the pictures are left and the students can say the verse with the pictures only.

THE PARABLE OF THE SOWER

I. OVERVIEW

Biblical Base: Luke 8:4-15

Memory Verse: *"He answered, 'Love the Lord your God with all your heart and with all your soul and with all your strength and with all your mind'; and, 'Love your neighbor as yourself.'"* (Luke 10:27)

Biblical Truth. True Christians don't let worries, problems or distractions keep them from trusting God.

Lesson Objective: To help the students reflect on the need to take care of their relationship with God, to grow spiritually, and to face difficulties without falling away from God.

II. TEACHER PREPARATION

The term "parable" was used in the Old Testament to describe any kind of story that was not to be taken literally; this also included fables, stories and riddles. Other Jewish teachers also used stories, but in general, their quality was not as good as the parables of Jesus.

Jesus' parables included a moral lesson or illustrated a truth. They were stories about common places, people and events. Jesus used them to illustrate the nature of the acts of God and the kind of response that people should give.

This parable is a simple description of the result of seeds being scattered on a field that had different soil types, both fertile and sterile. But the story itself says nothing about its meaning. Listeners were expected to ask, "What Does It Mean?"

Later, when the disciples asked Jesus what his parable meant, he began by making an overall statement about his use of parables. He said those who responded to his teachings had received knowledge according to God's purposes.

When Jesus spoke of "secrets," it referred to God's plans concerning the Kingdom that had been hidden for a long time, but were now being revealed to those he had chosen. Others refused to accept God's message, and that is why he now presented the truth in a veiled manner, so that if they didn't put in the effort to understand and accept, they would not become any wiser. This fulfilled the prophecy of Isaiah 6: 9-10 about those who don't understand the meaning of what they hear.

The language of the explanation of the parable differs in some details from Mark. Luke emphasizes the elements that he considers important for readers. The Word of God must be received with faith and perseverance if listeners are to be the kind of "soil" that produces good fruit.

In the hearts of some, the seed will never have opportunity to grow; while in others, growth will be interrupted because they will fail to persevere.

The principle revealed in this passage challenges us to receive the gospel message and to remain sensitive to the Holy Spirit for instruction.

The main goal, as a Sunday school teacher, is to help children come to know Jesus as their Savior. It's important to take advantage of this stage of childhood to sow the seed of the gospel, because it's at this age when the ground is very fertile and our commitment is to guide the child to establish a relationship with God.

Therefore, they need to understand that spiritual growth follows forgiveness of sins. To take care of your spiritual life requires nourishment and care, like a plant. Our Heavenly Father will provide that care in their lives through obedience to the Word of God and perseverance in prayer and worship.

Christians go through many difficulties that lead to spiritual failure, so you need to warn students of the dangers of not taking care of their personal relationship with God. Discuss with them the risks they may face in their spiritual life; perhaps discouragement due to problems they have with a friends in the church, or in sports, or at work.

Also, television programs, magazines or music that contradict the truths of God can be like thorns that damage their faith and keep them from seeing Jesus. Explain how dangerous it is to stop praying, reading the Bible and gathering to worship in a church.

III. LESSON DEVELOPMENT

Introduction

Prepare the classroom and welcome your students. Ask them to remember the previous lesson. The theme was praying and trusting in God. Ask: "Did you get an answer to prayer this week?" (Wait for replies.) Remind them that to trust in God is to wait knowing that he remains faithful to us.

Allow time for your students to put their gifts for

project "Operation Good Samaritan" in the basket. You can use the recommendation regarding this lesson that is at the beginning of this unit or use the following idea:

Bring to class a small potted plant and ask: "Do you know what this plant needs to live?" (Replies: water, sun and earth) "Do you think we could replace the soil with stones? (Wait for answers.) What would happen if it didn't get water or sunshine? (It would die.) Bring some seeds (beans, corn, etc.) and pass them around to your students and ask: "Have you ever sown (planted) seeds?"

Developing the Bible Story

Explain that today's story unfolds in Galilee during the busiest days of Jesus' ministry; villagers gathered to hear him teach. (Read the story aloud and have your students follow along on the worksheets that you give them.)

The Parable of the Sower

"A farmer went out to plant his field; some of his seeds fell on the road and the people who passed by stepped on them and the birds ate them. Other seeds fell where there were many stones: the plants sprouted, but soon died because they had no water. Others fell among thorns; the plants sprouted, but the thorns choked them and didn't let them grow. The rest of the seeds fell on good soil; the plants sprouted, grew and produced a crop that produced a hundred times more than what was planted."

"Look! Jesus is coming!" shouted a villager.

"And I see that some of our neighbors are already with him. Let's go so we can hear what he's saying."

Many villagers joined the crowd to hear the story Jesus was telling.

"A farmer went out to sow his seed," began Jesus. *"As he was scattering the seed, some fell along the path; it was trampled on, and the birds ate it up."*

The crowd looked at each other. Some of them were farmers and knew exactly what he was talking about, because this had happened in their fields.

"Some fell on rocky ground," Jesus continued, *"and when it came up, the plants withered because they had no moisture. Other seed fell among thorns, which grew up with it and choked the plants. Still other seed fell on good soil. It came up and yielded a crop, a hundred times more than was sown."*

"What does this parable mean?" the disciples asked.

"I am telling you some secrets about the kingdom of God" said Jesus. "You will understand, but some people will hear and won't know what it means."

"This story is like a riddle," they thought.

Later, Jesus' disciples asked him what the story meant, and so he said, *"This is the meaning of the parable: The seed is the Word of God. Those along the path are the ones who hear, and then the devil comes and takes away the Word from their hearts, so that they may not believe and be saved. Those on the rocky ground are the ones who receive the Word with joy when they hear it, but they have no root. They believe for a while, but in the time of testing they fall away. The seed that fell among thorns stands for those who hear, but as they go on their way they are choked by life's worries, riches and pleasures, and they don't mature."*

"Mmm," murmured the people. They had seen overgrown fields. Weeds don't let the seeds grow.

The disciples listened carefully until Jesus finished his explanation.

"But the seed on good soil stands for those with a noble and good heart, who hear the word, retain it, and by persevering produce a crop."

Life Application

Explain to the children that God expects to find in them hearts that are ready to hear the message and want to grow and produce fruit.

Activity: What Difference Does the Soil Make?

Give your students the worksheet entitled "What Difference Does the Soil Make?" (They will also need the back of the worksheet. If you make copies and cannot copy both sides on one sheet of paper, be sure to have the second page for them to cutout.) Ask them to look at the pictures of the two plants. Show them how to cut the page to discover what makes the difference between the two plants. Let them plant some seeds, take care of them and wait for the plants to germinate. When the plants have sprouted, let them tell others about it.

IV. ACTIVITIES

Activity: Who is What?

Give you students the worksheet with this section on it. Help your students remember the story to find the answers to this activity. Tell them: "You have learned that a parable is a story that uses a common thing or experience to explain a Biblical truth. Let's look at the parable again. Jesus told the disciples the meaning of each symbol in the story. Now, draw a line to connect the symbols with their meanings.

Activity: Avoid The Traps

Give your students the worksheet titled "Avoid The Traps." Let them use their Bibles to complete the activity.

A wise Christian avoids the dangers that would hurt their growth. Look up Luke 8:4-15 in your Bible. In the parable of the sower, what dangers or situations can become traps that would keep you from growing spiritually? (To listen, but not hear the truth; to allow difficulties to keep you from believing and growing; to let problems or activities capture your attention and thus neglect God.)

How do you avoid these dangers? (Truly listen to the Word of God; refuse to allow difficulties to get in the way of your relationship with God; keep God at the center of your life.)

Say, "What did Jesus say about those who are represented by the seed that falls on good soil?" (Those with a noble and good heart.) What do those that have a noble and good heart do? (Hear the word, retain it. They hear the word and put it into practice in their lives.) Ask you students if they have accepted Jesus Christ as their Savior. (If anyone says no, then give them the opportunity to ask Christ's forgiveness and pray with them.) Have your students make a list of what they should not do to care for their spiritual life, and another of what to do every day to grow spiritually.

Memory Verse

Write the verse on sheets of paper. Remove the vowels and leave blank spaces in their place. You can give each child a sheet or let them work in pairs. Explain that you have lost the vowels and you need them to write them in the blanks.

When they finish, give them a piece of paper with the entire verse on it so they can see if they did it correctly. While they are checking their work, have them recite the verse from memory.

At the end of the class, pray with the children, asking God to help each one of them keep their hearts clean for Him. And that they will always listen to God's Word and grow spiritually.

NOTES:

80

IS IT BAD TO BE RICH?

I. OVERVIEW

Biblical Base: Luke 16:13-15; Gal 5:22-23

Memory Verse: *"He answered, 'Love the Lord your God with all your heart and with all your soul and with all your strength and with all your mind'; and, 'Love your neighbor as yourself.'"* (Luke 10:27)

Biblical Truth: Money and material things are not bad, as long as they don't have the first place in our lives. Riches may be a sign of God's blessing (but not always).

Lesson Objective: To help the students discover that money and possessions are neither good nor bad; they just cannot be our priority.

II. TEACHER PREPARATION

Luke uses the parable of the "Rich Man and Lazarus" to address the Pharisees who loved wealth and mocked what Jesus said about this. They justified their materialistic attitudes, noting certain Old Testament scriptures and ignoring others. They taught that riches were a sign of God's favor. And if a person was poor, it was a sign of God's punishment.

This parable clearly contradicted the materialistic thinking of the Pharisees. Jesus' message was clear: There was a rich man who died and went to hell. The beggar named Lazarus died and the angels carried him to Abraham's side in heaven.

The parable rejects the idea that the rich have wealth because God rewards their righteousness. It also contradicts the common belief that poverty was a sign of sin. It's also important to note that Jesus was not condemning all who flourish. Likewise he didn't suggest that all those who were poor automatically inherit eternal life. His message was clear: "God knows (judges) our hearts."

Your students are aware of materialism that is in our world. They know that people place value on wealth and possessions. And they have doubts about why some people have an abundance and others have much need.

This parable makes them think about their own value system. The lesson will also help them understand that neither wealth nor poverty are indicators of a person's relationship with God. You will discover that the fruits of the Spirit are the only sure evidence of a good relationship with the Lord.

III. LESSON DEVELOPMENT

Introduction

Ask your students to tell about were some of the dangers they tried to avoid this week. Ask: "Do you feel discouraged?" (If they say yes, encourage them.)

Have you reached your target amount for "Operation Good Samaritan"? How do your students feel about the results of this project so far? Congratulate and celebrate their achievement with them.

Activity: Seeing What's Important

Give each of your students the worksheet titled "Seeing What's Important." Give your students a few minutes to look at the pictures on the worksheet before asking them to answer the questions. Ask: "How much can you tell about other people just by looking at them? Pretend that you are detectives. Look at the pictures of the three children. What do you know about them just by looking at the pictures? (There will be answers about color of their hair, clothes, etc...) "Do you know their age? Do you know if they love God or not?" (Allow them to discuss the answers to your questions.)

Ask: "If these children moved into your neighborhood, what would you like to know about them?" (Accept all answers.) "What if you find out that they discriminate against people because of their skin color, race or social class? Would your attitude change?"

Developing the Bible Story

Before reading the story, you may want to share some of the context found in the teacher preparation section so that children have a better understanding of the story.

Lazarus and the Rich Man

"No servant can serve two masters," Jesus said. *"You cannot serve both God and money."*

The Pharisees, who loved money, sneered at him. "He wouldn't say that if he had money," the Pharisees thought. "Besides, our teachers taught us that God rewards those who serve him. Our money shows that God is blessing us. Jesus thinks God wants His chosen people to be poor? Everyone knows that being poor is a punishment from God."

"What people value highly is detestable in God's sight," Jesus said.

A disciple said, "You know how proud the Pharisees are of their wealth. They believe that large amounts of money show that God is pleased with them."

"There was a rich man who was dressed in purple and fine linen and lived in luxury every day," said Jesus. *"At his gate was laid a beggar named Lazarus, covered with sores and*

longing to eat what fell from the rich man's table."

"What did the rich do to receive these blessings of God?" the Pharisees asked.

"I would like to know what Lazarus did to deserve such misery. I wouldn't want to be him," thought another.

Jesus continued his story. *"The time came when the beggar died and the angels carried him to Abraham's side. The rich man also died and was buried."*

"It probably was a glorious funeral!" thought the Pharisees. "But we are surprised that Lazarus was with Abraham. What is going on?" they asked.

Jesus continued. *"In Hades, where he was in torment, he looked up and saw Abraham far away, with Lazarus by his side."*

The Pharisees were amazed. "How could a beggar be with Abraham and a rich and blessed man be sent to hell?" This bothered the Pharisees.

Jesus continued telling his story: The rich man shouted, *"Father Abraham, have pity on me and send Lazarus to dip the tip of his finger in water and cool my tongue, because I am in agony in this fire."*

"But Abraham replied, 'Son, remember that in your lifetime you received your good things, while Lazarus received bad things, but now he is comforted here and you are in agony. And besides all this, between us and you a great chasm has been set in place, so that those who want to go from here to you cannot, nor can anyone cross over from there to us.'"

The rich man thought of his five brothers (who also had many possessions). *"Then I beg you, father, send Lazarus to my family, for I have five brothers. Let him warn them, so that they won't also come to this place of torment."*

Life Application

Ask: What was the difference between Lazarus, who went to heaven, and the rich man, who went to hell? (Lazarus was poor but loved God and obeyed God's commands. The rich man cared only for money.)

Read Luke 16:13 out loud and ask, "Does this verse tell us that people who have a lot of money cannot be Christians?" Tell your students that there is nothing wrong with having money, unless money and possessions are more important to you than God. Remind the children that the Lord commanded us to have no other gods before him.)

Say: "Does this parable teach us that being poor is a sign of being a follower of Jesus? Do poor people have assurance of eternal life to compensate them for their pain on earth?" (Answer: No. The Bible says clearly that we'll only inherit eternal life if we have a personal relationship with Christ. Neither wealth nor poverty are signs of our salvation. Read John 14:6 to your students.)

"How can money takes us away from following God? How can money help us?" (Let the children tell what they think. Remind them that if people or objects mean more to them than God, those things can be described as being their "lord.") "Think about who or what is most important in your life, and if they/it distracts you from God." Continue:

"How do we know when God is pleased or not with our life?" (Encourage them to think about how they can know if they are loving and obeying God.)

IV. ACTIVITIES

Activity: Who Said That?

Give each student the worksheet entitled "Who Said That." (Note: This worksheet has 2 sides, so if you are making copies, make sure to copy both sides, preferably on one sheet of paper. If that is not possible, then glue the two sheets together.) Say: "In this story, Jesus expresses some of the words that other Bible characters said. Look at the different verses to identify what words were said by which characters." (Have your students cut along the solid black line at the top of the square. Then students can work in pairs to get the answers. They can check their work by folding each triangular along the dotted lines.)

"Father Abraham, have pity on me and send Lazarus to dip the tip of his finger in water and cool my tongue, because I am in agony in this fire." (Luke 16:24) (The Rich Man)

"But Abraham replied, 'Son, remember that in your lifetime you received your good things, while Lazarus received bad things, but now he is comforted here and you are in agony." (Luke 16:25) (Abraham)

"... covered with sores and longing to eat what fell from the rich man's table." (Luke 16:21) (Lazarus)

"... God knows your hearts. What people value highly is detestable in God's sight." (Luke 16:15) (Jesus)

Activity: A Special Vision

Give your students the worksheet entitled "A Special Vision" (this is the back of the previous activity). Help your students complete this activity. They will need to find 1 Samuel 16-7b and Galatians 5:22-23 in their Bibles.

Memory Verse

Before class, cut several sheets of paper into four parts each. On eleven of those pieces, write one or two words of the verse: (1) He answered (2) Love the Lord 3) your God (4) with all your (5) heart and with (6) all your soul (7) and with all (8) your strength (9) and with all your mind (10) and Love your (11) neighbor as yourself. Fold each paper and put them in a bag. Take some additional pieces of paper and write words that are not from the verse on them. Fold them and toss them into the bag also, to mix up with others. The total number of papers should equal to the number of students in your class. If there are less than eleven children, regroup the words so that you have the same number of papers as students. Repeat the verse with your students until they have it memorized. Then invite everyone to take a paper out of the bag. Have them read their paper and see if the words are part of the verse they have learned.

Have those that have the words of the verse line up in the order of the verse. Verify that the words are correct and ask them to repeat the verse aloud. Those who have memorized the verse will receive a star on their "Verse of the Month Club" certificate.

GUIDE FOR UNIT VIII

JESUS' TEACHINGS ABOUT PRAYER

Bible Truth: Through the lessons of this unit, the student will learn the way Jesus taught his disciples to pray.

UNIT OBJECTIVE: That the students will comprehend the teaching of Jesus about prayer and will be able to:
- Understand and know by heart the "Lord's Prayer."
- Honor God every time he/she prays.
- Trust God, bringing to him his/her requests.
- Accept that the will of God must be first in our prayers.
- Learn to forgive others and ask God for forgiveness and protection.
- Recognize God as his/her heavenly father.
- Pray for others in the way Jesus taught us.

UNIT LESSONS
- Lesson 31: To pray is to honor God.
- Lesson 32: To pray is to present our needs to him.
- Lesson 33: To pray is an opportunity to forgive and to ask for forgiveness.
- Lesson 34: To pray is a way to ask for protection.

VERSE OF THE UNIT: *"This, then, is how you should pray: 'Our Father in heaven, hallowed be your name, your kingdom come, your will be done, on earth as it is in heaven. Give us today our daily bread. And forgive us our debts, as we also have forgiven our debtors. And lead us not into temptation, but deliver us from the evil one.'"* (Matthew 6:9-13)

It is possible that children who are in an advanced elementary class who have attended church have already recited the Lord's prayer in the worship service and have already memorized it by heart.

They must understand that praying the Lord's prayer is more than a simple religious exercise. They need to understand that prayer allows them to bring their needs to God. In this unit, the children will analyze this prayer as a model to praise God and to present their needs to him. When they learn the teachings of Jesus about prayer, the student will understand the importance of honoring God the father and to forgive others, as He has forgiven us. They will also learn that God delights when his children come to him. Finally, this unit will help them to know the importance of praying in the will of God.

Suggestions:
1. The challenge of memorization during this unit is for every child to learn the Lord's Prayer. To make this challenge easier, work with small parts of the Lord's Prayer each time. Highlight the verses that complement the lesson every week. Let them learn verse by verse, and then they can try repeating the whole prayer.

2. At the end of the unit, each student will be able to get a star for their certificate in the Verse of the Month Club. You can arrange a chart on the wall where everybody can see, with the names of your students. Highlight their improvement in their learning by awarding a star, a mark or a sticker.

3. During this unit of learning about Jesus and prayer, help the students understand that talking directly to God is a privilege. Help them not only feel the majesty and holiness of God, but also to trust him, bringing their needs to the Lord.

4. Tell them that you won't ask them to pray out loud, but they can if they want. Pray the Lord's Prayer all together so every single child can feel comfortable even if they don't know it by heart yet.

Necessary Materials:
Plain white paper, staples, construction paper. Cover the frame with colorful paper and place the Lord's Prayer in the center of the frame. Also make a big sign with the title "Jesus teaches us to pray." It's better if you have these materials ready for the first lesson.

Introduce new activities like writing their own prayers. You can help them try it on their own. For example: you can suggest the first phrase of the praise, and then let them finish it on their own. Be careful about being respectful of the privacy of your kids and their need of talking with God in their own way.

TO PRAY IS TO HONOR GOD

I. OVERVIEW

Biblical Base: Matthew 5-7

Memory Verse: "*This, then, is how you should pray: 'Our Father in heaven, hallowed be your name, your kingdom come, your will be done, on earth as it is in heaven. Give us today our daily bread. And forgive us our debts, as we also have forgiven our debtors. And lead us not into temptation, but deliver us from the evil one.'*" (Matthew 6:9-13)

Biblical Truth. Our prayers should always honor God.

Lesson Objective: To help the kids know how to honor God when they pray.

II. TEACHER PREPARATION

Chapters 5,6 and 7 of the gospel of Mathew record the well-known "Sermon on the mount," because Jesus preached/taught this while on a hill close to Capernaum. This paragraph is also found in Luke 6:20-49, with some differences made by God in the revelation to each writer.

Mathew wrote about the Lord's Prayer in the Sermon on the Mount. It appears that the audience was a mixed group of listeners. The first words of Jesus were addressed to the apostles; but there was a crowd listening to him. This sermon is one of the five biggest recorded in the gospel of Mathew, summarizing many days of preaching.

Jesus defines his attitude towards the law, challenges the pride and the hypocrisy of the leaders, and moves the attention towards the most important in the kingdom of God.

This sermon reflects the humble and sincere condition of the people, such as the prophets in the Old Testament had done, (Isaiah 57:15, 61:1-2; Psalm 51:10,16,17; 41:1), and describe the ideals in order to live a life that pleases God. Everything in the Sermon on the Mount need to be analyzed from the declaration of Jesus when he says,"The kingdom of God is starting."

While the sermon has teachings about a variety of subjects, this unit focuses on the teachings of Jesus about prayer. Jesus clearly condemn the practice of the hypocrites, who loved to show their spirituality. He also warns them about "vain repetitions" (Mathew 6:7-9).

In Jesus' example of prayer when he addresses God as "Father," he shows us that we can get close to him and that we can experience intimate relationship with God.

The phrase "Our Father in heaven, hallowed be your name" indicates that God, besides being almighty, holy and majestic, is also loving protector and he is close to us. This first part of the example prayer becomes a praise

that seeks to honor the name of God. Treating it with respect and reverence to his holiness is a way of honoring God. If we treat his name lightly in our prayers, without recognizing these attributes, we are not giving him the recognition of holy and God.

"Your kingdom come." This request was a plea for God to establish his government, his spiritual kingdom. In Jeremiah 30:3-8, God promised that restoration. The Jews prayed this way confidently, because they already knew the power of God to set them free from other kingdoms and slavery.

In Jesus' time, they were conquered by Rome, so they prayed for that. However, when Christians prayed that way, they were saying, we want the perfect kingdom of God to come, for the salvation of our souls.

"Your will be done." Ralph Earle says that Jesus repeated this third request in the Mount of Olives in Gethsemane (Luke 22:42). It is a trusting declaration that God's will be done in this world as it is in heaven. There is not a better prayer to be offered. We should take this as our personal prayer: may your will be done in my heart first as it is in heaven. Then may it will be done everywhere on the earth.

Most of the children know that prayer is one way to communicate with God to tell him whatever we want. Some people think that repeating prayers by heart pleases God. Others learn that praying is a way to ask for material items or other needs. The importance of this first lesson is the truth that true prayer is more than asking for material objects, wishes or repeating phrases.

The child could ask himself: Am I doing alright by repeating my praises or requests to God? Of course not. It isn't bad to come to the Lord with the same request; Jesus encourage us to persist in our prayers but he doesn't like vain repetitions of an insincere heart. This prayer that Jesus taught us could be an example for our own prayers. We must praise God in our prayers, pray for his kingdom in the world, for our needs and ask his help in our problems and conflicts.

What happen if a child has never known his father or if the father he has mistreats him? How can this child see his father without experiencing fear or anger against his father? Now days, many families don't follow the pattern of "dad," "mom" and "children"; family disintegration and child abuse and exploitation are happening all around the world. How can you show God the father to them? By teaching them the promises of comfort, mercy, satisfaction and peace that this passage mentions about.

Talk about the kind of love they experience from their parents; or think about the love you have for them as your class. In this messy world where there is often no protection, security or love, God shows himself as a father. The only thing he expects from us is obedience and praises to his holy name, and he wants us to be part of his kingdom.

III. LESSON DEVELOPMENT

Introduction

Ask: Who of you have told the parables of Jesus in your home last week? If you have done that, what were the answers of those who listened to you?

Develop the lesson using the activities from the student's notebook. Use the first activity to introduce the study about praying.

Activity: An important part of life

Have the kids find this activity in their worksheet; give them time to study the album pictures. Then ask them the questions from the right side of the page while you guide them through the story. Highlight how good it is to have someone come in prayer to give thanks and ask for help.

Ask: What is happening in each picture? (Let the kids identify them based on their own experiences.) What do these pictures have in common? (There is a person praying in each picture.) Why do you think these people are doing that? (Listen to their explanations about prayer.) Emphasize how important prayer is in our lives.

Developing the Bible Story

Explain briefly the meaning of "The Sermon on the Mount" and note the vocabulary words you will need. Write them on the board or on pieces of paper:

Abolish: Get rid of something.

Pharisee: Jewish leaders who gave high importance to law enforcement.

Hypocrite: Someone who claims to love God and follow him, but doesn't do it. Someone who tries to show that something is true that is not true, or vice versa. They do this to impress someone else.

Hallowed: Keep something holy, set apart for God.

Jesus teaches us to pray

Dramatize this dialogue with your class, and then talk about it.

"Look back!" said one of the disciples to another one. "The crowd following Jesus is huge." "Yes, the people have followed us everywhere we've been," said the other one. Jesus wanted to get to a place where everybody would be able to hear his teachings, so he went up to the mountain and he sat and started to teach them. He loved to explain about God's Kingdom to people. He told them who would be blessed.

So Jesus said, "Don't think that I have come to abolish the Law or the Prophets; I have not come to abolish them but to fulfill them. For truly I tell you, until heaven and earth disappear, not the smallest letter, not the least stroke of a pen, will by any means disappear from the Law until everything is accomplished."

"The Pharisees would be glad to hear that," thought the disciples. But Jesus had not finished. "For I tell you that unless your righteousness surpasses that of the Pharisees and the teachers of the law, you will certainly not enter the kingdom of heaven."

Some of the people from the crowd were jabbing each other and raising their eyebrows. "How is that possible?" they asked themselves. "Pharisees keep more rules than everyone else!" Jesus explained how love fulfills the law. Somebody who joined the crowd asked, "What did I miss?" "Jesus told us about everything," he was told, "murders, disagreements, about loving your enemies and helping the poor."

"When you pray, don't be as the hypocrites are," Jesus said, "for they love to pray standing in the synagogues and on the street corners, to be seen by others. If showing off is everything they want, truly I tell you, they have received their reward in full. But when you pray, go into your room, close the door and pray to your Father, who is unseen. Then your Father, who sees what is done in secret, will reward you. You don't have to worry about long and elaborate prayers. God doesn't get impressed by many words. After all, your Father knows what things you have need of, before you ask him. This, then, is how you should pray. 'Our Father in heaven, hallowed be your name, your kingdom come, your will be done, on earth as it is in heaven. Give us today our daily bread. And forgive us our debts, as we also have forgiven our debtors. And lead us not into temptation, but deliver us from the evil one. Amen.'" (Mathew 6:9-13)

IV. ACTIVITIES

Activity: A model to pray

Have the kids open their bibles to Mathew 6:9-10 and ask them to re-write those verses using their own words. What do you call God? (Father) That means that you see God as a loving and protective person and older than you, and you know that he is good, holy and perfect. Are you telling him that everything should be done as you want? (No, because he knows what to do, it should be his will and not mine.) That means that I know that God knows what is best for me, I show my respect by doing that.

Life Application

Ask them: How did the Pharisees feel about Jesus' teachings? (Angry, Happy, indifferent, amazed, confused, scared and worried.) Let the kids choose some of these words, and ask them why.

Jesus teaches us not to be like the hypocrites. Why? What do they do? (Let the kids comment on their thoughts or what they have learned.) Say: We don't pray to God to impress other people: neither do we use big words thinking that God will answer sooner.

Activity: Get a good start on your prayers.

This is the last activity. Work with the kids who have a hard time answering the questions.

Memory Verse

Read the Lord's Prayer directly from the bible. When you read it from the bible make sure to stick on the board a picture that represents each phrase. For example, when you say: "Our Father in heaven," stick the picture of the clouds. "hallowed be your name" - a bible with the word "God" o "Father"; "your kingdom come" - a crown; "your will be done, on earth" - children praying; "as it is in heaven" - An angel between clouds. Keep doing that with the rest of the verse. Repeat as many times as you consider enough. Then take the words out and repeat it using only the pictures.

NOTES:

TO PRAY IS TO PRESENT OUR NEEDS

I. OVERVIEW

Biblical Base: Matthew 6:11; 14:6-21

Memory Verse: "*This, then, is how you should pray: 'Our Father in heaven, hallowed be your name, your kingdom come, your will be done, on earth as it is in heaven. Give us today our daily bread. And forgive us our debts, as we also have forgiven our debtors. And lead us not into temptation, but deliver us from the evil one.'*" (Matthew 6:9-13)

Biblical Truth: When we have needs, we come to God through prayer, trusting that he hears us and that he will answer according to his will.

Lesson Objective: To help the kids trust that God will answer their needs when they pray.

II. TEACHER PREPARATION

In Matthew 14:6-12 we find four characters to study about.

The first one is Herod, who was the governor or King of Galilee, and he was celebrating his birthday. He was having an eastern party where only men were invited, and women were hired only to dance.

The second one is Herodias, the wife of Herod's step-brother. She lived with the king, and of course, that was adultery.

The third one is John the Baptist, Jesus' cousin, who condemned Herodias of adultery. She was very upset with John the Baptist because of this. She made her daughter Salome ask for John's head when Herod let her ask for a request as a reward for dancing at his birthday party. The king accepted her request because he said that he would please her with anything she would ask for, including half of his kingdom. So he sent someone to behead John.

The forth character is Jesus, who showed his humanity experiencing sadness because of what happened to John the Baptist. Many other times he was sad and cried, but this time he felt the need to be alone. In the bible we see that he went away alone in a boat. When people couldn't find Jesus, they started to search for him, because they already knew that he was the one who could meet their needs.

Tell your students that Jesus knows a lot about being sad (Matthew 14:13, John 11:35). Encourage them to seek Jesus as soon as they have a need in their hearts. God, who sees and knows everything, loves it when we trust in his love and power to solve any problem or need we have, he likes it when we pray to him. Remind them that Jesus is always ready to listen to us.

III. LESSON DEVELOPMENT

Introduction

Ask your students, "Have you called God 'Father' in your prayers? How do you feel when you do that?" Ask for volunteers to give a short testimony about what God means to them. Invite one of the children to pray for the lesson. Tell them that the prayer must be sincere and respectful to honor God the Father.

Start with a drama about the Bible Story (Matthew 14:12-21). One child will be Jesus, two children will be his disciples, and at least three more kids will be the sick people presented to Jesus. Chose a boy or girl to bring the bread and fish.

Jesus: (He is sitting and swaying back and forth, pretending to be in a boat on the ocean. He gets off the boat and gets close to the sick people.)

Sick people: (One could have chicken pox. Paint his/her face with lipstick or face-paint. Another could have a toothache: wrap his/her head with a cloth. Another could have a broken leg or arm, get a walking stick. They come close to Jesus and he heals them by touching them and they take off what makes them look sick.)

Disciples: (They go to Jesus and tell him) It's getting dark, so you should tell them to go back home to eat.

Jesus: You give them food to eat.

Disciples: We only have five loaves of bread and two fish.

Jesus: (While Jesus is blessing the bread and fish, and everybody else is praying, another kid adds more bread so everybody can eat.)

Thank the actors for their participation with applause. Help the kids understand that Jesus attended to at least two different kind of needs. The first one was health - he healed them because he had compassion for them. The second one was a basic need - food. Now, let's see what steps had been taken:

1. People went to Jesus because they needed healing and food.

2. They came to Jesus with their needs, and Jesus

answered their needs with compassion.

The bible doesn't mention that he didn't heal some of them, so we assume that Jesus healed everyone who came to him. Then he saw that they were hungry, so he provided food for them. People satisfied their hunger and there were left-overs afterwards.

Everyone - men, women, children and young people who came to Jesus got what they needed. After acting out the story, ask the kids to follow the Bible Story in their worksheets as you read it aloud, to reinforce the message.

Developing the Bible Story

Jesus Feeds 5000 People

"Have you heard the terrible news about John the Baptist?" asked one of the disciples with sadness on his face.

"Yes, we just heard about it," answered another disciple with a low voice.

"The dearest friend and cousin of Jesus, dead! I can hardly believe it!"

"What did Jesus do when he heard the news?" asked another disciple.

"He went away in a boat."

"Did anybody go with him?"

"No, he wanted to find a quiet place where he could be alone. However, after a little while people started looking for Jesus. They wanted to bring their sick relatives and friends to Jesus to be healed and to hear his teachings."

"Do you know where Jesus is? My brother is very sick!" cried a man.

"He is there! Over in that boat!"

Jesus came to the bay and stopped his boat on the beach. When he got out of his boat, he saw a huge crowd. He had compassion for them and healed those who were sick.

"I know that you can help me!" cried a woman.

"Jesus, come over here! Help me! Only you can do this," cried out another one. The crowd surrounded Jesus. As soon as he touched someone, somebody else would call out his name.

"Please, Jesus! Help me!"

About dinner time, the disciples went to Jesus to tell him, "This place is deserted and it's getting late. Tell the people to go and look for food in the closest towns; they must be getting hungry."

"They don't need to go," Jesus said to his disciples. "You give them food."

The disciple couldn't believe what they were hearing. "How are we going to feed a huge crowd? There are at least five thousand men, plus women and children. We don't have enough money to buy food for all of them. And we only have two loaves of bread and five fish."

"Bring those to me," Jesus said. The disciple gave Jesus the bread and the fish. Jesus told everybody to sit on the grass. Then he took the bread and fish, and raising his eyes to the heavens, he thanked God for the food. Then he divided the food into pieces, telling his disciples to start passing it out to the people.

Everybody ate, and afterwards they picked up twelve full baskets of left-overs.

Life Application

Activity: My Prayers

Grab the children's attention on this activity. Tell them to circle the reason for what they have prayed for:

- For someone they love who is sick;
- For money;
- For a friend who needs help;
- For a problem at school;
- For the church;
- For missionaries;
- For family.

IV. ACTIVITIES

Activity 2: Who cares?

Ask: "What problems or needs do children of your age have?" Tell them to write their answer on the packages in the basket and exchange their basket with someone else. Challenge the kids to pray for those needs they have in the basket.

Memory Verse

Read the verse several times. To make it fun, first read it aloud all together, then only girls and after that only boys. Finally, read all together again.

You could write phrases of the verse on each slice of bread (in the Bible story). Have them cut out the phrases and stick them on the wall or on the white-board/chalkboard. To finish the lesson, please take time to pray with them; you can always ask for volunteers to pray.

PRAYING IS AN OPPORTUNITY TO FORGIVE AND BE FORGIVEN

I. OVERVIEW

Biblical Base: Matthew 6: 12, 18:21-35

Memory Verse: *"This, then, is how you should pray: 'Our Father in heaven, hallowed be your name, your kingdom come, your will be done, on earth as it is in heaven. Give us today our daily bread. And forgive us our debts, as we also have forgiven our debtors. And lead us not into temptation, but deliver us from the evil one.'"* (Matthew 6:9-13)

Biblical Truth: Prayer can be a good way for us to ask God for forgiveness, as well as forgive those who have offended us.

Lesson Objective: To help the students understand that God answers our prayers when we ask for forgiveness and forgive those around us.

II. TEACHER PREPARATION

In the study passage (Matthew 18: 21-35), Peter asks, "Lord, how many times should I forgive my brother when he sins against me? Seven times?" While seven was a number of perfection among the Jews, Peter doesn't use it in this sense.

Among the Jews, it was a rule to not forgive someone more than three times. Revenge is natural in people who are vindictive; and therefore it is very difficult for them to forgive offenses.

In v. 22, the Lord expands the number of times we should forgive: seventy times seven. There is something very remarkable in these words, especially if they are related to Genesis 4:24 where they are used exactly the same. "If Cain shall be avenged seven times, Lamech seventy times seven." The righteous God punished sin in an exemplary manner.

Sinful man is exposed to divine justice, and therefore should be forgiving in abundance, especially because only the merciful obtain mercy. When Jesus tells Peter "seventy times seven," he wants him to know that he should always be willing to forgive. In the passage of the two debtors, Jesus tells a parable to them to show them the connection between the kingdom of heaven and forgiveness.

Ten thousand talents (v. 24) is calculated as approximately 60 million silver coins.

When ordering the man (v. 25), along with his wife and children, the Lord refers here to an ancient Hebrew custom of selling a man and his family to collect debts. We see this in Exodus 22: 3; Leviticus 25:39, 47; 2 Kings 4: 1.

In v. 26, the servant asks, "Have patience with me and I'll pay thee all" (Matthew 18:26). This shows us his need for forgiveness. In v. 27, we note that the source of salvation for a lost world is God's eternal mercy and compassion.

However in v. 28, the servant who had been forgiven would not forgive the person who owed him, and so he put that man into jail for the debt of a hundred silver coins. In v. 30, the attitude of humans is presented. God doesn't show mercy to those who don't show mercy; this is an eternal purpose of the Lord that no one can change. What God does with us is what he teaches us to do with our neighbor.

In v. 34, the servant is delivered to the torturers. This doesn't only refer to continued imprisonment, but the torture that accompanies it.

Jesus finished teaching by saying what his heavenly Father will do to us (v. 35). The kindness that God shows toward us is the pattern that we should follow in our relationship with others.

In the Lord's Prayer when the Lord says, "And forgive us our debts, as we forgive our debtors," it makes us reflect on how we were freely forgiven, and how we must in turn freely forgive others.

Forgiving seems simple, but it is difficult to heal the pain of offenses. We cannot forget or erase from our minds what happened, but we can ask the Lord to heal us. There will be a scar, but no pain or resentment needs to remain in our hearts once the Holy Spirit heals the wound. Only he changes the heart.

Often, forgiveness is not as simple as accepting an apology from someone who asks for our forgiveness. This can only be achieved if we believe that God can change it.

People are accustomed to getting revenge for the wrongs done to them. Compassion, mercy and forgiveness is a testament of the love of Christ in the heart; and with this we can impact others, because it shows that we are the true children of God. The best medicine for healing the wounds of offenses is the love of God in one's heart.

Tell your students the importance of the forgiveness of God for us, and our forgiveness to our neighbor. Perhaps some of them have resentment toward their parents for how they treated them. Or think about the problems children may be dealing with and reflect on those points. Pray with them if you see a need. Remember that you are their spiritual guide, and you have been given the beautiful privilege of caring for them.

III. LESSON DEVELOPMENT

Introduction

Prepare the classroom in advance and receive the students at the door, welcoming each one by name.

Ask: "Who prayed for what their partner wrote last week? Did anyone of you pray to God presenting a need?" (Have them share if God answered their prayers.)

Read the biblical story, "The unforgiving servant." Guide the students during class by reading it out loud. Clarify some situations or words that are not easily understood. (Allow children to ask questions.)

Write the letters of the word "FORGIVENESS" on the board out of order. Challenge the children to find what word they can form with these letters. When they find it, ask its meaning.

Say: "How many times do you think you can forgive someone who offends you?" (After they answer, read the Bible story together.)

Developing the Bible Story

The Unforgiving Servant

"Mom, how long do I have to forgive my brother?"

You're not the first to ask this. Did you know that Peter also did? He approached Jesus and asked him, "Lord, if a brother of the church does something against me, how often should I forgive him? Up to seven times?" Jesus answered, "I tell you, not seven times, but seventy times seven." We must forgive again and again; that is, forever. And for the disciples to understand this better, Jesus told them a parable:

"The kingdom of God works like something that happened some time in a far away country. A king summoned his employees to inform him what they owed him. When he started checking accounts, he saw an employee who owed him a lot of money. Since the employee didn't have any money to pay his debt, the king ordered him to be sold as a slave, along with his wife and children, and also to sell everything he had. This was so he could start paying back the debt with the money made.

But the employee knelt before the king and begged:

"Lord, have patience with me and I'll pay you everything." The king felt sorry for his employee and said, "Go quietly. I forgive you all that you owe me."

Leaving the palace of the king, that employee met a fellow who owed him 100 silver coins. He grabbed him by the neck and said, "Pay me back what you owe me."

This fellow knelt before him and begged, "Give me a little more time and I'll pay you!" But he refused and put him in jail until he paid the money he owed. Another fellow, seeing what had happened, went to tell the king.

Then the king asked to see the evil employee and said:

"How wicked you are! I forgave all that you owed me because you begged me. Why do you not have mercy on the other man as I had on you?"

The king was furious and ordered that the employee be punished until he paid all that was due. Jesus concluded: "So will my Father in heaven deal with each of you unless you forgive your brother sincerely."

Life Application

Ask, "Was the servant's attitude correct?" They will respond no. Ask: "Have you ever not wanted to forgive?" Read Matthew 6:12 and reflect on this verse. Explain what the will of God is for everyone: He expects us to be willing to ask for forgiveness and to forgive sincerely.

Explain the four steps of salvation:
1. Accept that we have sinned.
2. Repent of our sins.
3. Be willing to stop sinning.
4. Ask God for forgiveness and accept Jesus Christ as our Savior.

Discuss the importance of experiencing God's forgiveness. Refer to John 3:16-17 and indicate that if we have been forgiven, he tells us that we must also forgive others. If a student wishes to accept Jesus as their Savior, do so at this time.

IV. ACTIVITIES

Activity: The Right help at the right time

Give the students a few minutes to study the drawing, before doing what it says on the bottom of the page.

Say: "Study the scene, then connect the people who are threatened with the person who has the tools to help rescue them. People who have done wrong also need to be rescued."

Ask: "Why do you need to rescue people who have done wrong? What is in common between the people who don't have a relationship with Jesus and the people in the picture?" (They need someone to do something for them that they cannot do by themselves.) "How you can forgive those who have done wrong?"

Activity: As we forgive our debtors

Have the kids look up and read Matthew 6:12. Answer the questions and then write the text in their own words.

Activity: Did you forgive?

Ask the students to look up the activity and answer the questions

Memory Verse

Review the former verses (9, 10 and 11), encouraging the students to repeat them twice. Write this week's memory verse and have them read the words as you point them out. Play with them by changing the volume. Start by reading really softly and then louder.

TO PRAY IS TO ASK FOR PROTECTION

I. OVERVIEW

Biblical Base: Matthew 6:13, John 16-17.

Memory Verse *"This, then, is how you should pray: 'Our Father in heaven, hallowed be your name, your kingdom come, your will be done, on earth as it is in heaven. Give us today our daily bread. And forgive us our debts, as we also have forgiven our debtors. And lead us not into temptation, but deliver us from the evil one.'"* (Matthew 6:9-13)

Biblical Truth: We praise God because through prayer, we can tell him our fears and he will lift up our lives.

Lesson Objective: To help the students learn to give thanks to God for his care and ask for protection through prayer.

II. TEACHER PREPARATION

In these chapters (16 and 17), Jesus knew that he was soon going to die. Verse 16 contains one of his final conversations with his disciples.

At the time John was writing this Gospel (book), they had already faced persecution, and Jesus' words resounded in his ears. The time of Jesus' death was approaching and they must be ready. In this passage, Jesus warned it would not be easy to follow him; the Christian way was going to have a very high cost. Their expulsion from synagogues was something very hard for them; Jesus' good name, influence and everything needed in life was at stake.

Jesus explained that his departure was necessary to allow the arrival of salvation and comfort from the Holy Spirit. Pain and suffering would be great, but it would pass. The joy that would come afterwards would be great.

Chapter 17 is Jesus' prayer. It begins by asking to be glorified. With the term "glorification," Jesus was asking God for Jews and Gentiles to understand that he was the Messiah and his mission was to save the world from sin.

Jesus prayed for himself, for his disciples, as well as for future generations of disciples. Similarly, he referred to events that had not yet happened, as if they had already passed (vv. 10-11).

In Matthew 6:9-13, Jesus prays again. Jesus is teaching us to ask God to save us when we are going through difficult tests, and power to defeat the enemy.

Was it necessary that Christ die? What would have happened if he had not died?

Yes, it was necessary for Jesus to die for salvation and to make it possible for us to be in his presence. When he died, this became real through the Holy Spirit.

In our time, do we go through difficult situations?

Is there persecution in our country? Do you know someone who has been forbidden to attend school for being a Christian, or is in jail for preaching Christ?

Perhaps in the place where we live there is a certain degree of religious freedom, but in many places, persecution for religious reasons are a reality. In places like the East, this is a fact. Many people are still dying for preaching Jesus Christ and his message.

"More Christians have died in the twentieth century than in the nineteen centuries after the birth of Christ. In Indonesia, more than five hundred Christians have been killed.

In North Korea the church is hidden in underground caves, and Christians must hide to praise God. In Chechen, terrorists kidnap and kill Christians (International Mission Education Guide, Volume XVI, Year 2002).

How does Jesus' prayer help us get through these situations? Through prayer. Jesus teaches us to pray to God for protection in each of our difficulties.

In the Lord's Prayer, he teaches us to ask God for help in times of temptation, tests, or difficulties we may be experiencing. We must bring before God all our concerns, doubts and problems.

God can help us in the midst of difficulty.

III LESSON DEVELOPMENT

Introduction

Divide the class into two teams and give each a sheet of paper. Have them write five review questions based on this unit. Explain that each team will present their questions to the other group; and responses must be from the previous lessons.

Only give 3 minutes for this activity. (Remind students the content of the lessons by naming the titles.) Begin the game as soon as the teams have their questions ready. You can judge answers that are unclear. Give 10 points for each correct answer to keep the game interesting. Make it clear to students that the purpose of this review is fun and important ideas they have learned. You can reward both teams with candy or small awards to each student.

In the end, ask: "What did Jesus teach us about forgiving our debtors?" (We forgive those who trespass against us.)

Activity: Our best defense

Ask students to look at their activity sheet and ask: "What do all the objects in each category have in common?" Have them write the answers in the spaces. (They are used for protection. They are used to increase strength.) "In which category does prayer belong? Why? (Prayer belongs to both categories, because when we pray, God can give us both protection and strength.)

Developing the Bible Story

Jesus prays for his disciples

Read the story simultaneously with the children. While you are reading, stop wherever it is marked. Ask the question and let the kids talk about it.

"Where is Judas going?" asked one disciple to the other.

"Since he handles our money, maybe he is running an errand for Jesus," said the second disciple.

After Judas left, Jesus spoke to the disciples about what they would face in the future. He predicted his death and spoke about his resurrection.

"I've said all this so you would not stop trusting in me. You will be expelled from the synagogue; and the day will come when anyone who kills you will think he's doing God a favor."

Then Jesus began to pray, saying, "My Father, the time has come for you to show people how powerful I am. Thus, I also have shown them how great and wonderful you are. To everyone I showed how great and powerful you are, because I did everything you commanded me."

"Why does this prayer sound like his last?" some asked.

The disciples heard Jesus talking to God about them. "I have shown who you are to the followers you gave me. They were yours, and you gave them to me, and they have obeyed all I commanded them. I pray for them. I'm not praying for the people who don't accept me and just think about the things of this world. Instead, I pray for the followers who you gave me and they're yours. Heavenly Father, soon I won't be in the world, because I go where you are. But my followers will remain in this world. So I ask that you take care of them. While I was with them, I took care of them with the power that you gave me, and none stopped trusting me except Judas. I don't ask you to take them out of the world but that you protect them from Satan. I am not of this world, and neither are they. Your message is true; help them to listen and surrender completely to you."

Say: In the Lord's Prayer he taught us to pray "lead us not into temptation, but deliver us from evil" (Matt. 6:13).

Was Jesus asking God to keep the Christians from hearing or seeing the evil of this world? (No) He knew that his disciples would have to be in the world, and listen and see the evil around them to avoid it. If we know Jesus today, we are those disciples.

The disciples thought about Jesus' words: "I don't pray only for them but also for those who will believe in me when they hear your message."

They must have thought to themselves, "I wonder how many will believe us if Jesus is not here!" "Who will believe in our message? Not the religious leaders who are here!"

Who would be those who would believe through the disciples? (All the people of his time.) Who today believes through us? (Those that we know who testify.)

"Shortly after Jesus said this prayer, he and his disciples left the place where they had been. They went to an olive orchard. There, a band of soldiers led by Judas arrested Jesus and took him."

Life Application

Is there persecution in our country today? How can we help in these situations? (Have the children respond. You can give students a list of countries where there is persecution and have each of them pray during the week for a different country.)

Activities

Activity: God's Protection

Ask the children to think of situations in which they have had the protection of God, and write a prayer of praise for the care of the Lord. Remember that the four lessons speak about prayer.

Help them write some of their personal prayer requests. Ask, "Have you had prayer requests answered?" (That should also be noted on this part of the work.)

Memory Verse

This is the last section of the Lord's Prayer as a key verse, so children should have it already memorized.

If there are many students, divide them into two groups. Write the Lord's Prayer in paragraphs and distribute them among the children (without seeing what they have). They have to read (individual or as a group) the paragraph that you gave them, and say the words that are before or after (as you indicate). Remind them to put a star on their Verse of the Month Club certificate. The certificates will be given to those who have learned the three verses of the unit. Put them in a visible place in the classroom.

IN SEARCH OF TRUE WISDOM

Bible Truth: Loving, obeying, and knowing God are the secrets to true wisdom.

UNIT OBJECTIVE:
- That the students will learn that God teaches us to stay near him.
- That the students will learn that continual obedience to God is the secret to maintaining an intimate relationship with him.
- That the students will feel a desire to obey God at all times.
- That the students will seek and accept the guidance and help of God.
- That the students will learn to give God the best of their service and devotion.

UNIT LESSONS
- Lesson 35 - David, a conquering king.
- Lesson 36 - When God says "NO."
- Lesson 37 - Seeking God's wisdom.
- Lesson 38 - Solomon gives his best to God.
- Lesson 39 - Solomon turns from God.

UNIT VERSE: *"It is the Lord your God you must follow, and him you must revere. Keep his commands and obey him; serve him and hold fast to him."* (Deuteronomy 13:4)

At this stage of life, pre-adolescent students begin to reason abstractly. In pursuit of their own ideals and values, they begin to think for themselves, and often question the concepts of adults. Does this make sense? Do adults live what they teach ? Does this work in real life?

These lessons provide opportunities for students to make decisions based on biblical concepts, and help establish a foundation that will help them live close to God.

An analysis of the life of David and Solomon will serve as examples of devotion to God, and the dangers of disobedience. Students will be encouraged to give their best to God. Through David's life, they will see that it is important to seek the will of God, even if this is not what they would choose. Solomon's life teaches us the advantages of being faithful to God and the dangers of being apart from him.

Suggestion: Verse of the Month Club

1. Everyone can be a successful member of this club. Each month, students learn a verse or new passage. In the student worksheets in the first lesson of this unit, the child will find a certificate and a memory card for this section. Display certificates in a visible place as a reminder to learn the verses. Keep a record of student achievement. When the student can say the verse from memory, put a star on his certificate. You can offer small gifts as incentives for members who have learned their verses.

2. For Lesson 37, you need to bring a doll-shaped baby, a crown for a king (simple, you can use cardboard or paper) and the clothing of a soldier.

3. For lesson 38, write the text of the verse on pieces of cardboard (a word on each piece) to work with students in memorizing the text; the reading section will show you how.

4. Different ways to remember the text: Balloon Game: This activity will help students memorize verses. Do it when you have extra time. Materials needed: balloons or a beach ball. Students form a circle. The first person throws the ball in the air and says the beginning of the verse. The next student who catches the ball must say the second word, and so on. If the ball falls to the floor, they have to start over. Repetition is a good practice.

5. Write the memory verse on thick paper (need markers or paints); the children will cut each of the letters (let them work painting and decorating the words) to form the whole verse. When they have finished, look for a good place to place and remove until students are familiar with it.

6. Other activities: Plan a worship time with students during lesson 38, when the children have learned about the gift God gave Solomon. They can do this during the class or during children's church Invite students to tell about how they can use their talents to participate in this project. They can draw pictures on a banner, present something alone or as a choir. You can read some verses from Proverbs that teach us how to serve God.

DAVID, A CONQUERING KING

I. OVERVIEW

Bible Verse: 2 Samuel 5:1-25.

Memory Verse: *"It is the Lord your God you must follow, and him you must revere. Keep his commands and obey him; serve him and hold fast to him."* (Deuteronomy 13:4)

Biblical Truth: God guides the obedient.

Lesson Objective: To help students understand that God guides those who ask for his direction and are willing to obey.

II. TEACHER PREPARATION

David and Saul were in conflict for many years. Even after Saul's death, his followers continued with the battle. When at last the fight ended, David was named the new king of Israel. The Philistines (enemies of Israel) wanted to take advantage before David became powerful (2 Samuel 5: 1-25).

When David learned of their plans, before making any moves, he asked God for his guidance, and the Philistines were defeated. A year later, they made new plans of attack. But David repeated his strategy - he asked for God's guidance and God gave him a new plan which he obeyed, and once again he came out victorious.

David never feared, or acted hastily. He always sought God's guidance first. When we face problems in our lives, let's remember David, and do the same thing - ask God for his direction and obey everything that he commands us to do.

At this age, your students begin to seek independence, and don't always accept what their parents tell them. They want to behave according to their own convictions and thoughts. They want to do what they decide, and often experience the failures of their own decisions.

This is the right time for children to know the unconditional love of God and His perfect will for their lives. Keeping in mind that they are learning to read, encourage them to read on their own the corresponding biblical stories so that they will develop their faith as Christians.

III. LESSON DEVELOPMENT

Introduction

Draw a picture of the church on the board. Let the students add trees, sidewalks, paths, plants, parking, etc. When completed, give each child instructions in turn to follow, for example: "Go out the front door; Go down the sidewalk to the first tree; Turn left, now tell me, where are you? "

This activity emphasizes the importance of following the instructions we receive when we need to find a place or something in particular.

The following exercise can be done in or outside the classroom or outdoors. (You will need a handkerchief for each pair, to blindfold their eyes.)

Once the class is divided into pairs, one should be blindfolded and the other will instruct him/her behind their back and, without touching them, guide them to the place that you indicate. Example: "Walk five steps forward, turn left, continue walking, etc." Change the roles of the pairs so that both can participate and, once completed, share the experience they had during the game. Encourage them to explain how they felt when others guided them (fear, insecurity, trust in their partner, etc.).

Explain that many times we go through experiences like these when we obey God's instructions, but the difference is that we can fully trust in His divine direction.

Developing the Bible Story

"King Saul is dead!" shouted the people of Judah.

Then, the general of Saul's army made his son, Ish-Bosheth, king over Israel.

When Saul's son died, the leaders of Israel came to David and made him king. The people had a new king; but not everyone was happy with the news.

"Now is the time to attack Israel," Israel's enemies (the Philistines) said.

A general told his king, "Israel is weak, but David becomes more powerful every day." So the Philistines all went up to capture him.

Upon learning this, David went down to the fortress in search of a safe and quiet place; he needed time to meditate and pray. He knew he had to make a decision. The question was, what should he do?

And David inquired of the LORD, "Shall I go against the Philistines in battle? Will you deliver them into my hands?" God said to him, "Go, for I'll surely deliver the Philistines into your hands."

The victory was so fast that the Philistines fled without even stopping to get their idols. However, they didn't give up, but gathered in the valley of Rephaim to make a new plan of attack.

But David again went to God to ask what he should do. Then, the Lord gave David a secret plan for the war: "Don't go straight up to fight them, but circle around behind them and attack them in front of the poplar trees. As soon as you hear the sound of marching, move quickly, because that will mean the Lord has gone out in front of you to strike the Philistine army."

David did exactly as God commanded. He and his soldiers waited quietly near the trees. And when they heard the noise of their marching, they attacked. (2 Samuel 5)

Ask students to look up 2 Samuel 5:19 and have someone read it aloud. Then ask them:

"What does this passage tell us of David's secret strategy?" (Review the story and look for the instructions God gave him.)

David knew how important it was to follow God's direction. For that reason, he consulted Him first.

"In what kind of problems or situations do kids need to be guided?" (When they have temptations, problems with their friends or at school.)

Say: "Why do you think it is important for a Christian to seek God's will?" (Some answers: because he will help us make the right decisions. We believe that he is God and we want to do what he commands us. He knows more than us, etc.)

Read Proverbs 3:5-6, and point out that it mentions that sometimes it is difficult to know what God wants us to do, because He doesn't always speak clearly to us (as He spoke to David). Ask: "How does God guide us today?" (Through reading the Bible, messages from Christian leaders, listening to a worship song, etc.)

Tell the children to talk about the areas of their lives in which they need to be strengthen with God's direction (among friends, with parents, at school, with siblings, etc.). Write them on the board and let them pray for each other. End by asking God to guide each student and to help them recognize and obey him at all times.

Life Application
Activity: David's Secret Strategy

Say the following: "The Bible mentions David's secret strategy for being a good king and winning battles. Decrypt the secret message."

Answers:
* Accept God as your leader.
* Ask for his guidance.
* Follow his guidance.

Remind the students that we serve the same God who led David. We face different challenges than he faced, but in the same way we can seek God's will and follow his instructions. Give them time to answer the question at the end of the activity.

Say: "When you have to make a difficult decision, how will you decide what to do?" (Tell them to be prepared next week to tell about how they asked God for his guidance, and how he guided them. Remind them that seeking God's will is not always easy, as shown by the story of David. But God will guide those who follow him.)

Activity: The Recipe of a great leader

Ask the students to mention some people who have been great leaders. (The president of the country, athletes, teachers, etc.) Ask: "What did they do to be recognized?" (Write the answers on the board.)

Explain that in Old Testament times, the people of Israel decided to have a king. God wanted them to trust him because he knew what was best for them. But they wanted a king so that they would be like other nations. And God allowed them to have a king.

Ask the children to grab their worksheet and ask: "What characteristics do great leaders have?"

"How would you like to be Israel's leader? Make a "recipe" of the characteristics of the leader they would like to have." (Honesty, wisdom, goodness, etc.) Let them write on the "recipe card." Then, whoever wants to can show their recipe card.

Say: "Today's story is about David, the second king of Israel."

Memory Verse

Write this month's verse on the board. Then separate the students in the following ways: a group of those who have blue clothes; Others who have black shoes; Others who have white socks, etc. First say the text out loud, and then have each of the groups repeat it. This way it will be easy to memorize.

NOTES:

WHEN GOD SAYS "NO"

I. OVERVIEW

Bible Verse: 2 Samuel 7:1-29.

Memory Verse: *"It is the Lord your God you must follow, and him you must revere. Keep his commands and obey him; serve him and hold fast to him."* (Deuteronomy 13:4)

Biblical Truth: God doesn't always do what we ask him to do.

Lesson Objective: To help students accept God's authority when he says "NO."

II. TEACHER PREPARATION

God gave David victory over his enemies, and now the kingdom enjoyed times of peace. After years of conflict, the Israelites felt secure (2 Samuel 7:1-29).

David lived in a beautiful palace made of cedar wood. But he was ashamed that while he lived in such a place, the ark of the covenant was in a tent.

Nathan, a prophet of God, agreed with David in his plan to build a temple. David's request was good, but God said no. This is not to say that God rejected David, but that He was planning something even greater in David's life than allowing him the privilege of building a temple for him.

God revealed to Nathan the prophet that this was not his plan, and he went to tell David. God told David that his job was to unite and guide Israel, and to destroy their enemies. David accepted his role in God's plan and didn't try to go any further with his desire to build the temple.

Why did God say "no" to David? It's not known. Perhaps he wanted him to recognize that God can't be limited to being in one place. To the Israelites, the Ark of the Covenant signified the presence of God in the midst of them.

This lesson teaches us that in our walk with God, we often receive a "no" as a response to what we ask. Do we trust him when his answer goes against our wishes? Are we willing to wait for God's timing, as David did? Do we trust that he will do the best for us?

It is natural for children of this age, and adults for that matter, to get highly frustrated when they don't get what they want when they want it. We must learn to accept the Lord's answer at all times, even when He tells us NO, and to continue following Him, even if we don't understand the reason for His answer.

III. LESSON DEVELOPMENT
Introduction

Activity: The big "NO"
Who is your authority?

Ask the students to find this activity on their worksheet. On the blackboard write a large "NO" and ask the following questions and write down the different answers given by the children.

- Are there times when your parents say "no" to something you want to do? (Watch certain TV shows, buy certain kinds of clothes, have certain friendships, etc.)
- Why would they say NO? (Talk about this.)
- There are times when teachers say NO when you want to do something. Do you remember something for which your teacher said NO? (Chewing gum in class, talking we are talking, running down the aisles, etc. Discuss these reasons.)

There are times when police officers say NO to people, for example:
  - Crossing the street without looking.
  - Going through red traffic lights.
  - Not wearing a seat belt, etc.
  (Discuss these reasons.)

- Does God ever say NO to Christians? (Yes)
- When and why do you think God tells us NO sometimes? (When we are selfish, when we want something that doesn't benefit us, when what we desire may harm another person, etc. Explain that whenever God says NO, He does it for our good.)

Developing the Bible Story
The one who said "no" to the King

Tell your students that this story will teach them that when God says "NO," even kings have to accept it.

"At last there is peace in my kingdom," King David thought. "The army of Israel has defeated the Philistines, and they won't bother us for a while. Now I can enjoy my beautiful palace."

One day, Nathan the prophet visited King David and the king said to him, "Look, I live in a cedar house, while the Ark of God is in a tent. It doesn't seem right. I think I'll build a beautiful place for God."

"Do all that is in your heart, for the Lord is with you,"

answered Nathan.

"I'll have to make plans," David said.

But that night, the word of the Lord came to Nathan, and he immediately went to speak with David to communicate the message of God.

"God has given me a message for you, David," Nathan told him. "Thus says the LORD; Shall you build me a house where I'll dwell? I have never lived in a house from the day that I brought the children of Israel out of Egypt to this day, but walked in the tent and in the tabernacle. Did I ever ask you to build me a house?"

"God favors you, David," Nathan continued, "but he wants it to be one of your children and not you that builds a house for him." After the prophet Nathan left, David prayed,

"You have become great, O Lord God, because there is none like you, and there is no God beside you. I wanted to build this house for you, but you have said that it won't be me who does it. O sovereign Lord, you are God."

Life Application

Challenge the students to continue to seek the will of God when making choices during the week. Tell them to be prepared to tell you in what situation God said NO and answer the questions: How did they know that God told them NO? Was it something that was good as what David wanted to do? Why do you think God told them NO? How do they know what God wants them to do? (Reading the Bible, praying, asking the pastor or church leaders, etc.)

IV. ACTIVITIES

Activity: Why did God say "NO"?

Direct the student's attention towards this activity and ask for 6 volunteers to participate as actors.

SCENE 1

Characters: Matias, Sergio and Leonel.

These three friends meet at school during lunch time.

Matias: What do you think about Sunday school?

Sergio: It's AWESOME! I love what we learn from the Bible in every class.

Matias: Hey! I didn't know that God says no to important people like David. I thought He would be saying no just to kids like us.

Leonel: Yes, but what was wrong with wanting to build a temple for God?

Matias: That's not the point, Leonel.

Sergio: God often says yes. But when he says no, it is for some reason.

Matthias: Of course, even if we don't know that reason, God is sovereign. This means that He doesn't have to tell us why He says yes or no.

Leonel: I thought that God says no to prevent us from getting into trouble, like the Commandments that keep us from doing evil.

At the end of the scene, ask: Why do you think God sometimes says no to what we ask?

SCENE 2

Characters: Diana, Elizabeth and Liliana

The three girls meet in a house to do their homework. While Elizabeth and Liliana study, Diana sighs deeply and looks very sad.

Elizabeth: Diana, is something wrong?

Diana: Today I had a terrible day. I got a bad grade on my exam and I don't understand why.

Liliana: Maybe some of your answers were wrong.

Diana: Very funny! I know that my answers were wrong, but I thought that God would help me.

Liliana: What do you mean?

Diana: I knew we were going to have a test. I even took the books to my house to study. The problem was that I was watching a TV show...

Elizabeth: So you didn't study enough?

Diana: Well ... no. But when I went to school I started praying before I started the exam!

At the end of the scene, ask: Why do you think God didn't give Diana the correct answers? (Because she didn't do her part by preparing for the exam.)

Activity: Word Attack

Read the memory verse. Ask the students to work together with a list you will give them in order to define the key words in the memory verse.

"It is the Lord your God you must follow, and him you must revere. Keep his commands and obey him; serve him and hold fast to him." (Deuteronomy 13:4)

Define with the kids:
1. Follow - means to go behind, to imitate
2. Revere - means to look to God with love and respect.
3. Commands - are directions that one must follow
4. Obey - means to follow and accomplish the directions that are given to us by God each day.
5. Serve - means to work for someone.
6. Hold fast - means to not let go of or leave someone

Memory Verse

Prepare in advance a small paper to give to each student who wishes to participate in a memory verse contest. Tell them to write the verse, and give them time to do so. When they are done, check to see that they have written it out correctly, and if you want, you can give them a prize.

IN SEARCH OF GOD'S WISDOM

I. OVERVIEW

Biblical Base: 1 Kings 3:4-28, 4:29-34.

Memory Verse: *"It is the Lord your God you must follow, and him you must revere. Keep his commands and obey him; serve him and hold fast to him."* (Deuteronomy 13:4)

Biblical Truth: True wisdom comes only from God.

Lesson Objective: To help students discover that wisdom only comes from God.

II. TEACHER PREPARATION

Solomon and his leaders went to Gibeon to offer sacrifices to the Lord. (This proclaimed his dependence on God and his devotion to him.) Solomon had already offered a thousand sacrifices to God in that place. In this way, he showed his great gratitude for all the blessings he had received.

It was in that same place that God gave him the opportunity to obtain what he desired most in the world. Solomon thought about how he would lead his people, so he asked God for a heart to guide him well and make the right decisions. God was very pleased that he asked for this and promised to give him wisdom, riches, glory and a long life ... if he listened.

The incident with the two women who claimed to be the mother of the baby who was alive gives us an example of the wisdom that Solomon possessed. God gave him a special knowledge of human nature that helped him solve this difficult problem.

Solomon was a young man of twenty years old when he became king of Israel. He acknowledged that he didn't have the maturity or experience to make the right decisions. When God offered to give him what he asked, he only asked for wisdom to govern the people.

We can also ask God for this same wisdom (James 1: 5), which is available if we ask for it in prayer and with the right motive. Like Solomon, we must put it into action and apply it in all areas of our lives.

Notice that Solomon asked for wisdom to carry out his work, and didn't expect God to do it for him. We must ask the Lord for his wisdom to know what to do, and to have the courage to continue with it. We have to be brave enough to do what God wants to do through us.

Perhaps your students will never find themselves leading a nation, but there will be times in their lives in which they will face situations that will require them to make very important decisions. Be sure to awaken in them the earnest longing to receive this same wisdom.

III. LESSON DEVELOPMENT

Introduction

Activity: What I want most in the world

Ask them to look for this activity on their worksheet as you start reading:

"Professor Amanda had completed a research project, and arranged each of her notes in order. It began with the most popular answers, then the least likely ones. But her dog knocked them out of her hands and they were all mixed up. Do you want to help the teacher get them back in order? They can do it in the following way: number them from 1 to 11, with 1 being the most popular choice given by most people, then the less popular ones, and so on until all of them are completed."

(Encourage your students to read to each other their answers from the two lists.)

Developing the Bible Story

A wise choice

To further develop this lesson, use the following: a baby doll, a king's crown, and some soldier clothing.

Ask five volunteers to come to the front to participate in the following reading, assigning them the characters: Narrator, Solomon, soldier, 1st woman and 2nd woman.

Narrator: Solomon, the son of David, became king of Israel at the age of twenty. One night God appeared to him in a dream and said to him, "Ask me what you want me to give you."

Solomon: Since I am very young and don't know how

98

to solve problems, grant your servant an understanding heart, to judge your people and to discern between good and bad.

Narrator: People soon realized how much wisdom Solomon had. Many came to him to solve their problems.

Soldier: Salute King Solomon! Hail, O king Solomon, the wisest man in all the earth!

Solomon: Who came to see me today?

Soldier: Two women, my lord.

Solomon: Let them come!

1st woman: Ah, my Lord! This woman and I live in the same house, and I gave birth while I was with her in the house. It happened that on the third day of giving birth, she gave birth to her son too. One night, this woman's son died because she laid on him. She got up at midnight and took my son from my side while I was sleeping. She put him next to her and placed her dead son beside me.

2nd woman: No! That is not true. My son is the one who lives and her son is the one who has died!

1st woman: No, your son is the dead one and my son lives!

Solomon: Soldier, bring me a sword.

Narrator: Suddenly, there was great silence. How would King Solomon decide the truth?

Solomon: Cut the living child in two, and give half to one, and half to the other.

1st woman: No, my Lord! Give the living child to her and don't kill him.

2nd woman: Neither I nor you will have it, cut it in half!

Solomon: Deliver the living child to the first woman, and don't kill him; She is his mother.

Narrator: All Israel heard the judgment that the king had pronounced, and they revered him, because they saw that God had given him wisdom to judge. (From 1 Kings 3.)

Life Application

Discuss with the students what they learned in this lesson. Ask: "Where does wisdom come from?" (Let them express their thoughts.) Guide the discussion to help them understand that true wisdom comes from God.

Help them learn that God loves them and wants to help them in their problems.

Activity: Where does WISDOM come from?

Look at the drawing of this activity for the bible verses from the book of Proverbs that are hidden among all that is seen there. Talk about each verse as you find it:

- 2:6: "For the Lord gives wisdom; from his mouth come knowledge and understanding." (It is on the book on the upper part of the book shelf.)
- 9:10: "The fear of the Lord is the beginning of wisdom, and knowledge of the Holy One is understanding." (It is on the book that is on the floor, next to the box.)
- 10:23: "A fool finds pleasure in wicked schemes, but a person of understanding delights in wisdom." (It's on the desk drawer, between the leaves of the plant.)
- 15:33: "Wisdom's instruction is to fear the Lord, and humility comes before honor." (It is on the clock that is on the wall.)

Ask the children: "If true wisdom comes from God, how can we be wise?" (God gives us many resources. We can get it from the Bible, through prayer, church leaders, our parents and also learning from our mistakes.)

Ask: "What would you ask of God?" "Why did Solomon ask for wisdom?" (Discuss the difference between the two lists of activity 1.)

Encourage them to ask God for wisdom to make wise choices this week, and to be prepared to share their experiences in the next class.

Pray for the needs expressed by your students. Ask God to give wisdom to your children so they can make the right decisions.

IV. ACTIVITIES

Activity: Difficult Situations

Maybe some of the children are going through a difficult situation at home or with their friends. Tell your students to look up the Bible verses from Proverbs mentioned here and to do this activity as directed.

Memory Verse

Write the full text on the board, and after repeating it a few times, erase some key words.

As you progress through repetition and learning, erase the other words until the whole group learns it.

SOLOMON GIVES GOD HIS BEST

I. OVERVIEW

Biblical Base: 1 Kings 5:1.

Memory Verse: *"It is the Lord your God you must follow, and him you must revere. Keep his commands and obey him; serve him and hold fast to him."* (Deuteronomy 13:4)

Biblical Truth: God deserves the best we can give him.

Lesson Objective: To help the students learn the desire we should have for giving God our best.

II. TEACHER PREPARATION

When God told David that one of his sons was going to build the temple in his place, he began to gather the materials for the work (1 Kings 5: 1-6; 8: 1-30).

David made a trade pact with King Hiram of Tire to receive cedar wood and craftsmen. Solomon's wisdom was recognized when he arranged everything so that 30,000 workers, 70,000 road men, 80,000 bricklayers and 3,300 supervisors could work together in the great work. The temple was finished after seven years. But Solomon waited eleven months, until the end of the Feast of Tabernacles, to dedicate it to God. The ark of the covenant was already inside, placed in its place of honor. When the priests carried it in, a cloud that symbolized the presence of God filled the whole place. They could not finish the ceremony because the glory of God filled the temple. Solomon acknowledged that the completion of the temple was the fulfillment of a promise that God had made to David.

Students are surrounded by teachers, parents, grandparents and leaders who tell them how to lead their lives. Their ability is enriched and develops rapidly. When they do something that doesn't work very well, they practice it until perfecting it. They enjoy making use of their new skills, and feel proud when they do something right and receive recognition for it. Through this lesson, your students will learn to give their best to the Lord using their abilities, talents, and skills. They need to understand that God gave us his best when he sent Jesus Christ into the world.

III. LESSON DEVELOPMENT

Introduction

Activity: Who gave their best?

Have the students identify which actions are badly done or incorrect, and who is responsible for the mistake. (The person who left out some of the crayons, The one who didn't clean the tie well, the hairdresser, the seamstress.) Ask: "Did these people do their best?" (No)

"Sometimes we make mistakes, but this was probably an act of carelessness. How do you feel when you pay for something that was done wrong, or buy something and it doesn't work?" (Let down and angry.) "What does it mean to give your best? Who deserves our best?"

Developing the Bible Story

The Great Project

"David has crowned his son Solomon to be the king of Israel," King Hiram of Tire said. "He and I are good friends. I'll send a message welcoming Solomon."

When Solomon received the message from this king, he was very happy to know that he wanted to be friends with the people of Israel. "We can help each other," he thought.

Solomon also sent a message to Hiram. "You know that my father David could not build a house in the name of the Lord his God because of the wars in which he was wrapped up in, until the Lord put his enemies under his control. Now, the Lord my God has given me peace everywhere. I, therefore, have determined to build a house in the name of the Lord my God, according to what the Lord said to my father David, "Your son, whom I'll place on the throne after you, will build a house for my Name." "I want to use cedar wood from Lebanon for the temple," continued Solomon.

"Please have your men cut the trees. I'll pay whatever wages you say. My men will help, but as you know, we have no one who knows how to cut wood like your men." Then the king of Tire answered Solomon's message. "My men will cut down all the cedar and cypress you need," said Hiram. "They will carry the wood to the sea, tie them together to form rafts, and then they will transport them by sailing them to the place where you want them. There you will separate them and thus you will be able to take them to your palace. In payment, you will give me food for my house." So Hiram sent Solomon the cedar and cypress wood for the temple. As payment, he gave the king of Tire thousands of barrels of wheat and gallons of olive oil for food. So did Solomon and Hiram for many years. Solomon also needed stones for the foundations of the temple. So, he sent 70,000 haulers, 80,000 rock cutters and 3,300 supervisors to the mountains. These men cut and removed large rocks to make the foundation; worked the wood and prepared the rocks for the construction. Other workers did the interior finishing of the temple. For seven years, these people worked to build a house for God. When at last they were finished, Solomon gathered all the leaders of Israel. "Now is the time to bring the ark of Jehovah," he told them.

The priests carried the ark of the covenant of the Lord to a special place in the temple, the most holy place. The cherubim covered the ark with their outstretched wings. Inside the ark there were the two tablets of the law (10 Commandments) which Moses had placed inside at Horeb, where God made a covenant with the Israelites after they had left Egypt.

When the priests came out of the holy place, a cloud filled the temple of the Lord. They could not finish the service because the cloud prevented it; The glory of the Lord filled all with his presence. This cloud was the symbol of the Lord's presence in his temple. Solomon said, "The LORD has said that he will dwell in the darkness, but I have built Him a house to be in, a place where he can dwell forever." Then he turned to the people and said, "Blessed be the Lord, the God of Israel, who has promised to David my father what he has done with his hand." (From 1 Kings 5 and 8)

Life Application

Much later, the temple built by Solomon was destroyed, and a second was built under the leadership of Zerubbabel. Herod made improvements to this one, adding on to it, but the Romans later destroyed it.

Read 1 Corinthians 6:19. Emphasize that the Christians who form the church are the temple of God, since he lives within them. The children of God are the church, and they congregate in temples or buildings. Make a list of some the activities of your local congregation. Ask them: "What do you think will happen if the people who do these tasks neglect their responsibilities and don't do their jobs well?" (Guide the conversation to conclude that we should give our best to God.)

IV. ACTIVITIES

Activity: My Gift to God

Remind students of the list of tasks they did in the previous section. Ask: "Is the only way we can give God our best is by doing things in the church?" (No! We bring honor to him when we do our best in every activity and place.)

Ask: "Why did Solomon want to give God his best?" (To give him honor.) "How can you honor God with the best?" Tell the children to write a list of the gifts they can give to God on the boxes on the pages of this sheet. Challenge them to do the best they can during the week. Remind them that they must honor God.

The most beautiful way to show God how much we love Him is to do the best we can in all the circumstances of our lives. Encourage the students to say that they want to give God their best. Recognize their abilities and talents, and encourage them to always use them in the best way to honor God. Also, challenge them to perfect them.

Memory Verse

Write the text, word for word, on separate cards. Place the cards in the correct order on the board. Memorize the verse and review it with the class. Once it is learned, remove the cards from the board and mix them up, and then have the students, working as a team, place the words in the right order again on the board. Invite them to all belong to the Verse of the Month Club.

NOTES:

SOLOMON TURNS AWAY FROM GOD

I. OVERVIEW

Biblical Base: 1 Kings 11 & 12

Memory Verse: *"It is the Lord your God you must follow, and him you must revere. Keep his commands and obey him; serve him and hold fast to him."* (Deuteronomy 13:4)

Biblical Truth: Disobedience is the reason why we turn away from our relationship with God.

Lesson Objective: That the students will understand that even smart people can make mistakes and forget God, giving in to the bad influences He warns us about.

II. TEACHER PREPARATION

Solomon was doing very well. God had chosen him beforehand to rule Israel. He blessed him with wisdom, riches, a peaceful kingdom, the admiration of the neighboring kings, and success in all his affairs.

But Solomon didn't remain faithful to God. He thought it was politically beneficial to marry foreign women. The women brought with them their pagan beliefs, customs and idols. And to fulfill their desires, Solomon built places for them to worship their gods, and their worship of the true God became a simple ritual. Solomon's life stands as a warning against bad relationships with unbelievers, which can destroy the spiritual life of believers. God allowed Solomon to fall because of his disobedience.

Then Jeroboam came as a servant. He became the king's favorite, and soon was given great responsibilities. Jeroboam had a meeting with the prophet Ahijah, who broke his cloak into twelve pieces and gave ten to him. Those pieces represented the ten tribes that Jeroboam would one day govern. The other two tribes would be given to Solomon's son, just to keep God's promise to David.

Jeroboam was like David. God chose him to replace a disobedient king. Immediately, he tried to provoke an uproar to begin to reign. When that happened, Solomon tried to kill him, but Jeroboam escaped to Egypt and didn't return until Solomon died.

What causes the separation between a person and God? People move away from God, little by little, almost without noticing it. We must strive to live as Deuteronomy 13:4 says, "The Lord, your God, you will follow ..." and take seriously the warning of Proverbs 28:20: "The faithful man will receive many blessings, but he who wants to get rich in haste won't be free from guilt."

For a Christian, it is nice to remember the moment when he or she accepted Christ as their Lord and Savior. Some did so when they were children, others in adolescence and others as adults. But it is sad to hear someone say, "I accepted the Lord Jesus when I was young, but I turned away from him, and even came to think that God would never accept me again."

Pre-adolescent students are in a stage of spiritual development, and need to be taught the need to accept Christ as their personal Savior. They must learn that disobedience separates them from God, but that this is not the end. They can restore that relationship if they repent of the evil they have done. They also need to learn how to make wise decisions with God's help to avoid the dangers of what can separate them from Him.

III. LESSON DEVELOPMENT

Introduction

Activity: Danger Ahead!

Ask: "What in the drawing may present a danger to the boat?" (Give them time to be able to identify them and discuss the damage this would cause.) "What could keep us from God?" (Let them write the answers on the rocks and in the waves.) Some of the dangers would be: to stop reading the Bible, to not attend church, to allow friendships to influence us to do bad things, disobedience, etc.

Developing the Bible Story

Problems in the Palace

Let's see what happened in the life of Solomon:

"Is it true what we have heard from Solomon?" asked many people. "Is he as wise and rich as they say?"

From all parts of the world, people came to visit King Solomon: kings, queens, important people ... they all sought his advice, and he answered questions no one else could. But after he became very famous, he began to forget God's commands. He married foreign women, not caring that his heart started leaning towards their foreign gods. Solomon was not obedient to God. He made deals with foreign kings; he agreed to marry their daughters, and he ended up doing so with seven hundred wives and three hundred concubines (those who didn't belong to royalty or had great titles). When Solomon was old, his wives convinced him to worship pagan gods. In order to please his wives, he ordered places to be built to offer sacrifices to those gods. Solomon did evil in the sight of the Lord. Unlike his father David, he was not obedient to God. The Lord was angry because Solomon's heart had departed from Him.

On two occasions, the Lord appeared to him to tell him not to worship other gods, but he was disobedient and ignored God's warnings.

And God said to Solomon, "Because you have done this, and have not kept my covenant, and the statutes which I commanded you, I'll take away all the kingdom, and will give it to your servant. However, I won't do it while you are alive. For your father David's sake, I'll take it out of your son's hand."

The peace that prevailed among the people no longer existed. Other nations began to oppose Solomon. Even his own men turned against him, and one of them was Jeroboam.

Solomon had put him in charge of the workers who worked on the project to repair the walls around the city. One day as Jeroboam came out of Jerusalem, the prophet Ahijah found him on the road. He was covered with a new cloak, and they were alone in the field. The prophet took the cloak, cut it into twelve pieces, and said to Jeroboam, "Take ten pieces for you, for thus says the Lord, the God of Israel: 'I'll tear the kingdom out of Solomon's hands and give you ten tribes. He will keep a tribe for my servant David's sake and for Jerusalem's sake. I do this because he has left me and worshiped other gods, and has not walked in my ways to do what is right in front of my eyes and my statutes. You will be king of Israel if you listen to all that I command you, walking in my ways and doing what is right before my eyes, keeping my statutes, as my servant David did. I'll be with you.'"

When Solomon heard what had happened, he tried to kill Jeroboam, but he fled to Egypt and remained there until Solomon's death. Then Jeroboam returned to Israel.

When the Israelites heard that Jeroboam had returned, they proclaimed him their king. Only the tribe of Judah remained faithful to Rehoboam, the son of Solomon. Rehoboam gathered a great army of Judah to fight against Jeroboam, because he wanted to recover the territory that had belonged to his father Solomon and which Jeroboam now ruled.

And the LORD spoke to Shemaiah the man of God, saying, "Speak to Rehoboam, and say to him, 'This is what the LORD says. Don't go out to fight against your brothers, the children of Israel. Everyone should return to their own house, because this is my work.'" When they heard the words of God, everyone returned to his house according to what the Lord had said to them.

The reign of Solomon ended after forty years. His kingdom was divided and they didn't enjoy peace. Now his son Rehoboam didn't have a great kingdom to lead. If only Solomon had remembered the proverb he wrote: "The faithful man will receive many blessings." (Proverbs 28:20)

Life Application

Ask: "Does it cause you pain to have friends who aren't Christians?" (Let the children make their comments.) Say: "The Bible tells us about friendship with unbelievers. Look at 2 Corinthians 6:14; Proverbs 1:10-16 and Proverbs 4:14-16." (Invite a child to read.) Say: "The Bible warns us about what happens to us by having close friendships with non-Christians. How can we stay close to God?" (Reading the Bible, attending church, asking God for wisdom, having friends who are Christians.) Have someone read Deuteronomy 13:4. Explain: "If we do as this verse tells us, we'll remain close to God. We won't turn away from God as Solomon did."

IV. ACTIVITIES

Activity: Don't Ignore God's Warnings

Margaret received Jesus as her Savior when she was in third grade at school. She read her Bible, prayed, went to church and used her talents for God.

When she reached the sixth grade, her new neighbor Michael moved next door. She thought that if she tried to become his friend, she could talk about the Bible, church activities and Jesus. But Margaret began to listen to Michael's ideas, telling her that church was only for adults, and she began to believe this. She stopped praying, and read her Bible only when she went to church. And she began to do all the bad things Michael advised her.

What happened to Margaret and why?

What do you think of what she did?

Michael became more important for her than God. Even when she attended church on Sundays, she didn't worship or love the Lord. When the time came to attend high school, Margarita and Michael ended up going to different schools.

In English class, Margaret saw some of the classmates she had met in church camp as a child; they were Christians. One afternoon, they invited her to hang out with them and she agreed to go with them. She noticed how they treated each other and her. She thought how different they turned out to be. How did her new friends make her feel? Why were they different from Margaret?

Memory Verse

Review the text several times with your students. Organize a learning game by forming a circle. The first person will say the first word of the text, the second will say the first and second words, and so they will continue to add one word per participant, but repeating everything from the beginning.

This is the last lesson of the month. Put a star on the verse found in lesson 35 for the students who have memorized the verse.

GUIDE FOR UNIT X

ATTITUDES THAT JESUS TAUGHT

BIBLICAL TRUTH: Our attitudes and conduct must reflect what Jesus taught us.

UNIT OBJECTIVE:
- That the students will learn to make serving God with love their priority.
- That they will know that the attitudes and behavior Jesus taught us are totally different from those of non-Christians.
- That we should practice the teachings of Jesus.

UNIT LESSONS:
- Lesson 40 - Faced with a challenge.
- Lesson 41 - Let us love those who don't love us.
- Lesson 42 - The Mercy of Jesus.
- Lesson 43 - Let us follow the footsteps of Jesus.

UNIT VERSE: *"Love your enemies, do good to those who hate you, bless those who curse you, pray for those who mistreat you."* (Luke 6:27-28)

The teachings of Jesus in the Sermon on the Mount are a challenge for every Christian. The message is radical and very different from what children have heard in a non-Christian world. Ideas presented in cartoons, at school, by friends and even by adults, are often against our Christian beliefs.

Pre-adolescent students need to have a clear idea of what Christ expects of every Christian. The Sermon on the Mount exalts the attitudes and actions that the Christian should live. Children need to learn that trust in God is not compatible with worry.

The Sermon on the Mount will also teach us that the followers of Jesus Christ are to love their enemies. Christ gave us an example of love by the way he dealt with those who opposed him. This is already a great challenge, because we know that it is difficult to love those who don't love us.

Jesus Christ warns us of the danger of judging others. We'll learn that as we judge others, so shall we be judged. We need to build our lives on the basis of what Jesus taught us.

These lessons will allow you to practice Jesus' teachings in a safe environment. Although we'll see that following Jesus Christ won't always be easy, and that there are times when Christians suffer for what they believe, but in the process their lives will be strengthened and they will honor God.

He loves us and gave His life for us. Christians obey God because we love Him.

Suggestions:
Verse of the month Club
1. Everyone can be a successful member in this club. A sheet in the student's worksheets highlights these verses. They can take it home at the beginning of this unit. Suggest that they place it in a visible place so that they can remember to learn these verses.
2. The lessons in this unit suggest activities that will help students learn the verses. For example, for lesson 40, bring a soft ball to the class to use for memorizing the text.
3. When they can say the verse by memory, add a star to their Verse of the Month Club certificate. You can offer prizes as incentives. Keep track of what they have accomplished. Occasionally, review the other verses that have been memorized. The more they use them, the better they will remember them.
4. For Lesson 41, prepare a medium-sized box, line it with single-colored paper, and draw a bomb or dynamite on one side.

FACED WITH A CHALLENGE

I. OVERVIEW

Bible Verse: Mathew 6:25-34; Philippians 4:12-19

Memory Verse: *"Love your enemies, do good to those who hate you, bless those who curse you, pray for those who mistreat you."* (Luke 6:27-28)

Biblical Truth: Those who trust God have nothing to fear.

Lesson Objective: To help students learn that when we trust in God, he will help us with our worries.

II. TEACHER PREPARATION

When people say phrases such as "don't worry," and "don't be anxious," we don't want to accept them. We may think that this person doesn't know what we're going through. But in Matthew 6:25-34, Jesus mentioned these phrases five times.

He points out to us the tendency that we have to worry in certain situations. We want to control our own lives. We become uneasy when faced with circumstances we cannot solve. This takes away energy and doesn't let us achieve anything.

Trusting in the world around us and in our own abilities causes us anxiety. Instead of worrying, Jesus tells us that we must concentrate on serving God and being like him. This will allow us to enjoy his blessings. He encourages us to not worry about our basic needs. For the people who were with Jesus, this was very difficult, because many people were very poor.

To seek God first means to reflect our love for him at work and in our plans. Only then will we attain what will truly remain. The questions are: What are our priorities? Do we fully agree or completely disagree with God? Will we worry about food, clothing and what we have?

Paul was able to apply Jesus' teachings to his life. He wrote his letter to the Philippians while awaiting a verdict in jail. But he still rejoiced in those circumstances, because his trust was founded on God. The Philistines were part of God's answer to Paul's prayer (Philippians 4: 12-19).

Many adults think that the childhood is free of problems and concerns, compared to that of adults. But it is not so. There are children who do have concerns, and they feel weak and even have doubts about God's love for them.

Concern is interposed in man's relationship with God. It arises when attention is focused solely on the problem, regardless of the direction of the Lord. As we worry, we are denying that He can help us.

Children need to feel secure, and learn that by putting God as the top priority in their lives, he will control everything that happens to them.

Jesus' teachings in the Sermon on the Mount are a challenge for every Christian. One of them teaches us that we must love our enemies. Christ taught us by His example in loving those who opposed Him. This truth is a great challenge, since it's difficult to love those who don't love us.

Students need to be clear that trust in God is not compatible with worry. Jesus Christ also warns us of the danger of judging others, so that we won't be judged. We need to build our lives on the basis of what Jesus taught us.

These lessons will give us the opportunity to practice the teachings of Christ in a safe environment. However, we'll see that following Jesus is not always easy, and there are times when the Christian suffers for his faith. But in the process, your life will be strengthened and honor God. Let us not forget that God loves us and gave his life for us.

III. LESSON DEVELOPMENT

Introduction

Activity 1: Those who worry

People worry a lot about themselves, whether they are adults or kids. Have the children look at this activity in their worksheet and write their concerns on the shirt in each of the drawings.

Developing the Bible Story

Don't worry!

Read the story and have your students follow along

in their worksheets.

"Therefore I say to you; Don't be anxious about your life, what you will eat or what you will drink; or about your body, or what you will wear," Jesus said.

The disciples looked at each other. "Don't worry?" they thought. "We have lots of reasons to worry. We gave up work to follow Him! Our families need food, clothing and a place to live. Who will take care of them while we are following Jesus?"

The Lord clearly knew what his disciples were concerned about when he spoke to them. But he wanted them to know that they could trust that he would take care of them and their families.

Jesus continued with his sermon: "Is not life more than food, and the body more than clothes? Look at the birds of the air; they don't sow or reap or store away in barns, and yet your heavenly Father feeds them. Are you not much more valuable than they? Can any one of you by worrying add a single hour to your life? And why do you worry about clothes? See how the flowers of the field grow. They don't labor or spin. Yet I tell you that not even Solomon in all his splendor was dressed like one of these. If that is how God clothes the grass of the field, which is here today and tomorrow is thrown into the fire, will he not much more clothe you—you of little faith?

So don't worry, saying, 'What shall we eat?' or 'What shall we drink?' or 'What shall we wear?' For the pagans run after all these things, and your heavenly Father knows that you need them. But seek first his kingdom and his righteousness, and all these things will be given to you as well. Therefore don't worry about tomorrow, for tomorrow will worry about itself. Each day has enough trouble of its own."

Years later, Paul became a follower of Jesus' teachings. While in prison, he wrote a letter to his friends in Philippi. He didn't know if he would get out of that place alive, but he wanted his friends to trust in God no matter what happened.

"I know what it is to be in need, and I know what it is to have plenty," Paul wrote in his letter. "I have learned the secret of being content in any and every situation, whether well fed or hungry, whether living in plenty or in want. My God will meet all your needs according to the riches of his glory in Christ Jesus."

(From Matthew 6 and Philippians 4.)

Life Application

Activity: Review Questions

Tell the class to think about their concerns. Ask: "Do you want to give them to God?"

Encourage them to trust God instead of worrying, and to prepare themselves to do just that.

Ask the following review questions; help them answer them on their worksheet.

1. What did Jesus tell people they should not do? (Worry, struggle)
2. What worried the disciples? (Food and clothing)
3. Jesus said that the disciples had little … (faith)
4. What did Jesus tell the disciples to look for? (God's kingdom)
5. Where was Paul when he wrote a letter to his friends in Philippi? (In jail)
6. What did Paul want his friends to know? (That he trusted God, no matter what happened.)

IV. ACTIVITIES

Activity: God's treasure chest

Have the children think of what won't be found in heaven, and write them in the "treasure chest of the world"; And then think of what we'll find in heaven, and write those things in the "treasure chest of God."

Read Matthew 6:25 and 33. Help them compare what is eternal, that is what we can keep in the treasure chest of God, to that which is temporary, which we can store in the treasure chest of the world. (Offerings or spend everything on oneself, go to church or stay at home watching TV, etc.)

Remind them of the different decisions that David and Solomon made, and the consequences of those who sought God first and those who acted without consulting God. Write down the worries they have on the clothes of "the Worried." And ask God to help them be winners.

Memory Verse

Prepare in advance a soft-textured ball. Review the memory verse together with the students several times. Then throw the ball to one of them to repeat the verse. Once they have said the memory verse, they will throw the ball to a classmate so that they can say the verse, and so on. You can spend a set amount of time doing this activity, or finish after everyone has participated.

LOVING THOSE WHO DON'T LOVE US

I. OVERVIEW

Bible Verse: Matthew 5:38-48; 6:47-56; Luke 22:51-53

Memory Verse: *"Love your enemies, do good to those who hate you, bless those who curse you, pray for those who mistreat you."* (Luke 6:27-28)

Biblical Truth: Jesus teaches us to love the entire world, even our enemies.

Lesson Objective: To help the students understand that Jesus teaches us to love our enemies.

II. TEACHER PREPARATION

To love our enemies means to forgive, without wanting to retaliate or seek revenge on them. It is feeling peaceful instead of feeling vengeful.

We can only truly forgive if God is put first in our life and in our heart. Through Him, the love that we experience is pure. God surrendered everything when He sent His son, Jesus Christ. To receive this unmerited gift, we should also love our neighbors.

This love isn't just about feeling good around someone. The perfect love that Jesus tells us to have isn't only a feeling, but a willingness of the heart to love and to be kind, refusing to fuel our hurt, affliction and resentment.

With God's help, we can overcome resentment, anger, and vengeance, or whatever else is interfering with us loving our brothers. All of these things affect our life. The approach that Jesus showed when loving our brothers is to show mercy and forgiveness. It isn't a passive response towards the bad; in deciding to respond with love, mercy and forgiveness, we demonstrate being free from sin and the freedom to choose what is right.

Jesus gave us an example of how we should treat our enemies when they arrested him and Judas betrayed him with a kiss. Even though this was a way to greet a friend, it was also the signal that identified Jesus so he could be arrested.

Even though Judas had joined forces with the enemy, Jesus continued to call him "friend." To welcome a traitor with friendly words is like Jesus saying "Judas, I haven't changed. The one who changed is you, but the way to grace and forgiveness is always open" (Matthew 26:47-56).

Peter's immediate reaction right before the arrest of Jesus was to attack his enemies. He cut off the ear of the servant of the high priest; but Jesus healed him; he didn't want violence. Jesus healed the one that wanted to kill Him. What kind of love is that?

During this time in their lives, children hope that life is fair to them. If they are friendly to someone, they assume they'll receive friendliness in return; but on the contrary, if someone hurts them, they seek revenge.

Your students need to understand what Jesus was saying when he said, "Love your enemies." Love from the Lord isn't just a feeling; it demands action on our part.

It's hard to forgive someone who has done us wrong, when it seems that they don't deserve it.

Your students also need to know that not loving or not forgiving interferes with their relationship with God. You can't love God and not love your brothers/sisters.

Jesus' teachings about "turning the other cheek" or "walking the second mile" doesn't mean that people should take advantage of others. The children need to validate their rights, but should learn to forgive and not retaliate against people who have hurt them.

III. LESSON DEVELOPMENT

Introduction

Activity: Would you love someone like this?

Ask: "Why do you think these people are wanted?" Have them write their answers on the lines under each picture. Each picture represents someone who could be an enemy. The first is a dangerous man; the second is a neighbor that gets irritated when kids come in his yard and make too much noise; the third is some friends who are angry with each other.

Have the students write why each case could represent an enemy. And in the blank square, have them draw someone they consider an enemy. Make sure to tell the students not to mention any real names of people.

Ask them to write about an occasion when someone hurt them. They can refer to the same person(s) they drew. Ask them: "How did you react?"

"What happens between us and God when we hate someone?" (Help them understand that if we hate someone and we don't forgive them, this will affect our relationship with God. To love God means to love our neighbors, including our enemies.)

Developing the Bible Story

While Jesus went around preaching and healing people, some religious leaders didn't agree with what He spoke about or what He did. They became his enemies and plotted to kill him.

One night, Jesus went to the Garden of Gethsemane to pray; when he returned, he found his disciples sleeping.

"Are you still sleeping? Look, they come, and the Son of Man is delivered into the hands of sinners. Rise! Let us go! Here comes my betrayer!" said Jesus.

Suddenly, lots of people with spears and sticks appeared. Judas came close to Jesus and said, "Greetings, Rabbi!" Then he gave him a kiss on the cheek, the same way that friends greeted each other in those days. This was the signal that Judas said would show which one was Jesus. How terrible that one of the disciples had become His enemy. But Jesus said to him "Do what you came for, friend."

Then the men surrounded Jesus and arrested him. His other disciples couldn't believe what was happening and wanted to defend him; Peter even took out his sword and cut off the ear of the servant of the high priest. This isn't what Jesus had wanted to happen. He knew his mission, he knew that they would arrest him and then crucify him, but he also wanted to protect his disciples. "Put your sword back in its place," Jesus said to him, "for all who draw the sword will die by the sword. Do you think I cannot call on my Father, and he will at once put at my disposal more than twelve legions of angels? But how then would the Scriptures be fulfilled that say it must happen in this way?"

After all of this, Jesus did something surprising; he touched the ear of the high priest's servant and healed it. Afterwards he said to his enemies, "Am I leading a rebellion, that you have come with swords and clubs? Every day I was with you in the temple courts, and you didn't lay a hand on me. But this is your hour – when darkness reigns." All of His disciples fled in fear for their lives, leaving him alone. Later, they understood what Jesus wanted to say that night when he said, "Love your enemies" (Matthew 5, 26 and Luke 22).

Life Application

Activity 2: What does this mean?

Ask a volunteer to read Matthew 5:44. Explain the meaning of the words "Enemy" and "Mercy."

Enemy: A person, group or country who has bad desires and attitudes towards a person, group or country, and is always looking to hurt the other.

Mercy: Compassion that helps us forgive. To do what is right to an enemy, especially when it's not expected.

Ask "Who were Jesus' enemies?" (Mention how the disciples reacted to Jesus' enemies.) "How did Jesus act in front of his enemies?" (He called Judas His friend and healed the ear of someone who wanted to kill him.) "In Matthew 5:38-48, Jesus teaches us to love our enemies. If we love God and understand His love towards others, we can experience this type of caring towards others."

"What kind of love does God talk to us about?" (It's not only a feeling, it's an action. It's not to say that our enemies will begin to like us, but at least we can forgive those who have hurt us. In order to love in this way, it is necessary to have God's power. We can suffer from loving like this, but our love towards others shouldn't change; this is the kind of love that pleases God. It's quite possible that our enemies won't change and perhaps we won't get their love in exchange, however you are obeying God's wishes.

Tell your students that in Jesus' times the people practiced a rule that said, "An eye for an eye." Write these words on the whiteboard/blackboard and ask: "What do you think this means?" (Compare the attitude that sometimes kids have while playing, or they want to seek revenge on someone who has hurt them.)

Say: "Jesus taught us to love our neighbors. He said that we should forgive our enemies. Think about someone who it has been hard to forgive, and ask God to help you love and forgive that person. How can we show this kind of love to someone?"

IV. ACTIVITIES

Memory Verse

Prepare beforehand a medium-size box covered with a picture of a bomb or dynamite. Recite the verse with the students (Luke 6:27-28). Organize them in a circle and have them pass the box between them. When you clap, they are to pass the box around. When you stop clapping, they must stop passing the box.

Turn your back to them and start to clap and they must pass the box. When you stop clapping, turn around to see who has the box. The student that has the box in their hands when you stop clapping will need to recite the verse from memory. If the student doesn't know the verse all the way, you can help them by giving them a couple of words and help them finish the verse.

To end the lesson, ask a student to pray and thank God that they were able to have class and that they will be able to come back again.

THE MERCY OF JESUS

I. OVERVIEW

Biblical Verse: Matthew 5-7

Memory Verse: *"Love your enemies, do good to those who hate you, bless those who curse you, pray for those who mistreat you."* (Luke 6:27-28)

Biblical Truth: Jesus teaches us to have mercy on our neighbors and to not judge them unfairly for something they've done wrong.

Lesson Objective: To help the students learn to have mercy on others and to not judge them unfairly for their wrongdoings.

II. TEACHER PREPARATION

The Sermon on the Mount teaches us about three areas of our relationships. First, our relationship with God. While we only see the outside of people, God sees what's on the inside; He sees our hearts. The problem with judging others is that we put ourselves above others as judges, and that role is only God's.

Secondly, the Sermon on the Mount teaches us about our relationship with others. When we look for faults in others, we will see an attitude in ourselves that lacks love and forgiveness. Jesus shows us how to love and forgive others like he loves and forgives us.

Thirdly, the Sermon on the Mount teaches us about our relationship with ourselves. We can't help others if we judge and speak badly of them; this attitude comes from our own selfishness, since we need to feel superior. Jesus asked us, "How can you condemn others and be blind to your own faults?"

In Matthew 7:2, Jesus tells us, "For in the same way you judge others, you will be judged, and with the measure you use, it will be measured to you." He isn't teaching us to overlook the sin; but what condemns us is the despicable attitude and the lack of love that we have when we condemn others. Jesus loves the sinner but hates the sin.

How do we not judge others? God has provided us with His forgiveness, so we owe it to God to see the good in others and respond with the love of a forgiver towards every sin committed.

Children form concepts and ideas of other people, just like the world that's around them. At this age, they develop the capacity to think for themselves, and they start to see good and bad in the world. For kids, the bad demands punishment.

They need to learn to establish a difference between judging and condemning; and to know all of the facts to make that kind of decision.

In this lesson, they will learn how to show mercy in place of condemning others. God wants us to forgive others with love like we experienced when He forgave us.

III. LESSON DEVELOPMENT

Introduction

Ask two volunteer to read Matthew 26:75 and 27:1-5. Analyze the passages with the class and observe the different ways that Peter and Judas betrayed Jesus.

Emphasize to the children that even though these men were Jesus' disciples, in a moment of weakness they both acted like His enemies. In both cases, the men had the opportunity to realize what they had done, and now they have to choose what they will do as they face the sins they committed. (Give the students an opportunity to analyze who made the better decision.) Let them recount an experience where they forgave someone or they were forgiven.

Activity: Who is who?

Ask the students to find this activity on their worksheet and trace a line between each person and the prize they think each person won.

Easily the first impression the kids will have is based on the appearances of the people in the pictures. For example: the child in the wheel chair could be an admirable artist; the strong, young man could be a great athlete; the child with the spectacles could be the computer genius.

Narrate the following stories so the students will understand that first impressions aren't always correct.

The great athlete:

Carla was born with a mental limitation. Even though she's never been able to walk, she loves sports. Her father takes her to lots of different games and practices. One day she entered a wheel-chair race that was being held in the youth Olympics. Can you imagine who won?

The computer genius

Luis is a strong and attractive young man; his dad is a high school football coach. His friends all thought that he would join the youth football league, but Luis doesn't enjoy rough games. He prefers the computer. He actually joined a computer club at his school. One day he took part in a competition to see who could create the best computer game. Do you know who won?

The admirable artist:

Mario has glasses with thick lenses because he has problems seeing. He always goes around with a pencil tucked behind his ear because it makes him look smart. But he doesn't like to read; he only enjoys reading when there are lots of pictures. He loves drawing pictures in his folders. One day the art teacher told him that there was going to be an art competition at the Municipal Library. He suggested that Mario enter the competition. Who do you think won?

Now, have the kids draw a line between the child and the real prize they won and ask them, "What happens if we judge people too quickly without getting to know them at all?" (We draw wrong conclusions and we can hurt people s feelings or hurt their reputation, etc.)

Ask them "Is everything as it seems?" Have the students discuss how easy it is to judge things incorrectly. Ask them to mention some examples of situations in their lives when they have judged things wrongly.

Whatever ideas we have about people can be right or wrong if we don't have all of the details, and in this way we can be unfair. Remember the words of Jesus Christ, "Do not judge, or you too will be judged. For in the same way you judge others, you will be judged, and with the measure you use, it will be measured to you" (Matthew 7:1-2a).

Developing the Bible Story

Jesus went through the grain fields on the Sabbath. His disciples were hungry and began to pick some heads of grain and eat them. When the Pharisees, who had been following Jesus and spying on him, saw this they said to him, "Look! Your disciples are doing what is unlawful on the Sabbath." Jesus knew that the Pharisees didn't care that the disciples were hungry. They didn't feel love nor did they care very much about circumstances; the only thing they cared about was carrying out the law and the authority that it gave them.

Jesus reminded them of the story of David when he was escaping from King Saul: "Haven't you read what David did when he and his companions were hungry? He entered the house of God, and he and his companions ate the consecrated bread – which was not lawful for them to do, but only for the priests. Or haven't you read in the Law how the priests desecrated the temple on the Sabbath and yet were innocent? If you had known what these words mean, 'I desire mercy, not sacrifice,' you would not have condemned the innocent. For the Son of Man is Lord of the Sabbath."

The Pharisees stopped their discussion with Jesus but He knew they hadn't changed their way of thinking; they would keep trying to find faults with Jesus and try to find a way to destroy him.

(Matthew 7 and 12)

Life Application

Help the students understand that God wants to forgive them for the wrong they have done, but they need to repent and ask for forgiveness. Explain that every day we make decisions in our lives. If we fail, we can ask God to forgive us and He will show His love and mercy to each one of us.

IV. ACTIVITIES

Activity: What does it mean?

Ask two volunteers to read the meanings of the words "to condemn" and "to judge."

To condemn:

To say that a person or something is wrong. // To accuse, to blame. // To punish or sentence.

To judge:

A person that has enough knowledge to give an opinion of something // To blame or critique. // To think or suppose something.

Use this as a base to talk about the different ways that people judge. Read Matthew 7:1-2 and ask them what they think about what Jesus says about judging.

Read Matthew 7:5 and ask them to imagine what Jesus wanted to teach us by saying, "Take the plank out of your own eye and then you will see clearly to remove the speck from your brother's eye." Ask: "Have you seen Jesus' sense of humor?" Ask them to draw a picture of the verse and encourage them to practice love and forgiveness during the week.

Activity 3: Biblical commentary for students

Ask a student to read out loud what this activity says. Then tell them all to write a letter to God to give thanks for having sent his Son Jesus Christ to save us.

Memory Verse

If any of the kids know how to play an instrument, encourage them to accompany the group by putting a beat to the text to help them memorize it. The more people accompany the more fun it will be.

FOLLOWING JESUS' STEPS

I. OVERVIEW

Biblical Base: Matthew 7:24.

Memory Verse: *"Love your enemies, do good to those who hate you, bless those who curse you, pray for those who mistreat you.* (Luke 6:27-28)

Biblical Truth: Wise people follow the teachings of Jesus.

Lesson Objective: To help the students understand that if we follow the teachings of Jesus, we too can be wise.

II. TEACHER PREPARATION

In the Sermon on the Mount, Jesus gave guidelines for the Christian lifestyle. He finished with a story that illustrates the importance of practicing His teaching, and the consequences for not doing so. For those who don't believe, it may not be until late in life that they figure out the consequences for defying God ... a life in ruins.

Jesus told a story about two men who built their own houses: one was wise and one was foolish. The wise one was a carpenter and knew that his house would need a sturdy foundation to be able to withstand the weather conditions in Palestine. Most years it was very dry, however when the rains came, they came in storms and destroyed everything that didn't stand firm.

The key to the story is that the wise man built his life on Christ, who should be our foundation as well. The foolish man built his life on the morals and ideas of the world. Each of the men encountered storms and troubled times in their lives, but at the end of it all, the house (the life) that the wise man built stood firm and the house that the foolish man built perished.

The young students that attend your class regularly should already have a pretty good spiritual foundation that they can base their decisions on and obey God. Problems come up when people don't act according to what they've heard. Many have heard, but few obey.

To follow Christ means to carry out His teachings. This doesn't mean that one will always have success when facing hard times. They should understand that obeying God doesn't guarantee a life free of problems. There will come a time when their beliefs are challenged. They need to discover that true security comes from God, and that the world will pass away, but the love of God is forever

III. LESSON DEVELOPMENT

Introduction

Remind the students that sometimes we judge people we don't know incorrectly. Ask them to look at their shoes and the shoes of their classmates. Say, "There's an old saying, 'You can't really understand another person until you've walked a mile in their shoes.' What do you think this saying means in regards to judging people?" (That if we haven't gone though someone's situation, we don't have the right to judge or criticize them. God wants us to love them and forgive the shortcomings of others.)

Activity: Signs of the times

Ask someone to read the page in their activity sheet.

Ask: "Do you like that there's always someone telling you what to do? Do you know someone who has broken the rules and wasn't punished? What happens if people ignore rule breaking?" (Let them discuss the consequences of ignoring what you're told to do.) Then ask, "What are some rules that parents give to children? What about the rules at school? What happens when you don't obey? Why does it annoy some people to follow rules? Why do you think there are so many rules?" (So, we are safe and away from danger, to help us get along well with others, take care of our environment, etc.)

Say, "Many rules exist but how can we decide which ones are important?" (Let them answer. Show them that some people violate the rules. But if they don't think they are important, they may suffer terrible consequences ... even death.)

Continue, "In the story that we'll be reading today, we'll see what happens to people who don't pay attention to important rules. And also what happens to those who obey Jesus."

Developing the Bible Story

Building blocks

Divide the class into two groups. Have the first group build a house on a firm foundation and the second group build a house on a towel. Let the groups discuss what would happen if the house had a "bad time." Ask them to try to move the towel without making the house fall. They probably can't do it as it will shake enough to fall. Talk about what happened and why.

Is everything secure?

Ask the students to read along in their worksheet while you read, or let them take turns reading aloud.

Jesus had dedicated many hours to teaching His disciples and the rest of the people who would listen to him. He told them not to worry about their food or clothing. He reminded them that God loved them all and would supply their every need.

He also told them to love their enemies; for if they only loved the people that loved them, they weren't any better than the people who didn't love God.

He also told them not to judge others unfairly. He reminded them that they should take a look at their own wrong doings before telling others about theirs.

Jesus knew that people forgot his teachings easily. Because of this, he told them this story:

"Therefore everyone who hears these words of mine and puts them into practice is like a wise man who built his house on the rock. The rain came down, the streams rose, and the winds blew and beat against that house; yet it didn't fall, because it had its foundation on the rock. But everyone who hears these words of mine and doesn't put them into practice is like a foolish man who built his house on sand. The rain came down, the streams rose, and the winds blew and beat against that house, and it fell with a great crash."

If Jesus was here today telling the same story he would probably say something like this…

Two friends met up and this was the dialogue:

"Hey, Hugo! What's going on?" asked John.

"Hiya, John! What's new with you?" responded Hugo.

"Do you remember that house that I was planning on building? Well I finally found a good foundation, a solid rock, where I can build it. I've worked a long time on building it and soon, once I'm finished, I can move in!" said John.

"Wow!! How great is that!" responded Hugo. "I've also been building a new house. I found a sandy place where it's easy to build. I'll be done building soon and then I'll be able to move in. Yeah, I guess I didn't really take too much time to plan it, but I think it's going to be great!

"Yeah, probably," said John, "I just hope your house can resist the strong winds and rain."

"John, there is one difference between you and I," continued Hugo, "I want to do everything the fastest and easiest way. I mean, my house is practically done. You'll figure it out pretty soon." And he left. Both men finished building their houses and moved in. Soon the rains came and the winds blew strongly and the waters hit the houses crazily. John's house withstood the strong winds, rain and floods because he built his house on the rock. But Hugo's house fell.

In His story, Jesus warned those who listened that it was important to love God and build their lives on His teachings. If they didn't, they wouldn't feel secure when they faced difficulties; they would collapse, just like the foolish man's house.

When Jesus finished his story, the people admired the way he taught because he taught with authority, not like scribes. (Matthew 7)

Ask the class: "What do you think Jesus wanted to show His followers?" (Let the children respond and show them that He wasn't necessarily showing us how to build a house but how to build our lives.)

Life Application

Ask them to find James 1:22-23 in their Bibles and have everyone read aloud. Ask, "What similarities can you find between this verse and with Jesus' story about the wise man and the foolish man? (Each of them talk about the importance of not just hearing the Word of God but obeying it.)

"What is James trying to say with regards to the men who only hear the Word but don't follow it?" (The foolish man who built his house on the sand deceived himself by thinking he was safe in building his house there. Some people deceive themselves into thinking that they shouldn't do what God says.) During their discussion, show that those people deceive themselves when they don't follow the Truth.

Memory verse

Challenge the students to say their Bible verse by memory. Give a star to each student who can do it.

Show that it is easier to listen to the teachings of Jesus than to live them. He shows us how we should live. Explain to them that if they have disobeyed God, now is a great time to ask for forgiveness.

Lead them in a prayer of confession. Allow them to have a private moment talking with, God confessing what they've done wrong. Ask the Lord to help them live according to what Jesus taught and not just to hear the Word.

IV. ACTIVITIES

Signs of the times

Tell the students to look at the signals that are on their worksheet. Ask them, "What would happen if people ignored these?"

Activity: Biblical Commentary for students

Have a volunteer read Matthew 7:24-29 and another read what the next activity is. Have everyone draw two houses, one built on the rock, that is Christ, and one not built on the rock.

GUIDE FOR UNIT XI

ELISHA, A COMPASSIONATE MAN

BIBLE TRUTH: God worked through His followers to show compassion to everyone who needed it, no matter their social class, belief, nationality or gender.

UNIT OBJECTIVE:
- For the students to learn that the prophet Elisha was used as an instrument of God to have compassion on other people.
- To learn that God hopes that we show compassion for the needy, for the believers, for those who want to do harm to us, and for those who have a lot of material items but are missing something.

UNIT LESSONS:
- » Lesson 44 - Compassion for the needy
- » Lesson 45 - Compassion for the believers
- » Lesson 46 - Compassion for authority
- » Lesson 47 - Compassion for our enemies

UNIT VERSE: "*Therefore, as we have opportunity, let us do good to all people, especially to those who belong to the family of believers.*" (Galatians 6:10)

Nowadays, hardly anyone shows compassion to others; it's for this reason that children show indifference to respecting others.

The prophet Elisha is a good role model for kids, because God used him to do acts of mercy and compassion. That's why sometimes they call him the "compassionate prophet." He spent time with people of all types and always treated them kindly and compassionately, just like the widow and the military commander.

While the students study the compassionate acts of Elisha towards the needy, they can learn that God hopes that they too will demonstrate kindness and compassion to others. Through this lesson, they will learn and practice new ways of being kind to others.

However, you should emphasize the differences between acts of compassion that Christians do, and acts that others do for recognition.

Christians don't respond out of pity, but because they feel sincere love towards others. Their compassion shows love to God and God towards them.

By doing acts of kindness and mercy, Christians help others discover the love of God.

Suggestions:
1. There is a principal teaching that says: "He who hears, forgets; he who sees, remembers; but he who does, learns." That's why children look for things in the lessons that they can use to show compassion to the needy people that they know.
2. In the same way, it's possible that each class can carry out a project to show compassion towards someone. Remember that this unit consists of four lessons, so you have a whole month to plan and execute the project.
3. A suggestion for the project could be a canned food drive (no perishables) or other kind of things that you can give to a family in need. Motivate the kids in this project: name the project something catchy to attract the kids. This is important so they remember what they are doing. However, don't just do this; talk with the students to see if they have another idea that would be just as good.
4. Be aware that in the Christian life, compassion should become a way of life, a practice that's more practical than theoretical.
5. Verse of the Month Club: It's very important that the students learn this unit's verse. Take some time to plan different activities for each class, with the end result being that the student doesn't fight to learn it. Remember to put a star in the student's certificate when they have memorized the text.

COMPASSION FOR THE NEEDY

I. OVERVIEW

Bible Reference: 2 Kings 4:1-7
Memory Verse: *"Therefore, as we have opportunity, let us do good to all people, especially to those who belong to the family of believers."* (Galatians 6:10)
Biblical Truth: God uses his followers to show compassion to those in need.
Lesson Objective: To help the students recognize that God can have compassion on those who are needy through the people who are willing to serve.

II. TEACHER PREPARATION

Elisha was the successor of Elijah, prophet of Jehovah. Elisha was called by God when he was out plowing his land (1 Kings 19). Maybe he was someone who had lots of money. In his ministry, he took an active part in Israel's public issues, he preached and performed miracles. Out of all of the prophets, only Elisha predicted several of Christ's miracles, which makes us remember his goodness.

Elisha was God's prophet, and God declared things through his life. People of all classes sought out his help. Many recognized him as someone important, but Elisha didn't let this divert his attention from his ministry and what the people needed.

The husband of a widow had acquired a debt that he couldn't pay before he died. During this time, widows didn't have a source of income because they weren't allowed to work outside of the home, so she couldn't pay the debt.

According to the law (Leviticus 25:38-42), a creditor could take the debtor's family as slaves for a period of time, up to 50 years, and that way pay the debt. The widow wanted to save her children from their similar destiny.

"Compassion" is a strange concept today, especially for kids who, far from practicing it, have the tendency to think only of themselves. Not only are they predominantly thinking about themselves, but they are quick to judge others and think poorly of those who are different. It's a psychological trait or characteristic of children.

During Biblical time, where this passage comes from, compassion was reduced and limited by laws and certain social prejudices. However, Elisha knew exactly who had called him and why; he was to serve the Living God. He was to proclaim His message and show a lifestyle that conformed to His divine will.

Many of Elisha's follower's forgot the word of Jehovah, but he preached it. Many didn't live according to what God wanted, but Elisha did; and the city with their customs, didn't show compassion. As a result, Elisha decided to show compassion to those who needed or asked for it.

"What can I do for you?" With this question, Elisha made his personality obvious. We should imitate his attitude in our lives, even when the world in which we live is not compassionate, and instead is selfish, cruel and plain mean. God calls us to be different and to carry out His will.

III. LESSON DEVELOPMENT
Introduction

Fuel (gas, diesel, oil, etc.) is very much a valued product in our lives; it moves vehicles and is used in almost every industry. It comes from a very necessary liquid and it just gets more and more expensive. In the same way, oil was very precious to the Jews, because they used it for light and to heat their home in the night. It was also used to anoint; people in the medical field used it and people also used it to cook with as well. It had many uses and that is why it is very valuable.

Read with your students the passage in 2 Kings 4:1-7 and interact with them by asking them questions about: what happened, where it happened, the characters, etc. You can also talk about the attitudes of the widow and of Elisha, Elisha's availability to help – but not doing the whole thing himself, he let the widow do her part too – and Elisha's ability to listen.

Divide your students into equal groups and ask them this question: "What was it that motivated Elisha to help the widow?" Then, let each group discuss their answers and finally have a spokesperson from each group tell everyone their group's answer.

Ask the students to get into pairs. (They can work by themselves if they'd like.) Have them make a list of different needs that their community may have, and then have them come up with possible solutions to those problems. Ask everyone to read their list to the class.

Have the students think about their lists and consider them while keeping in mind that God uses people who are willing and able to serve him, just like he used Elisha. In this way God blesses the needy.

Pray with them that God can use each of them to have compassion on the less fortunate.

Activity: Why doesn't anyone do anything?
What is compassion?

Help the student understand through this activity. Have them use the code to fill in the blank spaces on top of the numbers and they will figure out the meaning of the word "compassion": To love enough to help someone.

Developing the Bible Story
What can I do for you?

Knock, knock! Elisha hurried over to see who was at the door. He recognized the woman immediately; she was the widow of one of his friends.

"What's going on?" Elisha asked.

"Your servant, my husband, is dead, and you know that he revered the Lord. But now his creditor is coming to take my two boys as his slaves," she said.

Her husband owed a lot of money when he died. The law said that people who were owed money were allowed to take the debtor's family as their slaves, until their work paid for the debt. Elisha knew that the widow had no money.

Elisha replied to her, "How can I help you? Tell me, what do you have in your house?"

"Your servant has nothing there at all," she said, "except a little oil."

Elisha said, "Go around and ask all your neighbors for empty jars. Don't ask for just a few. Then go inside and shut the door behind you and your sons. Pour oil into all the jars, and as each is filled, put it to one side."

The widow thought to herself, "What will this little bit of oil do for me now?" But, she closed the door and gathered her sons and told them what Elisha had told her. They went from house to house asking their neighbors for all of the empty jars they could get. Once they were back at their house, the widow asked her sons to please bring her a jar. As they brought the jars to her, she kept pouring. She told them that as each one got full to move it aside so they didn't get in the way. The sons saw how many empty jars they had all over the house and said "How is it possible that with so little oil we can fill all of these?" But they obeyed their mother's instructions anyway.

One of the sons passed a jar to his mother and attentively watched how she took what little oil they had and started to fill the empty jar. When it was full of oil, the other son took it away to make room for another jar that his brother brought.

They filled jar after jar. Their mother kept pouring the oil every empty jar she got. "Bring me another jar." But her son replied, "There is not a jar left." Then the oil stopped flowing. She went and told the man of God, and he said, "Go, sell the oil and pay your debts. You and your sons can live on what is left."

Life Application
Hope project

Help the students plan this project, something they can call Hope, to help others out this month. Ask them to bring canned foods, or another type of food that is imperishable, to every class for the rest of the month. If the church is collecting baskets of love at this time, the class can donate half of the food to this cause. Otherwise, they can offer the food to whatever family or group they choose.

IV. ACTIVITIES
Activity: Show compassion to the needy

Have the children find this activity in their activity sheet. Divide the class into three groups and give each group the beginning of a story. Have them read it and then ask them to think about and then discuss the following questions before they write the end of the story.
1. Who has a need in this story?
2. What is that need?
3. What can someone do to show this person compassion?

Tell the children that they should now finish the stories. Make sure to tell them that by working together with God they can show compassion to others.

Story #1 - "There is a student in the class who uses hearing aids to help him hear; he also uses very thick glasses. Some students make fun of him. They say that he sounds weird when he talks." (This little boy obviously is in need, since he already is confronted with physical impairments. God loves him, but he also needs friends who accept him for who he is.)

The children can show him compassion by inviting him to join a group of friends; or ask the ones that do make fun of him to not do it anymore. Emphasize that we shouldn't blame anyone for having physical impediments.

Story #2 - The father of a little neighbor girl lost his job. The little girl has a new baby sister. (Everyone has a need here. The father lost his job and the mom just had a baby. It's harder for students to think of what they can do in this situation. But if the little girl is younger, they could offer to take her to and bring her home from school, or the bus stop. They could also play with her while the mother rests or watches the baby.)

Story #3 - "A lady lives by herself in the neighborhood. She doesn't come outside often. A nurse visits her house once a week to see how she's doing. Sometimes she sits in front of her house and watches the people pass. Every once in a while she yells at kids that come into her yard." (This lady has a need. She can't come outside often and she is lonely.) The students can show her compassion by visiting her when she sits in front of her house. They could bring her the mail, or bring her flowers and small gifts.

Let the children read the ending to their stories.

Memory Verse

In this unit the children will be learning a new verse, it's quite short. Challenge them to learn it quickly. You can think of games and activities to make it easy to learn.

COMPASSION FOR THE BELIEVERS

I. OVERVIEW

Bible Verse: 2 Kings 4:8-37, 8:1-6
Memory Verse: *"Therefore, as we have opportunity, let us do good to all people, especially to those who belong to the family of believers."* (Galatians 6:10)
Biblical Truth: Jesus teaches us to have mercy on our neighbors, and to not judge them unfairly for something they've done wrong.
Lesson Objective: To help the student understand the need to show compassion to others who believe in Christ.

II. TEACHER PREPARATION

In the previous lesson, we learned that Elisha was Elijah's successor as Jehovah's prophet (1 Kings 19). In another place, Shunem was situated on the slope of a hill in front of the valley of Jezreel. Elisha met a woman there and they hit it off.

In verse 13, we see the expression, "I have a home among my own people" which could mean "my city will take care of my every need."

The Shunammite's husband was probably very conservative in his religion. We assume this because she said in verse 23, "Why go to him today? It's not the New Moon or the Sabbath. It's all right," she said. She saddled the donkey and left to go find help.

There are several things that indicate that the Shunammite woman and her family had lots of money. They described her as an important woman (verse 8). She had the ability to make room in her house for guests (verse 9). She had followers and helpers that worked for them (verses 18, 19, 22 and 24); all in addition to her religious life. She recognized Elisha as a man of God. They also knew about religious traditions. However, this didn't mean that they lived a life without needs and problems; instances where they would need help and encouragement would still arise.

Even today there are brothers and sisters in the church that are exposed to difficulties and difficult trials; things that may make them trip in their faith in God. These strong Christians also need encouragement and people who listen to them, people that help feed their hungry spirit. This is something that we should always remember and put into practice.

III. LESSON DEVELOPMENT

Introduction

With the help of your students, write on the board or on a piece of paper, a list of needs or problems that they know of in their congregation, whether a person, family, or level of leadership in the church.

You can initiate the activity like a brainstorm. (You can check out what this consists of on the next page under Activities.). Start with the question: "What needs are there throughout our church?" It's important that you, as the teacher, are wise and know how to guide the activity so there aren't jokes about people or students prying into people's private lives.

Read with your students the passage in 2 Kings 4:8-37. You can use the reading technique called "jump over to…" (Activities next page)

Interact with the kids to see if they have understood the story that you just read. Ask them to give you ideas of how to help the needs of the people you talked about earlier. Help them come up with ideas in order for them to carry out their ideas.

Another idea for this activity is to provide them with materials like paper, crayons, pencils, glue, etc. so they can make cards and give them to the pastor of the church, declaring their support of him in ministry.

Developing the Bible Story

One day a woman said to her husband, "I know that this man Elisha who often comes our way is a holy man of God. Let's make a small room on the roof and put a bed and a table in it, as well as a chair and a lamp for him. Then he can stay there whenever he comes to us." The husband paid people to build this room.

"Elisha! Welcome again! Come in, I have a surprise for you!" said the Shunammite woman. She took the prophet to a room she had prepared for him. Elisha had stayed with this family many times.

"Whenever you come to visit Shunem, you are welcome to stay here," she said to Elisha. Elisha thought about the woman and her loving ways towards him and he wanted to give her something in return. He called his servant Gehazi, "Call the Shunammite. Tell her, 'You have gone to all this trouble for us. Now what can be done for you?" She replied, "I have a home among my own people."

"What can be done for her?" Elisha asked. Gehazi said, "She has no son, and her husband is old." Then Elisha said, "Call her." So he called her, and she stood in the doorway. "About this time next year," Elisha said, "you will hold a son in your arms." The woman had wanted a son, but she thought it would be an impossible thing.

But the woman became pregnant, and the next year about that same time she gave birth to a son, just as Elisha had told her. She was so happy to be a mother! The child grew, and one day he went out to his father, who was with the reapers. He said to his father, "My head hurts! My head hurts!" His father told a servant, "Carry him to his mother." After the servant had lifted him up and carried him to his mother, the boy sat on her lap until noon, and then he died. The mother was inconsolable and went to find Elisha. She went as fast as she could to where he was.

Elisha saw her coming from far away and he sent Gehazi to meet her and see if everything was okay, but he didn't say to ask about her son. She wanted to tell Elisha directly, but he gave Gehazi his staff as a symbol of his prophetic authority. "Tuck your cloak into your belt, take my staff in your hand and run. Don't greet anyone you meet, and if anyone greets you, don't answer. Lay my staff on the boy's face."

When they got to the house, Gehazi did as he was told to do and went back to Elisha to tell him that the boy had not woken up.

When Elisha reached the house, there was the boy lying dead on his couch. He went in, shut the door, and prayed to the Lord. Then he got on the bed and lay beside the boy. As he stretched himself out beside him, the boy's body grew warm. Elisha turned away and walked back and forth in the room and then got on the bed and stretched out beside him once more. The boy sneezed seven times and opened his eyes. Elisha summoned Gehazi and said, "Call the Shunammite." And he did. When she came, he said, "Take your son."

Sometime after, God told Elisha that he was bringing a drought. There would be nothing to eat. Elisha remembered the compassion of the Shunammite woman and went to go warn them. "Get up, take yourself and your household away to live where you can, because God has declared a famine in this land for the next seven years," Elisha told them.

So she and her family left. After seven years, they returned, only to find their home and possessions had been taken. She went to the king to beg for her house and land. The king was talking to Gehazi and he told the king who she was and her story. Once the king heard this, he ordered that all her belongings be returned to her. (2 Kings 4 and 8)

Life Application

Activity: Who needs compassion?

Tell the children that in this picture they'll find people who need compassion. Have them circle them.

Activity: Showing compassion to my church family

Have the students look at the picture on their activity sheet and ask them, "How can people show compassion to these people?"

- Square 1: Explain that sometimes pastors feel lonely. They listen to others people's problems and sometimes feel as if they aren't able to help them out. People criticize them unjustly. A way to show them compassion is to tell them you love them and are praying for them.
- Square 2: Someone could hold the door open for the lady.
- Square 3: The church can provide things that will help the family start their new life. Write on the board "What needs does our local church have?" (Write the answers on the board as well.)
- Square 4: Have the children write or draw how they can help someone at church.

Once everyone has finished, have them share and explain their answer for square 4. Invite them to put these ideas into practice this week.

IV. ACTIVITIES

"Brainstorm". Write a question on the board (something that has to do with compassion) and have the kids think of answers. Write each answer down on the board. Children can expand on others' ideas. Have them do their own brainstorms.

"Jump over to…" Consists of someone starting to read the Bible passage and whenever they are ready they can say "Jump over to…Ana" and then Ana will pick up reading where they left off. This goes on and on. This activity is a great way to involve each student while maintaining their attention. If someone gets called in and they don't know where they are supposed to pick up, have them do something silly as a "punishment."

Finish the class with prayer asking the Lord to help the class make their ideas and thoughts about showing compassion a reality. Remember to pray for your pastors and other ministers involved in your church.

Memory Verse

To know if the children have memorized the text, ask the following questions: "When should we do good to all?" (When we have the opportunity.) "Especially who?" (Those who belong to the family of faith.)

COMPASSION FOR AUTHORITY

I. OVERVIEW

Bible Verse: 2 Kings 5:1-15.

Memory Verse: *"Therefore, as we have opportunity, let us do good to all people, especially to those who belong to the family of believers."* (Galatians 6:10)

Biblical Truth: God uses His followers to demonstrate to those who have been put in a place of power that He is the only true God.

Lesson Objective: To help the students learn that it is also necessary to show compassion to those who have been placed in a place of power.

II. TEACHER PREPARATION

Naaman was a distinguished captain of the armed forces in Aram (Syria) and he had leprosy. One of his Hebrew slaves felt a lot of compassion for him, and she told him that from what she had heard, there was a prophet in Israel who could cure him.

Because the national security depended on Naaman, it was necessary that he be healed. So, the king of Syria sent Naaman with a letter to the king of Israel so he could be healed. This king didn't have the power to heal him and he was scared when Naaman came to him. He was sure the king of Syria was trying to have an excuse to start a war with Israel.

Right then, Elisha came in. His sure and strong words, "Have the man come to me," was a big contrast to the weak words of the king, "Am I God?" The king of Israel wasn't close to God, but the prophet was.

Naaman hurried to Elisha's house and hoped that the prophet would salute him with all the respect that his great position deserved, and that he would be healed quickly and magically. But it wasn't like that at all. Elisha sent his servant with a message to him. "Go, wash yourself seven times in the Jordan River, and your flesh will be restored and you will be cleansed" (v. 10).

Naaman got really mad. Did this prophet not understand that the leader of Syria's armed forces was here on his porch? And he wants me to wash myself in the muddy waters of the Jordan? Why not the cleaner rivers of Syria? (Obviously, Naaman had forgotten that he had already tried all of the resources Syria had to offer.)

His servants reminded him that he had been willing to trying anything to be healed, so why not try this simple act? Finally, he decided he had nothing to lose, and as soon as he did it, he was healed, and his skin became clean like that of a young boy. No one doubted that this was a supernatural gift from God. Elisha rejected the gifts that Naaman offered him. He knew that if he accepted them, the miracle wouldn't be of God anymore but of himself,

and he wanted to show Naaman that the grace of God isn't something that you win, buy or that you even deserve.

God calls us to have compassion on everyone equally. It's easier to see the needs of the sick, those that have suffered through accidents, people who have physical disabilities or those who are poor. Despite these, sometimes behind the outward appearances of the wealthy, and those who hold high positions, hide other realities: empty lives, needs that they try to fill with material objects, big houses, and cars; appearances that are just masks hiding what is really there.

Sometimes we think of powerful people only as people who have a lot of money, positions in the government or big company owners. But there are other people who have authority like professors, parents and pastors.

The thing that puts us all in the same social level (the rich and poor, educated people and not, sick and healed, etc.) is the unavoidable need for Christ in our lives (Romans 3:23). Regardless of what social class we are in, we all need Christ.

As Christians, we should always show compassion, towards the wealthy, the important, etc. because even though they have a lot, many are missing something very important, the presence of Christ in their hearts.

LESSON DEVELOPMENT

Introduction

Developing the Bible Story

Are you kidding me?!

"Oh no!" cried the young servant girl. "Leprosy? No!" Naaman, her master, had a terrible disease and no one could cure it. She said to her mistress, "If only my master would see the prophet who is in Samaria! He would cure him of his leprosy." Naaman's wife commented to him what the servant had told her.

"Could he really help me?" Naaman asked her. He went to ask the king if he could go to Israel to find this prophet Elisha. The king of Syria said, "By all means, go.

I'll send a letter to the king of Israel."

Naaman went to Israel with his servants, horses and chariots. The letter he took to the king said, "With this letter I am sending my servant Naaman to you so that you may cure him of his leprosy." As soon as the king of Israel read the letter, he tore his robes and said, "Am I God? Can I kill and bring back life? Why does this fellow send someone to me to be cured of his leprosy? See how he is trying to pick a quarrel with me!"

When Elisha, the man of God, heard that the king of Israel had torn his robes, he sent him this message: "Why have you torn your robes? Have the man come to me and he will know that there is a prophet in Israel." So Naaman went with his horses and chariots and stopped at the door of Elisha's house. Elisha sent a messenger to say to him, "Go, wash yourself seven times in the Jordan, and your flesh will be restored and you will be cleansed."

But Naaman went away angry and said, "I thought that he would surely come out to me and stand and call on the name of the LORD his God, wave his hand over the spot and cure me of my leprosy.

Are not Abana and Pharpar, the rivers of Damascus, better than all the waters of Israel? Couldn't I wash in them and be cleansed?" So he turned and went off in a rage.

Naaman's servants cared for and loved their master and wished that he would be cured. They knew he had already tried everything and nothing had healed him, so they said, "My father, if the prophet had told you to do some great thing, would you not have done it? How much more, then, when he tells you, 'Wash and be cleansed!'"

So Naaman went down and dipped himself in the Jordan River seven times, as the man of God had told him, and his flesh was restored and became clean like that of a young boy.

Then Naaman and all his attendants went back to the man of God. He stood before him and said, "Now I know that there is no God in all the world except in Israel."

Naaman was so excited that Elisha had compassion on him that he tried to give him lots of gifts, but the prophet refused because he wanted Naaman to understand that it wasn't he who healed him, but God. And that no one could buy favor in the eyes of the Lord. (2 Kings 5)

Life Application

Give the students some paper, glue, markers and newspapers or magazines they can cut.

Tell them to think of people they admire, maybe they have some authority over them or they're famous, their parents, etc. Have them draw and decorate the person/people on the paper. When they are done, let them make a kind of mural with all of the pictures. You can hang it on the wall or the board. Once everything is hung up, you can have the kids talk about who they drew and why.

IV. ACTIVITIES

Activity: What would have happened?

Ask the kids to think about what would have happened to the characters in the bible story if no one had showed anyone compassion. Read each question and let the children express their ideas and feelings. What would have happened ...

1. If the servant hadn't cared enough to talk to Naaman's wife?
2. If Naaman's wife hadn't cared enough to tell him what the servant said?
3. If Elisha hadn't told Naaman what to do?
4. If the king of Syria hadn't given Naaman permission to visit Israel?
5. If the servants of Naaman had let their master leave after not wanting to wash himself in the Jordan?

Activity: Compassion for those who have power and authority

Have the students find this on their activity sheet and have them write answers to each of these questions:

1. Who are people that have power and authority? (Kings and queens, presidents, teachers, pastors, parents, etc.)
2. Why do people with power and authority need compassion? (Because sometimes they feel alone. They have problems just like the rest of the people, some have lots of money but money doesn't buy everything; for instance health or happiness. We all need Christian compassion.)
3. How can we be compassionate towards them? (We can write them letters of appreciation, etc.)

Project Hope

Collect all of the foodstuffs from the kids that they brought. Congratulate them for bringing in food to help others. Remind them that God is using them to show compassion to others.

Memory Verse

Tear papers into strips and write one word of the verse on each of them. (It may be easiest for this exercise to just use whole pieces of paper, or even half, and write one word per sheet.) Fold them in half. Invite everyone who wants to to participate. Have each student choose a piece of paper and tape them up on the board in the correct order.

For the end-of-class prayer, ask the Lord to help the students to show compassion to others.

COMPASSION FOR OUR ENEMIES

I. OVERVIEW

Biblical Base: 2 Kings 6:8-23, Matthew 5:44.
Memory Verse: *"Therefore, as we have opportunity, let us do good to all people, especially to those who belong to the family of believers."* (Galatians 6:10)
Biblical Truth: God wants His followers to show compassion to everyone; even to those who wish to hurt us.
Lesson Objective: To help the students understand the necessity of showing compassion to others, including those who want to hurt us.

II. TEACHER PREPARATION

The King of Syria was at war against Israel, being the aggressors. Israel had found themselves happy and peaceful with Syria, but Syria continually pestered them with armed forces entering their land. They went to the border of Israel to rob, kill and take their people captive.

Soon, everything started to fall apart for the Syrians. Israel counted on their divinely inspired intelligence system. God would tell Elisha where the Syrians would appear for their next attack, and Elisha would then tell the king. This happened so often that the King of Syria thought that one of his officers was a spy. But they all denied it and told him that it was coming from the prophet Elisha; that he found out everything they were doing and told the king of Israel.

The king of Syria sent spies to find Elisha, and when they returned they said, "He is in Dothan." Dothan was north of Samaria, not too far from the territories that the Syrians occupied. By the next morning, the Syrians had already surrounded the city. The only thing they needed to do was capture Elisha. With so many horses and chariots, they though the it wouldn't be difficult to trap the prophet. The plan was so easy, but apparently the Syrians had forgotten about the God of Israel.

When Elisha's servant saw the Syrian army surrounding the city, he hurried to tell him. But Elisha wasn't worried, he was sure that God was in control of the situation. He responded, "Those who are with us are more than those who are with them." Elisha knew that God always took care of His city, no matter what kind of danger or insecurity it faced.

Afterwards, his servant had a vision where he saw a heavenly army all around the Syrians. Compared to God's army, the Syrians were nothing.

When the Syrian army started to advance, Elisha prayed that God would blind them. Then, Elisha lead the Syrians to Samaria, where the king (probably Jeroboam) and the Israel army waited for them. After Elisha prayed that their eyes be open, the Syrians realized that they were in Samaria. The king of Israel found himself anxious to seek revenge, but he followed Elisha's advice. (It must have been so hard for him to prepare a grand banquet in honor of his enemies.)

But Elisha knew something the king of Israel didn't.

Hostility only brings about more hostility, and war provokes more war. The advice that he gave turned out to be the wisest. The attacks against Israel finally stopped. The act of compassion that Elisha showed brought peace to his country.

One of the most radical concepts that Jesus preached, and that he asked his followers to practice, was love and compassion towards one's enemies. The meaning of the word "enemy" is widely used. It doesn't only mean the hatred that is represented by evil villains, but it also means those people who look for ways to hurt us, sometimes with reason, sometimes without.

The commandment that Jesus gave us was clear and doesn't give room to doubt: We should love. Children know other kids from school or in the neighborhood that annoy them, make fun of them, hurt them, and pester them. These are enemies to our kids and hopefully through this lesson they'll learn that through the eyes of God, they can love them and have compassion on them.

III. LESSON DEVELOPMENT

Introduction

"BUT THEY'RE THE ENEMY?!"

Have the students look at the activity sheet of today's story. This is a play. Assign the students to read certain parts and have everyone read out loud. If there are too many children who want to participate, have someone be the narrator to set the scene; otherwise you read it.

Characters: Syrian king, guards, Syrian soldiers, first officer, second officer, Elisha, Elisha's servant, other soldiers (optional)

ACT I

(In a Syrian army camp. A scared soldier enters. You can tell by his face how scared he is. He bows in front of the king.)

Syrian soldier: Your highness! The ambush against Israel has failed, again!

Syrian king: (angrily) AGAIN?! There has to be a spy among our men that is communicating our plans to the Israeli king. Go call all of the officers immediately! We'll discover who our spy is!

Syrian soldier: Yes, your majesty! I'll go right away! (He leaves and returns with the officers.)

Syrian king: Will you not tell me which of us is on the

side of the king of Israel?

First officer: None of us, my lord the king. Elisha, the prophet who is in Israel, tells the king of Israel the very words you speak in your bedroom.

Second officer: Yes, your majesty! This prophet knows exactly where we are going to attack. His God reveals to him our plans, then he shows them to the king of Israel.

Syrian king: Go, find out where he is so I can send men and capture him.

(The officers leave and the king writes on a piece of parchment. The first officer enters and bows before the king.)

Syrian king: Have you found where the prophet Elisha is?

First officer: Yes, he is in Dothan!

Syrian king: Dothan? Surround the city right now!

First officer: Yes, your majesty! (He leaves.)

Syrian king: (claps his hand together and smiles evilly) Elisha, I'll make you my prisoner soon enough!

ACT II

(Early in the morning in Dothan, Elisha's servant goes to the well to bring in water. He realizes that the entire city is surrounded by the Syrian army. He hurries to tell Elisha.

Elisha's servant: Master, the city is surrounded by the Syrian army! They're going to kill us! Oh my lord, what shall we do?

Elisha: Don't be afraid. Those who are with us are more than those who are with them. (Elisha bows his head and starts to pray.) Oh Lord, open his eyes so that he may see.

Elisha's servant: (looks around him in awe, rubs his eyes) I can't believe what I'm seeing! There are other horses and other chariots on the hills surrounding the Syrians. They are so bright, like they're on fire!

Elisha: (looks to the sky and prays) Strike these people with blindness.

(The Syrian soldiers begin to trip on the road, they have no idea where they are going.)

Elisha: (walks close to the first officer) This is not the road and this is not the city. Follow me and I'll lead you to the man you are looking for.

First officer: (Orders his men) Follow me.

(Elisha guides them to the king of Israel and prays once more.)

Elisha: Oh, Lord, open their eyes so they may see.

First officer: (looks around) Where are we?

Second officer: It looks like Samaria, but it couldn't be!

Israel king: Should we kill them, my lord?

Elisha: Don't kill them. Would you kill men you have captured with your own sword or bow? Set food and water before them so that they may eat and drink and then go back to their master.

First official: Did you hear that?? They are going to give us something to eat and then let us leave freely and return home!

Second official: What kind of people are these? (2 Kings 6)

Life Application

Help the students think of some ways that they can put this lesson into practice. Talk about how to show compassion to those who need help, and how to show compassion and forgive those who hurt us.

Organize the group into a circle where they are comfortable and can talk. Lead a conversation in which the kids can talk about experiences they've had. This can be a motivation to ask questions like: "What has been done to you that resulted in a painful situation for you?" "What do you dislike that they do to you?" "What would you never do to your best friends, siblings or your parents?" "What could they do that you would never forgive them for?"

It's very important to keep in mind:

1. If you're trying to get them to open sensitive parts of their heart, it could take a little work. Be creative and wise in order to do it correctly, not forcefully.
2. As previously mentioned, this is working with sensitive parts of kids' emotions. Your kids could start talking about and remembering delicate facts and things that are very significant in their personal, family and spiritual lives. Be wise and professional when you direct the conversation in order to assimilate and manage the information that could come up.

IV. ACTIVITIES
Activity: Who doesn't deserve compassion?

Ask the students to look at the pictures on this activity page. Ask them: "Who do you think doesn't deserve compassion?" (The students could mention the people in the pictures: the one that is stealing the wallet, or the person yelling at the mailman.) "Why don't these people deserve compassion?" (Let the students respond.) "How do you think we should treat people who don't deserve compassion?" (Talk about how God treats people much better than what they deserve. This is the grace of God.) Because we are His children, He wants us to treat people better than they deserve too.

Activity: Official board

It's important for the kids to feel compassion for the needy. Challenge them to think of a plan that would help them show compassion to others, and have them write it next to this activity. Invite them to be the "messenger of Mercy".

Memory Verse

Have the kids who are ready repeat Galatians 6:10 in unison. Ask a volunteer to explain the meaning of the verse.

Project Hope

It's time for the kids to give the food they brought for Project Hope. If it's possible, invite a representative of the church (pastor or superintendent) to visit the class and accept the gift.

GUIDE FOR UNIT XII

CHRISTMAS ACCORDING TO ...

BIBLICAL TRUTH: God fulfilled His promise of sending a Savior for humanity: Jesus Christ

UNIT OBJECTIVES
- That the students will learn the signs and messages that God showed us through the history of His people, with the purpose of showing us that He would send a Savior.
- That they will understand how God prepared His people to receive the promised Messiah.
- That they will understand the significance of Jesus becoming human like us, to save us.
- That they will recognize God's mercy revealed to us through Jesus.
- To help the students give God everything they are and everything they have.

UNIT LESSONS:
- » Lesson 48 - Christmas according to the Patriarchs and the Prophets
- » Lesson 49 - Christmas according to Zechariah and Elizabeth
- » Lesson 50 - Christmas according to Mary and Joseph
- » Lesson 51 - Christmas according to Simeon and Anna
- » Lesson 52 - Give everything to God!

UNIT VERSE: *"She will give birth to a son, and you are to give him the name Jesus, because he will save his people from their sins."* (Matthew 1:21)

Suggestions:
1. Collect clothes and sheets to prepare the set design for lesson 50.
2. To dramatize the bible story in lesson 5, you'll need a baby doll to represent baby Jesus.
3. Prepare small cards for the kids for one of the activities in lesson 52. You'll also need a box (you can decorate it) that says "Heaven's Bank" to use in another activity.

Since it is the Christmas season, the class room should be decorated in order to contribute to the student's learning. The most important thing is that it be simple for the first Christians that we'll learn about this month. Ask the students to actively participate in the decorating.

If the group doesn't have its own classroom, the Christmas ornaments that they make can be for church or their own homes. This activity can take place in someone's home if possible, with the objective of facilitating teamwork and togetherness.

They can also make decorations with flour and salt; mix equal parts of both products. Add water and mix until the dough is consistent. Then, take it out and make ornaments using cookie cutters with a Christmas theme. Let the dough dry so that the students can paint and decorate them with glitter and glue.

Another easy ornament to make is the star of David. You can make it using popsicle sticks. Make two triangles, glue them so they form a star and then decorate them with glitter or whatever else you want.

Christmastime is a special time of year to demonstrate the love we profess as Christians to people that we know from church and also to those who don't know Jesus yet.

Start (if you can) with a party "Celebrating the Savior"; the kids should come dressed up like their favorite person from the Christmas story. Have the party at your house or a student's house. After playing games and eating, sing some Christmas carols and read the Bible story of Christmas. At the end, say a prayer where each student can voluntarily thank God for the Christmas season. The party to celebrate the Savior can continue developing in the following weeks coming up to Christmas Eve, when the students, you and some of the families can decide to visit senior homes to sing some carols to them and bring them cards that the students made. You could also visit children's shelters to bring them toys, books and cookies. Assume this as the challenge for Christmas, you'll only need a good plan and some creativity. The Holy Spirit wants to change these children's lives!

CHRISTMAS ACCORDING TO THE PATRIARCHS AND THE PROPHETS

I. OVERVIEW

Biblical Base: Genesis 12:1-3; Isaiah 7:14, 9:1-7, 40:1-5; Micah 5:2

Memory Verse: *"She will give birth to a son, and you are to give him the name Jesus, because he will save his people from their sins."* (Matthew 1:21)

Biblical Truth: God had a plan to save the world, and he prepared his people throughout history for the coming of Jesus.

Lesson Objective: To know the signs and messages that God showed his people throughout history, with the purpose of making known the coming of the Savior.

II. TEACHER PREPARATION

Abraham. In this passage we start the story of one of the most famous men in humanity: Abraham, God's friend (James 2:23); who started with the name Abram, which means "father is high or the father loves" (The Study Bible - God Speaks Today).

God's promise to His friend was clear: "I'll make you into a great nation and I'll bless you. I'll make your name great, and you will be a blessing. I'll bless those who bless you, and whoever curses you I'll curse; and all peoples on earth will be blessed through you." (Genesis 12:2-3)

It's true that His promise was clear, but at the same time, it resulted in something absurd. Who would have thought that Abraham would start the line of descendants that would produce Jesus, the Savior of the world? (Look at Matthew 1 at the genealogy of Jesus.) Who could have imagined that, knowing that Abram and his wife Sarah couldn't have children? But God always keeps His promises, and Abram believed God.

Isaiah, called the prophet of faith, started his prophetic ministry in the year 740 B.C. This date is important because it shows us how God, almost three quarters of a century before Jesus was even born, reminded us through his prophet of the covenant of salvation he made with Abraham.

God's promise through Isaiah about the virgin birth of a child whose name would be Emmanuel, "God with Us," reveals that He had a plan of salvation for His people all along. Even with Israel's disobedience, God's love was always present, and the biggest expression of love was the presence of His son in the world. Isaiah's prophecies are directly fulfilled by Christ's birth.

In the book of Micah appears a message from the Lord that records the promise made to His servant David: "You will never fail to have a successor on the throne of Israel" (1 Kings 2:4).

Micah doesn't mention "Emmanuel" like Isaiah, but he does reference the Lord of Israel: "He will stand and shepherd his flock in the strength of the Lord, in the majesty of the name of the Lord his God and they will live securely, for then his greatness will reach to the ends of the earth. And he will be our peace." (Micah 5:4-5)

From the descendants of David would come the King of kings and Lord of lords, Jesus Christ (Matthew 1:1).

Why did God give some "clues" to His servants like Isaiah and Micah about His plan of salvation?

If something could assure us, it's that man fell in Eden, and since then God had a plan to save us all. He had chosen us even before He made the Earth (Ephesians 1:4).

The loyalty of God will be forever, even though His time isn't the same as ours (Psalm 90:4). In His time he keeps His promises, like He did with his greatest promise: the Promised Messiah.

III. LESSON DEVELOPMENT

Introduction

Friendship and Review

Give the students an opportunity to share their testimony about how they showed compassion to someone last week. Ask them, "How many of you showed compassion to someone?" "How did you feel before?" "How did you feel after?" "How was it received?"

Developing the Bible Story

Interviews for Christmas

Assign students for each of the roles of this drama.

Reporter: God has been planning Christmas for a long time. Peter said that Jesus was chosen to come to this world before it was even created (Peter 1:20). After Jesus came, God helped the writers of the New Testament find the clues in the Old Testament. We're going to talk to one of the most well-known patriarchs and a couple of prophets who personally received hints or clues from God.

Abraham: Okay, who would have thought? Everything I know is what God told me: "I'll make you into a great nation and I'll bless you; I'll make your name great, and you will be a blessing. I'll bless those who bless you, and whoever curses you I'll curse; and all peoples on earth will be blessed through you" (Genesis 12:2-3).

You guys can imagine how crazy this sounded in the beginning. I mean, my wife and I didn't even have kids! Generations later, out of my family, Jesus was born. He is the Son of God. This is the most amazing thing I could have ever imagined!

Reporter: I can imagine! Thank you, Abraham. My next guest is Isaiah, the prophet. Welcome, Isaiah!

Isaiah: It's incredible to see the way that God moves and acts, I knew of Abraham, I'm one of his descendants. God let his family grow and become many large nations. When I was ministering, the people were always scared that they were going to be destroyed. The Lord inspired me to speak to them about hope. So I told them: "Therefore the Lord himself will give you a sign: The virgin will be with child and will give birth to a son, and will call him Immanuel." (Isaiah 7:14) And he also said: "For to us a child is born, to us a son is given, and the government will be on his shoulders. And he will be called Wonderful Counselor, Mighty God, Everlasting Father, Prince of Peace" (Isaiah 9:6).

Reporter: I've heard of these in stories and Christmas songs.

Isaiah: And you can see why. They describe Jesus perfectly! He came hundreds of years after my time. God used my messages to give hope to his people during this time! If we would turn towards God, He would protect us. But, there's something even better! The Son used my words to help other people recognize that Jesus fulfilled the prophecies in a special way.

And one more thing! He also told the people of Israel about a man who would prepare the way for the coming King. This person would say: "In the wilderness prepare the way for the Lord; make straight in the desert a highway for our God" (Isaiah 40:3).

Reporter: Many years later, Matthew saw that these words described John the Baptist, who prepared the people to hear the message that Jesus brought. Thank you, Isaiah. My last guest today is the prophet Micah.

Micah: Thank you! It's a pleasure to be here. Isn't it amazing how great God is? Just like Isaiah, I also lived in times of trouble. Israel had divided into two nations. I warned them that their sin would destroy them.

Reporter: How terrible!

Micah: Yes, it was. God was tired of us. But he gave us an opportunity to return to Him. Bethlehem was a tiny town, but important people came out of it, like Naomi, Ruth and even David! I said, "But you, Bethlehem Ephrathah, though you are small among the clans of Judah, out of you will come for me one who will be ruler over Israel, whose origins are from of old, from ancient times" (Micah 5:2).

Reporter: So you were the prophet that gave Herod's men the idea to look for Jesus there!

Micah: All of that happened a long time after my time on earth. But I was the one who prophesied about where Jesus would be born.

Reporter: Incredible! It's no surprise why Matthew and the other New Testament authors were so excited about what they found in the Old Testament. They found the clues that helped people see that Jesus really was the Son of God. His coming to Earth was the last piece of our puzzle.

After finishing the drama, ask the students "Why do you think these passages talk specifically about Jesus?"

Life Application

Emphasize to the students the importance of carrying out promises that they've made to others or to God.

In this moment, they can comment about some promise that they made to someone that they didn't keep so they can realize their emotions with respect to this situation. They can also talk about a promise someone else made to them that they didn't keep.

You can remind them of some promises that Jesus made and kept, like the coming of the Holy Spirit, his presence will be with us to the end of the world, and others.

IV. ACTIVITIES

Activity: Verse of the Month Club Challenge

Challenge the students to keep working on memorizing for the Verse of the Month Club. Remind them that they will have to learn a new verse every month:

December: Matthew 1:21

January: John 11:27

February: 1 Corinthians 10:31.

Help them prepare their ornaments and other decorations for the classroom.

LESSON 49

CHRISTMAS ACCORDING TO ZECHARIAH AND ELIZABETH

I. OVERVIEW

Biblical Base: Isaiah 40:1-5; Matthew 3; Mark 1:1-14; Luke 1:5-25, 1:39-45, 5:57-80

Memory Verse: *"She will give birth to a son, and you are to give him the name Jesus, because he will save his people from their sins."* (Matthew 1:21)

Biblical Truth: God prepared for the coming of Jesus Christ through His obedient people.

Lesson Objective: To help the students comprehend how God prepared his people to receive the promised Messiah.

II. TEACHER PREPARATION

Zachariah and Elizabeth were irreproachably obedient to God's law. Both had asked God for a son, even though they lived in a time where very few people believed in the Lord's power.

Then came the angel Gabriel and he told Zachariah that his wife Elizabeth would give birth to a baby, whom they would call John; and the baby, even in Elizabeth's womb, would be filled with the Holy Spirit. Even though this promise came from an angel, Zachariah doubted it was true because Elizabeth was far too old to be having children.

Because of Zachariah's inability to believe, the angel made him mute until his son was born.

When the baby was born, their neighbors and family members wanted to call him Zechariah like his father. Even though this was customary in their town, Zechariah and Elizabeth were sure that they had to name their son John, just like the angel had prophesied. This showed the people that this child was very special, that God's hand was on him.

When John was an adult, he was a prophet whose message was about repenting from sin, and many people came to hear him.

John baptized people in water, but he taught that the Messiah would come and baptize them in the Holy Spirit and fire. He was the first to recognize that Jesus was the promised Messiah.

The promises of God are clear, and there isn't any doubt that he will reward the honesty and loyalty of His children (Psalms 5:11b-12; Psalms 92:12-15).

In the example of Zachariah and Elizabeth, Luke talks about the two characteristics that God's children should have:

To be upright in the sight of God and obedient to His every law.

It's interesting to think about how a priest – Zechariah, surrounded by a religious structure and living in a period where people doubted the power of God, because of the social and political oppression – remained upright and obedient in the sight of the Lord. No matter what was going on around them, Zechariah and Elizabeth maintained their loyalty to God. How many Zechariah's and Elizabeth's do we need today?

Even through our social difficulties, our economic situation, and cultural pressure, we need to remain upright in the sight of God and obedient to His every law (Luke 1:6).

The calling of God is that we be a people who can make a difference, not people who are following the world's models (Romans 12:2).

III. LESSON DEVELOPMENT

Introduction

Read with your students the Bible Story "Preparing the way for the Savior."

"Is it true that one day we'll have a son?" Elizabeth asked Zechariah.

"I don't know, we are so old already and we've prayed for this for so long," responded Zechariah. Zechariah was a loyal priest who served while Herod was the king of Judea. He and his wife were righteous before God.

One day when it was Zechariah' turn to enter the sanctuary and burn incense, an angel of the Lord appeared to him. Seeing him, Zechariah was startled and scared, but the angel said, "Don't be afraid, Zechariah; your prayer has been heard. Your wife Elizabeth will bear a son, and you are to give him the name John. He will be a joy and delight to you, and many will rejoice because of his birth, for he will be great in the sight of the Lord. Many of the people of Israel will he bring back to the Lord their God. And he will make ready a people prepared for the Lord."

Zechariah asked the angel, "How can this be? I'm already old and so is my wife."

Responding, the angel said, "I am Gabriel. I stand in the presence of God, and I have been sent to speak to you to tell you this good news. And now you will be silent and not able to speak until the day this happens, because you didn't believe my words, which will come

125

true at their proper time."

"What happened to Zechariah?" people asked.

"He's excited! Look at the way he is moving his arms back and forth like that."

"Actually I think he's trying to tell us something," said someone.

When he had finished his responsibilities at the temple, Zechariah went home with his wife Elizabeth. One day she came home with good news. "Zechariah, we're going to have a child! God has answered our prayers." Six months later, Mary, a relative of Elizabeth's, went to go visit her. When Elizabeth heard Mary enter her home and greet her, the baby leaped in her womb, and Elizabeth was filled with the Holy Spirit. In a loud voice she exclaimed, "Blessed are you among women, and blessed is the child you will bear!" Mary stayed with Elizabeth for three months. When the time came, Elizabeth gave birth to a baby boy, just like the angel told her. The neighbors and family members celebrated with her.

"What will you call him?" they asked her.

"Maybe you should name him Zechariah like his father," suggested the men.

"No! His name is John," said Elizabeth.

The neighbors and family members said, "Why? There is no one in your family with that name." Then they asked the father what he thought they should name the baby, and he asked for a tablet and wrote on it, "His name is John." At that very instant, Zechariah could talk and he blessed God.

John lived in the desert until he appeared publicly to Israel. His clothing was made of camel skin and he had a leather belt, and he ate locusts and wild honey. When it was time, he began to preach, "Repent, for the kingdom of heaven is near."

He also said that he was the prophet to whom Isaiah was referring to when he said, "In the desert prepare the way for the Lord; make straight in the wilderness a highway for our God." All of the people from Jerusalem, Judea and from around the Jordan came to hear John preach.

Talk to the kids about God having prepared his people even before Jesus came.

Ask them how people get ready for Christmas.

Life Application
Activity: Christmas Lists

Have the children find this activity on their activity sheet, and talk about preparations that they make to get ready to celebrate Christmas

Say: "What is that you do with your family to get ready for Christmas?" (Bake cookies, clean the house, decorate, go shopping, etc.)

"How did God prepare for the first Christmas?" (First He chose a family that would give birth to His Son, the family of Abraham; God chose the people He knew would help Him.)

"Do you know how God did that?"

Ask the kids to answer the questions they find on their activity sheet, writing the answers on the blank lines.

Discover who I am

Preparing the world for the birth of Jesus wasn't all the God had to do. He also had to prepare someone to preach about Jesus.

-My clothes are made of camel skin.
-My belt is made out of animal skin.
-My food consists of locusts and wild honey.
-One of the things I must do is baptize.

"Who am I?"

Activity: John the Baptist

To review the story, ask the students to answer the following questions on their activity worksheet.

1. Who visited Zechariah in the temple and told him he'd have a son? (Luke 1:11) – An angel
2. What did the angel tell Zechariah he had to name his son? (Luke 1:13) – John
3. What name did the people think the baby should have? (Luke 1:59) – Zechariah
4. Who was John's mother? (Luke 1:13) – Elizabeth
5. What did John eat? (Matthew 3:4) – Locusts and wild honey.
6. What did John come to do? (Luke 3:4) – Prepare a way for Jesus.
7. What did John tell the people to do? (Matthew 3:2) – Repent
8. What did John do with water? (Luke 3:16) – Baptize
9. What kingdom did John say was near? (Matthew 3:2) – The kingdom of heaven
10. What did John say the one coming after him would baptize them with? (Luke 3:16) – The Holy Spirit
11. Where did John live? (Luke 1:80) – In the desert
12. What prophet talked about someone coming out of the desert? (Lucas 3:4) – Isaiah
13. With what did John baptize? (Luke 3:16) – Water

(Get a little gift for the child who answers the most questions correctly.)

IV. ACTIVITIES
Pass the gift

Practice the verse of the month (Matthew 1:21). Ask the children to sit in a circle. While you play music, have the students pass a present around the circle. When you stop the music, the child who is holding the gift should recite the verse in order to keep playing.

Ask them who they talked to this week about the prophecies that spoke about Jesus' coming. Thank God for sending John the Baptist to prepare the world for when Jesus came. Pray for the students to remember the real reason for Christmas while they prepare to celebrate.

CHRISTMAS ACCORDING TO MARY AND JOSEPH

I. OVERVIEW

Biblical Base: Matthew 1:18-25; Luke 1:26-38, 2:1-20; Philippians 2:5-8

Memory Verse: *"She will give birth to a son, and you are to give him the name Jesus, because he will save his people from their sins."* (Matthew 1:21)

Biblical Truth: During the Christmas season, we remember that Jesus, other than being God, came to the Earth as a human to save humanity.

Lesson Objective: To help the students comprehend the significance that Jesus became a human like us to save us, and invite them to thank Jesus for having come to Earth. And something very important: help them to accept Jesus as their Savior.

II. TEACHER PREPARATION

At this age, it's very well possible that your students have participated in many activities revolving around the life and ministry of Jesus. But it's probable that they haven't known about the full incarnation; Jesus was fully man and fully God.

Jesus, being fully God, didn't need to come to Earth to die for us humans. But because of his love for us, he became fully man, physically suffering until finally giving his life for ours on the cross.

The book of Matthew starts off with Jesus' genealogy, then he writes about the events of Jesus' birth.

The birth of Jesus Christ

Matthew tells us that Mary and Joseph were engaged to be married, but didn't live together yet. Back then, an engagement was a lot more serious than today. Legally, they were married. They only lacked being married before the church and living together.

Mary was expecting a child conceived by the Holy Spirit's power. But Joseph found that hard to believe. Joseph, being a righteous man, didn't want to divorce her publicly, so he decided to leave her secretly. That was until an angel of the Lord came to him and explained what had happened. Joseph then understood and took care of Mary and the baby.

In Matthew 1:22-23, we can see that Jesus came to fulfill the promises made by God to his people Israel (Isaiah 7:14). These verses show us that he was the long-awaited Messiah.

God as man

This was a marvelous miracle that doesn't have a scientific explanation. Jesus, with the exception of being born without original sin because he was conceived by the Holy Spirit, was completely human and completely God.

The Bible teaches us the humanity of Jesus, in that he ate, drank, was hungry, thirsty, tired, he got angry, he had problems, was tempted, felt pain, not to mention was crucified and killed without even deserving it. By doing the last thing mentioned, he took our place.

And we see the godliness of Jesus when he spoke with divine authority; he claimed the power of forgiving sins (Mark 2:5-12), he accepted adoration for his name (Matthew 14:3), He is the son of the Living God (Matthew 16:16-17).

The Gospel of Luke talks about Jesus' childhood. Luke adds in another story about Jesus' infancy that proves his humanity, and it's the testimony of the shepherds. In Luke 2:8-20, an angel comes to them and announces the coming of Jesus to Earth, and immediately, the shepherds leave in search of this baby King. They were happily surprised to find a baby sleeping in the manger.

We can make a summary of Jesus' life from Philippians 2:5-11, where Paul writes to the people of Philippi and reminds them of Christ's humility and the exaltation He deserves. Jesus renounced everything that was naturally his and humbled himself all the way to the cross, where he died because he loves us so much, so Heaven and Earth would kneel and worship Him.

What would have happened if Jesus didn't come to Earth? God would be the same, but how would things be for us?

It was necessary for us that Jesus came to Earth so we could receive salvation; it's thanks to his sacrifice that we have this precious gift. We should be forever grateful to Jesus for coming and sacrificing his life for us.

It wasn't his obligation to give his life, but he did so to show us His love. And thanks be to Him, we no longer have to make sacrifices to God to pardon our sins; we don't have to suffer or die for our sins.

What is so important about Jesus becoming man? He

became a man which allows him to understand us fully; he gave us a model to follow, and gave us a goal: to be like him.

Jesus was tempted by everything and he never sinned. He cried, he laughed, suffered, was exposed to harsh weather, was hungry, he ate, he rested, was exposed emotionally and physically to human fragility, pressures, and human aspects of life. The difference between him and other human beings is that even through all of this, he never once sinned.

III. LESSON DEVELOPMENT

Introduction

Greet and hug the kids as they come to class; give a special welcome to the kids who are here for the first time. Explain that today they will be participating in a drama of one of the most important stories in the whole world. You'll need volunteers to do it. Ask the kids to look at their activity sheet for this lesson. Bring costumes and scene settings that you deem necessary, and ask them to participate in the play. (They can read their roles, no memorization required!)

Developing the Bible Story:

In the still of the night

Characters: Narrator, Mary, Joseph, angel, angel choir, innkeeper and shepherds.

Scene 1: (Mary and Joseph are talking excitedly)

Mary: Joseph! Something marvelous has happened!

Joseph: What happened?

Mary: An angel came to me and told me "Greetings, you who are highly favored! The Lord is with you!"

Joseph: And you weren't frightened?

Mary: At the beginning I was, but the angel told me, "Don't be afraid, Mary, you have found favor with God. You will be with child and give birth to a son, and you are to give him the name Jesus."

Joseph: Wait just a moment!! You can't be pregnant! We haven't even gotten married yet!

Mary: Yes I know, but this isn't a normal baby. The angel told me, "The Holy Spirit will come upon you, and the power of the Most High will overshadow you. So the holy one to be born will be called the Son of God."

Joseph: (with sadness) But, Mary! Did you even stop to think, how could God have a son? I need time to think about this. (Talking to himself) I suppose Mary and I'll have to break off our engagement.

Scene 2: (Joseph is sleeping. The angel appears in his dreams.)

Narrator: Joseph went to sleep, concerned and confused. While he slept, an angel appeared in his dreams.

Angel: Joseph son of David, don't be afraid to take Mary home as your wife, because what is conceived in her is of the Holy Spirit. She will give birth to a son, and you are to give him the name Jesus, because he will save his people from their sins.

Narrator: All this took place to fulfill what the Lord had said through the prophet: "The virgin will be with child and will give birth to a son, and they will call him Immanuel – which means, 'God with us.'" When Joseph woke up, he did what the angel told him and took Mary as his wife.

It was time to pay taxes and the king had ordered that everyone return to the place where he was born to pay and be present for the census.

Joseph: Mary, we need to go to Bethlehem. My family is there. You know that David is my ancestor.

Scene 3: (Mary and Joseph have traveled to Bethlehem. The innkeeper talks to them.)

Innkeeper: All of Bethlehem is full of people coming to register for the census. The inn is completely full. I hope no one else comes that I have to tell them that I have no more room. Oh…just my luck, another person knocking at the door.

Joseph: Do you have a room available?

Innkeeper: I'm sorry, but the inn is full. You'll have to find another place.

Joseph: We've come from Nazareth. My wife is about to have our baby and she is so tired. You don't have any place where we could rest for a bit?

Innkeeper: I already told you, no! My inn is full. I'd like to help you but…no. Wait a minute, I have an idea. If you want, you can stay in the stable out back. It's all that I can offer you.

Joseph: The stable. Okay, that's fine, thank you.

Scene 4: (Mary and Joseph and the baby are in the corner of the stable. The shepherds have sat down around their campfire when the angels appear.)

Narrator: While they were there, the time came for the baby to be born, and she gave birth to her firstborn, a son. She wrapped him in cloths and placed him in a manger.

In the same region, there was a group of shepherd that were keeping watch on their flocks at night. An angel appeared to them.

Shepherds (scared): What is this? Who are you? Please don't hurt us!

Angel: Don't be afraid. I bring you good news of great joy that will be for all the people. Today in the town of David a Savior has been born to you, he is Christ the Lord. This will be a sign to you: You will find a baby wrapped in cloths and lying in a manger.

Narrator: Suddenly a great company of the heavenly host appeared with the angel, praising God and they said:

Angels: Glory to God in the highest, and on earth peace to men on whom his favor rests.

Narrator: Then the angels left.

Shepherds: Let's go to Bethlehem and see what the Lord has told us.

Narrator: The went quickly and found Mary and Joseph, and the baby asleep in the manger.

The End

Ask the following questions:

According to the angel: What would the shepherds find in the manger? (a baby)

Who was that baby? (Jesus)

Why was he called Jesus? (Because he would save his people from their sins.)

Why do you think the shepherds went to worship Jesus? (Because he was the long-awaited Messiah, and they were so excited that the prophecies were finally coming true.)

Life Application

Much of the Christmas celebration that the children enjoy can happen throughout the year. Now that Christmas is almost over, challenge the children to maintain an active Christmas spirit. The Christmas stories are always appropriate to read. Talking about the birth of Jesus and showing good will towards other, this is something we should be doing constantly.

Say: "What could you do to show others the true meaning of Christmas? What can you use to help your non-believing friends learn why Christians celebrate Christmas?" (Remind them that as Jesus grew up, he showed us how to live our lives in a way that exalts God. Finally, he died and was raised from the dead so that we too can have eternal life.

IV. ACTIVITIES

Activity: Look at yourself

Tell the students to look at their activity for the section with mirror. Hand out colored pencils to each student and ask them to write or draw words of gratitude to God, because Jesus became a man because he loved us. Also, ask them to think about what happened to them last week. It can be something happy or sad (a birthday party, a trip to the park with their parents, a hard chore they did, something painful that happened to them, a problem they encountered at school, etc.) Tell them that in the mirror they can draw this situation that they saw. When they are done, ask who would like to share what they drew/wrote. Let everyone who wants to talk; but don't make them.

Read Hebrews 2:16-18. Jesus, the Son of God, came to the Earth to be a human and went through everything we go through as humans. Make reference to stories told to children. Jesus, being fully human, understands when we feel happy, sad, scared, mad, or hurt, because he felt these and more. That's why he died on the cross, as if he was at fault for loving each of us. Jesus should be the role model we all follow.

Ask someone to pray, thanking Jesus for becoming human and saving us. Ask that he helps us to be thankful that he knows the same feelings as us. Ask that he helps us when we go through difficult situations.

Activity: Verse of the Month Club

Direct the students to do this activity. Their activity sheet has instructions for them to follow.

NOTES:

CHRISTMAS ACCORDING TO SIMEON AND ANNA

I. OVERVIEW

Biblical Base: Luke 2:21-40

Memory Verse: *"She will give birth to a son, and you are to give him the name Jesus, because he will save his people from their sins."* (Matthew 1:21)

Biblical Truth: Jesus, being the promised Messiah and also being God, came to help us know our Father.

Lesson Objective: To help the students recognize the mercy of God in revealing his love to us through Jesus, our Messiah.

III. TEACHER PREPARATION

Something that was characteristic of Joseph and Mary's life was their obedience to the Word of God. Because of this, Jesus was eight days old when they had him circumcised, and when he was 40 days old, they took him to the temple to present him to the Lord. When they went to the temple, they also brought a sacrifice offering that Mary offered, to be pure after Jesus' birth, just like the law said (Exodus 3:2-12 and Leviticus 12).

When Joseph, Mary and Jesus reached the temple, they met two people, Simeon and Anna.

The first was a righteous and pious man who had waited for the rescue of his people. Simeon had received a promise from God that, "He wouldn't die until he saw the promised Messiah in person."

In the temple, Simeon held the baby tenderly in his arms, the baby who would save his nation. In Jesus, Simeon could see two promises that had been kept: (1) the coming of the promised Messiah, and (2) the work of the Holy Spirit, in that he got to see the promised Messiah in person before he died.

And God was faithful to keep His promises, so Simeon lifted up his prayer, now called the Song or Prophecy of Simeon. In Latin, it's called Nuncdimittis which means "Now you dismiss." Simeon could now leave ... God had kept his promises.

The second person that Jesus' family met was Anna. Even though she was older, her relationship with God let her see that this child, born only 40 days ago, was to be the Savior. As she began to give thanks to God, she talked about Jesus to all of the people who waited for the promise of freedom for their people.

Even though the promise was clear, with respect to the coming of the Messiah, no one knew that on that day in the temple, the baby Jesus was the Savior they were waiting for. But God, with all his mercy, revealed it to Simeon and Anna, his faithful servants.

In this early stage of Jesus' life, we learn important aspects for our own lives. On the one hand, the obedience of Joseph and Mary with respect to God's law for his people, i.e., the dedication of their firstborn and the sacrifice to be pure after childbirth (Exodus 3:2-12 and Leviticus 12).

The loyalty of God became a reality through this experience for Simeon and Anna. We remember that in the earlier lessons, God had revealed to different people, like Isaiah, Micah and Zechariah, that He would send a Messiah to rescue his people.

Simeon, like Anna, knew this promise well; and God in His loyalty and mercy let them meet the promised Messiah because God always keeps His promises.

When a person has a personal and profound encounter with Christ, something happens as a result,. Their life changes radically, so much so that their spirit doesn't keep quiet and they want to tell everyone how Jesus has changed their life.

After her encounter with the baby Jesus, Anna told everyone about the promise coming true (Luke 2:38). Simeon, like Anna, would never be the same either ... the Holy Spirit had guided them to meet Jesus.

III. LESSON DEVELOPMENT

Introduction

Start the class by asking the students how they feel about Jesus, the son of God, being born as a child like them. Tell them the story of Simeon and Anna meeting Jesus in the temple. A great way to tell the story is that you can dress up like Simeon or Anna. Remember that they were both old in age; get a doll that can represent the baby Jesus and you can hold Him in your arms. You can use him for both of your roles. Impact the lives of the kids!

When you are done with the story, remind the students that Christmas isn't just for Christians, that Jesus came to save the whole world (John 3:16-17).

Write your opinion

Challenge the children to think about how they could teach someone the true meaning of Christmas. If you wish, you can make this activity more attractive by having the children explain it to each other or take turns explaining it to you. Assume the role of someone who thinks we celebrate Christmas just to have a party and to give and receive gifts, and have them try to explain to you the true meaning of the holiday. Challenge some of them with questions. That way the real convictions of the students will come to light and this will help them to reinforce their belief with respect to personal evangelism, beliefs in Christmas and others.

Celebrate together

To finish the class, debate with the students to see if they believe that Christmas should be celebrated throughout the whole year.

Developing the Bible Story

A long-awaited welcome

It feels like just yesterday they were on their way to Bethlehem. Now the baby Jesus already is 40 days old. Joseph and Mary took him to Jerusalem to present him to the Lord. They went on their way to the temple. Now there was a man in Jerusalem called Simeon, who was righteous and devout. It had been revealed to him by the Holy Spirit that he would not die before he had seen the Lord's Christ. Moved by the Spirit, he went into the temple courts. When the parents brought in the child Jesus to do for him what the custom of the Law required, he said, "This baby is unlike any other. This baby is very special because he is the promised one." He took him in his arms and praised God, saying, "Sovereign Lord, as you have promised, you now can dismiss your servant in peace. For my eyes have seen your salvation, which you have prepared in the sight of all people, a light for revelation to the Gentiles and for glory to your people Israel."

Then Simeon blessed them and said to Mary, "This child is destined to cause the falling and rising of many in Israel, and to be a sign that will be spoken against, so that the thoughts of many hearts will be revealed. And a sword will pierce your own soul too. Always remember how special he is."

Anna, the prophetess, was also in the temple that day, she was very old. She never left the temple but worshiped night and day, fasting and praying.

When she saw Mary, Joseph and Jesus, she approached them and recognized Jesus. "This is the baby that we've been waiting for God to send," she said. "Glory to God! Because he has sent the one he promised! I must tell everyone that is near!"

Mary and Joseph were astounded by what she said about Jesus. An angel had come to them and said that he would be called the Son of God. When he was born, some shepherds came from afar and told of a choir of angels announcing his birth and that this was good news for all people. And now Simeon and Anna had recognized the baby as God's chosen one. When Joseph and Mary had done everything required by the Law of the Lord, they returned to Galilee to their own town of Nazareth. (Luke 2)

Life Application

With the students, thank God for faithfully keeping His promise to send a Savior to rescue us.

Remind them of Simeon and Anna's experiences with the baby Jesus. This would be a great time to invite anyone who wishes to have a personal encounter with Jesus or to reaffirm in them the calling we all have to tell everyone about Christ. Anna is a great example of acting on the calling that each of us Christians have.

I

V. ACTIVITIES

Activity: Express your point of view

Christmas isn't just for Christians, for Jesus came to save the whole world so that we can all believe in him and accept him as our personal savior. But there are still many people that don't have even the slightest idea that this is what it's all about. Help the students find the answers to the questions that the non-believers can pose. Then discuss them as a group.

To make this activity more inviting to the kids, have some kids act out what this would be like. Have them tell what they think/believe about Christmas; how would they answers these questions? What evidence could they give? They can write their questions on a piece of paper.

Child 1: I like to give and receive gifts and also have parties at school. For me, this is the real reason we celebrate in December. Why would I throw Jesus into all of that? (Without Jesus' existence we wouldn't celebrate his birth.)

Child 2: Yeah, so maybe Christmas really is Jesus' birthday. So what? (Jesus isn't just another person, he's fully God and fully human. Just imagine that the Son of God was just a little, defenseless baby. This shows us that He really does love us. He came to the Earth to show us His great love.)

Child 3: Clearly, Jesus was a great person. But how can we really know that he was God's son? (Through the story, God gave hope to His people that He would send a Savior. He prepared a path for Jesus when He called John the Baptist. Angles announced his birth to Mary, Joseph and shepherds saying he was the promised one. Jesus' birth fulfilled the prophecies exactly. Then, his ministry and resurrection shows us that he truly is the Son of God. We know that this is true, when you have a personal relationship with Him.)

Make note that even though the birth of Jesus was to bring happiness to everyone, some people don't love him. Sometimes telling the story isn't enough. We can pray for those who don't know, and show them the love of God through how we treat them. But God has given enough evidence that Jesus is His Son. Tell them, "Today we are going to find more evidence that God sent His son to save all the people."

Activity: Celebrating together

Help the children figure out how to act on this activity. Invite them to prepare to talk about their testimony next week - about how they talked to others about the real reason for the season.

Memory Verse

Write the verse on the board but take out the first and last word and where they can find the verse; ask volunteers to complete the verse.

Finish class with a moment of prayer where each child can give thanks to God for sending His son Jesus to save us, and that He has revealed this truth to us in the Bible.

GIVE EVERYTHING TO GOD!

I. OVERVIEW

Biblical Base: Mark 12:41-44

Memory Verse: *"For if the willingness is there, the gift is acceptable according to what one has, not according to what he doesn't have."* (2 Corinthians 8:12)

Biblical Truth: The will of God is that we give ourselves to him, completely, without conditions.

Lesson Objective: To help the students give everything they have to God.

II. TEACHER PREPARATION

After debating with the priests, the scribes, the Pharisees and the Sadducees, and preaching to the multitudes of people who followed him, Jesus wanted to rest. He sat down opposite the place where people brought their offerings. He watched a lot of people come and bring their offerings. But of all the people who gave their offerings, Jesus spoke to his disciples about a poor widow who came to give her money. She deposited in the offering only two very small copper coins, worth only a fraction of a penny. With this action of the widow, Jesus taught a big lesson about giving. She gave all that she had, everything she had to live on (v. 44).

In the verses prior to this, Jesus denounced the scribes for giving a hard time to the widows and their well-being (v .40).

To give is a characteristic of humans that has lost its meaning in our egotistical society. The Christian message that says that God wants us to give Him everything is always poorly interpreted.

This story of the widow and her copper coins clearly shows us the love we should have when we give. Her decision to give everything she had should be an example to us in our materialistic society.

III. LESSON DEVELOPMENT

Introduction

Remind the students about the past lessons about Christmas.

Activity: What's important to me

After reviewing the earlier lessons, have the students write on a piece of paper 10 objects or things of value that are very important to them, and have them write then on their activity sheet.

When they are done, give them another piece of paper and ask them to write, of the 10 objects, what would they be willing to give to a friend.

Lastly, ask them, "Of that list, what would you give to a stranger?"

Talk with them about why it's hard to give things of value away to someone they don't know, and what they think God wants them to give to Him.

Developing the Bible Story

The tiny, powerful coins

Ask for two volunteers to read the parts of Mony and Dolly, and if you can, bring something they can dress up in to look more like money. This way you can better impact the kids.

Start the drama off by telling the students about the two little coins that belonged to the widow that she took out of her purse while she walked. The coins begin to talk:

Mony: Dolly! It's so great to see you again, where have you been?

Dolly: I've been around! I'm always being passed around without stopping. Last week I was even in the purse of a tax collector!

Mony: Seriously? Are you kidding me? Tell me, what kind of coins did you meet?

Dolly: I met some coins made of platinum and some dinaris. Those other coins made fun of me and said I didn't make a difference, I was only copper.

Mony: Yeah, I get it. I've also gone through a similar situation. It's been a couple weeks, but a while ago my owner was a man of power. He had coins of gold in his purse. And you know what? That gold coin didn't even want to talk to me!

Dolly: It's okay, I guess, here we are in the market again. I wonder who we'll belong to next.

Mony: Who knows?! But I'm ready for a new adventure!

Dolly: You know what's interesting? This lady that we belong to now, she doesn't have any other coins, only us.

Mony: That's true, it's just the two of us in here.

Dolly: We are only two simple copper coins. She can't buy much with only us. Do you think we're all she has?

Mony: I don't believe it! Everyone in the world has more money than two simple copper coins, but what can someone buy with only two copper coins?

Dolly: Well, look at her clothes, they're ripped and torn.

Mony: And you know what, we are moving a lot, this lady is going really fast! I wonder where we're going!

The coins sit still for a while.

Ask the students:

"What do you think is directing the woman? What do you think she is going to do with the money?" Tell the following story of the widow who gave everything.

It was late in the afternoon when the lady rushed through the marketplace. She paused every once in a while to look at the food. She wanted so much to stop and enjoy a piece of grape dessert or one of the fresh cheeses. All of this reminded her she hadn't eaten all week, just a small piece of bread! It was all she had in her house.

She opened her hands to look at the only coins she had, they were only copper. She put them back inside her pocket of her tattered clothes so she wouldn't lose them. Her thoughts were concentrated on her small coins. "I wish I had more to bring to God, but this is all I have." She was thankful to the Lord that she even had these two small coins to offer.

When she arrived at the temple, she quickly went up the stairs. She went to a patio where the women went to deposit their offerings. There were lots of people in the temple that day. While she deposited her copper coins, she saw that in the offering box there were lots of gold and silver coins. Her coins looked so small and insignificant in comparison to the others. Her eyes filled with tears and her heart was content to have brought everything she had to God. After having given her offering, she left the temple. But, while she was the temple, someone watched everything she did. It was Jesus and he called his disciples and said, "I tell you the truth, this poor widow has put more into the offering than all the others. They all gave out of their wealth; but she, out of her poverty, put in everything – all she had to live on."

The small coins return to the front.

Mony: Did you see where we're at?

Dolly: Yes! We're in the temple offering! It's the first time I've ever been here.

Mony: Me too! I thought we would end up in the marketplace.

Dolly: That lady was really hungry; I imagined we'd stay there too.

Mony: Then, why did she bring us here??

Dolly: (softly) Don't tell anyone but I think we are an offering to God. We were all the money that lady had and she gave us to God. Don't you feel important, Mony?

Mony: Obviously! But I feel uncomfortable being surrounded by all of these silver and gold coins.

Dolly: But, you know what, Mony? There are things that are more important than silver or gold!

Mony: I think you're right!

To finish off this part of the lesson have a student read Mark 12:41-44. When they are done reading ask them, "Why do you think the widow gave her only two coins to God? Why did Jesus say that these two copper coins were worth more than silver or gold?"

Life Application

Just like the widow, God wants us to give everything to Him. When we invite Him to reign in our lives, we are also saying that He reigns over every part of our lives, everything we are and everything we have. We are giving everything to Him, without conditions.

Are we ready to give everything to God, without conditions? Us giving our entire life to God is a great present for him; it's the greatest offering and nothing could pay for it, not even all the silver and gold in the world.

IV. ACTIVITIES

Activity: We accept deposits

Invite the students to fill out a check to "Heaven's bank." Once they are finished, they can deposit them into the box that you prepared beforehand. When everyone has made a deposit, pray with them that they too can bring their lives to God, everything they are and have.

Memory Verse

To make memorizing more enjoyable for the students, you can try out the following: Write the verse on the board and have the kids read it out loud. Then in the middle of the verse they can lower their voice so that no one can hear them.

NOTES:

www.ingramcontent.com/pod-product-compliance
Lightning Source LLC
Chambersburg PA
CBHW081541040426
42448CB00015B/3174